Time Out Guides Limited
Universal House
251 Tottenham Court Road
London W1T 7AB
Tel + 44 (0)20 7813 3000
Fax + 44 (0)20 7813 6001
Email guides@timeout.com
www.timeout.com

Editorial

Editors Emma Howarth, Anna Norman
Deputy Editor Yolanda Zappaterra
Copy Editors Simon Coppock, Jan Fuscoe
Listings Checkers Alex Brown, Kohinor Sahota
Proofreader Tamsin Shelton
Indexer Jackie Brind

Managing Director Peter Fiennes
Editorial Director Sarah Guy
Series Editor Cath Phillips
Business Manager Dan Allen
Editorial Manager Holly Pick
Assistant Management Accountant Ija Krasnikova

Design

Art Director Scott Moore
Art Editor Pinelope Kourmouzoglou
Senior Designer Henry Elphick
Graphic Designers Kei Ishimaru, Nicola Wilson
Ad Designer Jodi Sher

Picture Desk

Picture Editor Jael Marschner
Deputy Picture Editor Lynn Chambers
Picture Researcher Gemma Walters
Picture Desk Assistant Marzena Zoladz
Picture Librarian Christina Theisen

Advertising

Commercial Director Mark Phillips
Sales Manager Alison Wallen
Advertising Sales Ben Holt, Matt Peel, Jason Trotman
Copy Controller Alison Bourke

Marketing

Marketing Manager Yvonne Poon
Sales & Marketing Director,
North America & Latin America Lisa Levinson
Senior Publishing Brand Manager Luthfa Begum
Marketing Designer Anthony Huggins

Production

Group Production Director Mark Lamond
Production Manager Brendan McKeown
Production Controller Damian Bennett
Production Coordinator Kelly Fenlon

Time Out Group

Chairman Tony Elliott
Chief Executive Officer David King
Group General Manager/Director Nichola Coulthard
Time Out Communications Ltd MD David Pepper
Time Out International Ltd MD Cathy Runciman
Time Out Magazine Ltd Publisher/Managing Director Mark Elliott
Group IT Director Simon Chappell
Head of Marketing Catherine Demajo

Contributors
Brighton Elizabeth Winding; **Oxford** Rachel Williams; **Bristol** Emma Howarth; **Woodbridge** Sarah Guy; **Rye** Sarah Guy; **Lewes** Rachel Williams; **Grantchester** Simon Coppock; **White Horse Hill** Yolanda Zappaterra; **Ashwell** Yolanda Zappaterra; **Henley-on-Thames** Daniel Smith; **West Wittering** Hugh Graham, Elizabeth Winding; **Camber Sands** Hugh Graham, Yolanda Zappaterra; **Dungeness** Hugh Graham, Kate Riordan; **Botany Bay** Jessica Cargill Thompson, Hugh Graham; **Littlehampton** Rachel Williams; **Whitstable** Jon Lynes; **Leigh-on-Sea** Ruth Jarvis; **Mersea Island** Andrew Shields; **Burnham Beeches** Jon Lynes; **Salcey Forest** Alex Barlow; **RHS Wisley** Simon Coppock; **Westonbirt Arboretum** Kate Riordan; **Conservation Volunteering** Ronnie Haydon; **The Stour Estuary** Daniel Smith; **Surrey Hills** Llama Trek Lucy Smallwood; **Hell-Fire Caves** Alex Barlow; **Hever Castle** Hugh Graham; **LASSCO Three Pigeons** Ruth Jarvis; **Windsor Great Park** Emma Howarth **Cambridge** Daniel Kamb; **Constable Country** Andrew Shields; **Cheltenham Literature Festival** Kate Riordan; **Snape Maltings & Aldeburgh** James Mullighan; **Goodwood** Lucy Smallwood; **Polo** Andrew Shields; **A Round of Golf** Andrew Shields; **Harrison's Rocks** Daniel Neilson; **SNO!zone Milton Keynes** Candice Pires; **Sequoia at the Grove** Yolanda Zappaterra; **Bath Thermae Spa** Emma Howarth; **The Haybarn** Emma Howarth; **The Spa at Pennyhill Park Hotel** Sarah Guy; **The Vineyard Spa** Lucy Smallwood; **Calcot Manor** Kate Riordan; **Middle Farm, Glynde** Maisie Tomlinson; **Novelli's Academy** Alexi Duggins; **Mrs Tee's Wild Mushrooms** Lucy Smallwood; **Pick Your Own** Yolanda Zappaterra; **The Bluebell Railway** Lucy Smallwood; **Blackdown Farm's Rural Rides** Maisie Tomlinson; **Beachy Head** Daniel Neilson; **Hot-air ballooning** Candice Pires; **Hayling Island** Rachel Williams, Meryl O'Rourke; **Roald Dahl Museum & Story Centre** Cathy Limb; **The Lodge** Ronnie Haydon; **The Living Rainforest** Poppy Cogan. **FIVE and TEN features were written by** Alex Barlow, Poppy Cogan, Hugh Graham, Sarah Guy, Phil Harriss, Fiona McAuslan, Candice Pires, Andrew Shields, Yolanda Zappaterra.

The Editors would like to thank Damian Bennett, Simon Cook, Sarah Ellison, Sarah Guy, Ronnie Haydon, Ruth Jarvis, Jenni Muir, Meryl O'Rourke, Cath Phillips, Mark Phillips, Kate Riordon, Patrick Welch, Elizabeth Winding.

Backcover photography by Michel Muller, Britta Jaschinski, Jonathan Perugia and Heloise Bergman.

Photography pages 3, 6 (left), 46, 56, 57, 139 Nerida Howard; pages 5, 7 (right), 14, 15, 16, 35, 36, 39, 62/63, 80, 87, 88, 89, 95, 96, 107, 114/115, 121, 123, 125, 133, 145, 157, 158, 159, 162/163, 172, 173, 202/ 203, 205, 206, 207, 208, 213, 214, 239, 240, 241, 248/249, 256, 257, 262, 263, 265 Jonathan Perugia; pages 6 (right), 9, 44/45, 66, 67, 69, 70, 71, 75, 77, 90/91, 93, 153, 216 (left), 221 Britta Jaschinski; pages 7 (left), 167, 168 Centaur Photographic; pages 10/11, 21, 25, 28, 34, 50, 51, 58/59, 61, 102, 103, 113, 226/227, 235, 236, 237, 267, 268 Heloise Bergman; pages 13, 222 (right), 223 Scott Wishart; pages 32, 48, 87, 178/179, 110, 199, 230, 247 Alamy; page 41 CCC Tourism; page 83 (top left) Kent Tourism; page 83 Jael Marschner; page 105 (bottom) Paul Groom; page 120 English Heritage Photo Library; page 122 Leeds Castle Foundation; page 129 (top) NTPL/Vera Collingwood; page 129 (bottom) Andreas von Einsiedel; page 130 (top) Tony Tree, courtesy of The Charston Trust; page 130 (bottom) NTPL/Robet Morris; page 131 (top left) NTPL/Mike Williams; page 131 (top right) NTPL/Penny Tweedie; page 131 (bottom) NTPL/John Miller; pages 132, 133 English Heritage; pages 136/137 De La Warr Pavilion; page 146 Chris George; pages 148, 149 Latitude Festival; page 150 Keith Saunders; page 152 Bernard Holmes; page 161 Becky Thomson; page 161 (bottom right) Michel Muller; page 165 John Colley; pages 169, 170 Cranfield Golf Academy; page 174 Jamie Harris; page 175 Alan Bone; page 180 Action Images/Ascot Racecourse; page 181 Empics Sport/PA Photos/Epsom Downs; page 182/183 Thermae Spa; page 215 Christina Theisen; pages 215 (bottom), 219 (right) Jitka Hynkova; page 217 (left), 219 (left) Alys Tomlinson; pages 216 (right), 217 (right) Natalie Pecht; page 222 (top left) Graig Deane; page 222 (bottom left) Rogan MacDonald; page 229 Tove K. Breitstein; page 234 Rick Tomlinson; pages 243, 245 (bottom right) Daniel Nielson; page 245 Adam Monaghan; pages 258 (top left), 259 The Aspinall Foundation; page 258 (bottom left) Tracey Smith; page 258 (bottom) Dave Rolfe.

The following images were provided by the featured establishments/artists: pages 54, 97, 98, 99, 104, 105, 117, 118, 119, 126/127, 141, 155, 160, 177, 185, 186, 187, 188, 189, 191, 192, 193, 194, 196, 197, 200, 201, 209, 210, 211, 224, 225, 251, 252, 246, 254, 261.

About the guide

This book is divided up into eleven different sections, arranged by theme – starting with day trips to towns and cities outside London, and finishing with ideas for days out with children. On top of the varied chapters within each section, we have also included round-ups of popular trips, or variations on a theme, in our FIVE and TEN features. The map section on pages 278-280 shows the location of each destination.

TELEPHONE NUMBERS
All phone numbers listed in this guide assume that you are calling from within Britain (and, specifically, London). If you're calling from abroad, dial your international access code, then 44 for the UK; follow that with the phone number, dropping the first zero of the area code.

DISCLAIMER
While every effort has been made to ensure the accuracy of information within this guide, the publishers cannot accept responsibility for any errors it may contain. Businesses can change their arrangements at any time, so, before you go out of your way, we strongly advise you phone ahead to check opening times, prices and other particulars.

ADVERTISERS
The recommendations in *Great Days Out from London* are based on experiences of Time Out journalists. No payment or PR invitation has secured inclusion or influenced content. The editors select which venues and activities are listed in this guide, and the list was compiled before any advertising space was sold.

LET US KNOW WHAT YOU THINK
We welcome tips for days trips you consider we should include in future editions and take note of your criticism of our choices. You can email us at guides@timeout.com.

Contents

Introduction................................9
Indexes....................................270
Map..278
Map key...................................280

TOWNS & CITIES   10

Brighton....................................13
FIVE One-off shops.........................19
Oxford......................................20
Bristol.....................................25
Woodbridge..................................31
Rye...33
Lewes.......................................35
FIVE Shopping extravaganzas.................41
FIVE Village customs........................43

COUNTRY   44

Grantchester................................46
White Horse Hill............................48
TEN Perfect country pubs....................53
Ashwell.....................................55
Henley-on-Thames............................58

COAST   62

West Wittering..............................65
Camber Sands................................69
FIVE Retro ice-cream parlours...............72

Dungeness...................................73
Botany Bay..................................76
Littlehampton...............................79
FIVE Retro resorts..........................81
Whitstable..................................82
TEN Beach activities........................85
Leigh-on-Sea................................86
Mersea Island...............................87

NATURE   90

Burnham Beeches.............................92
Salcey Forest...............................95
TEN Gardens.................................97
RHS Wisley.................................101
Westonbirt Arboretum.......................104
Conservation Volunteering..................106
The Stour Estuary..........................108
TEN Natural encounters.....................109
Surrye Hills Llama Trek....................112

HISTORY   114

The Hell-Fire Caves........................116
Hever Castle...............................117
Stonehenge & Avebury.......................120
Down House.................................121
FIVE Castles...............................122
LASSCO Three
  Pigeons..................................124
Battle.....................................126
TEN Stately homes..........................129
Windsor Great Park.........................134

CULTURE — 136

Cambridge 138
FIVE Galleries 143
Constable Country 144
TEN Architectural marvels 146
FIVE Festivals 148
Garsington Opera 150
FIVE Works of art 151
Cheltenham Literature Festival 155
Snape Maltings & Aldeburgh 156
FIVE Sculpture parks 160

SPORT/ACTIVE — 162

Goodwood 164
Polo 167
A Round of Golf 169
Harrison's Rocks 171
FIVE Learn to… 174
FIVE Spectator sports 175
SNO!zone Milton Keynes 177
FIVE Places to fly a kite 178
FIVE Days at the races 180

RELAXATION — 182

Sequoia at the Grove 185
Bath Thermae Spa 188
The Haybarn 190
The Spa at Pennyhill Park Hotel 192
The Vineyard Spa 195
FIVE Soothing sunsets 198
Calcot Manor 200

FOOD & DRINK — 202

Middle Farm, Glynde 205
Daylesford Organic Farm Shop 209
Novelli's Academy 212
TEN Food markets 215
Mrs Tee's Wild Mushrooms 220
Pick Your Own 222
FIVE PYO farms 223
FIVE Seasonal food events 224

JOURNEYS — 226

FIVE Transport rentals 229
The Bluebell Railway 230
FIVE Scenic drives 233
FIVE Boat trips 234
Blackdown Farm's Rural Rides 235
FIVE Bike rides 239
Beachy Head 243
Hot-air ballooning 246

CHILDREN — 248

TEN Theme parks and
    adventure playgrounds 251
Hayling Island 255
Hollycombe Steam Fair 256
FIVE Animal adventures 258
Roald Dahl Museum & Story Centre 260
FIVE Model villages 262
The Lodge 264
FIVE Mazes 266
The Living Rainforest 267

Introduction

All Londoners know – and visitors soon find out – that their lists of things to do in the capital will never be fully realised; that there's an endless source of activites of all kinds. Yet, sometimes, you need to escape the Big Smoke – to free yourself from the chaos, the noise, the grime, or simply for the sake of a change of scene and to see or do something out of the realms of zones 1-6. Whether it's an impromptu escape, an excursion waiting to happen or a special plan for a future trip, Time Out's *Great Days Out from London* aims to provide you with the ideas, inspiration and impetus for an easy, enjoyable and fulfilling day out.

We've tried to include a good mix of places and experiences within the 11 themed sections of the guide, some of which make classic (although not necessarily obvious) day trips (pottering around the antiques shops of Rye; embracing Tudor mania at Hever Castle; hiding in the dunes of Camber Sands), some of which are more quirky (a trip to Hell-Fire Caves; trekking with llamas in the Surrey Hills), some of which are culturally or physically stimulating (sculpture parks; Snape Maltings concert hall; climbing Harrison's Rocks), others of which are escapes of a calming, reviving or grounding nature (day spas; Westonbirt Arboretum; foraging for wild mushrooms). We've also tried to offer some alternative slants on well-trodden destinations (Cambridge from a cultural angle; Bath from a roof-top pool), as well as seasonal tips on making the most of good weather (or hiding from bad) and on annual festivals, or activities to do in the school holidays. What's more, we've provided information on the best eating and shopping options outside the capital.

One thing all the days out listed here have in common is that they are all within two hours' reach of London and largely hassle-free; most are reachable by train and the majority don't have to be planned in advance.

So, whether you're in the mood for browsing out-of-town shops, enjoying a pub lunch in the country, seeing some world-class art, or an animal safari with the kids, this guide will provide the ideas and direction to realise that great day out from London.

Towns & Cities

Brighton 13

FIVE One-off shops 19

Oxford 20

Bristol 25

Woodbridge 31

Rye 33

Lewes 35

FIVE Shopping extravaganzas 41

FIVE Village customs 43

Brighton

Louche Brighton mixes classic seaside with a vibrant shopping scene.

With its bracing sea air and whiff of scandal, Brighton has been a favoured day-trip for Londoners ever since the 19th century, when the pleasure-loving Prince Regent decamped here to escape his father's watchful eye. Its Regency heyday left a rich legacy of stately seafront terraces and squares to rival those of Bath, but Brighton's soul leans irresistibly towards the bohemian; far more to its taste are the elaborate domes and minarets of the Royal Pavilion (01273 290900, www.royalpavilion.org.uk) – the Prince's ornate, outlandish country farmhouse-turned-mock-Mughal palace.

This is a city that shuns the mainstream and embraces counterculture, with an ebullient gay scene and a packed arts calendar, culminating in the three-week arts extravaganza of the Brighton Festival (01273 709709, www.brightonfestival.org). It's also home to a laid-back but fiercely independent shopping scene, encompassing flea markets, art galleries, jewellery shops, delis and idiosyncratic boutiques – perfect for a leisurely day of browsing and café-hopping, at a pace unthinkable on Oxford Street. Which means you'll be in exactly the right frame of mind to sample some of the city's excellent bars and restaurants before heading back to London.

Wherever your wanderings in Brighton take you, all roads lead irresistibly down to the sea, and its famous pebbly beach. The bare frame of the ruined West Pier is a lonely, starkly beautiful local landmark, while brash, brassy Brighton Pier is a riotous welter of flashing fairground rides, candyfloss kiosks and hook-a-duck booths, where kids shriek on the dodgems, coins teeter on the two-penny falls and Elvis croons softly in the background.

At dusk, linger at the seafront to watch flocks of starlings swarm around the pier, then head for dinner or cocktails before boarding the train back to London – with one last look over the sea for romantics, or a quick paddle for the brave.

NORTH LAINE

Head left out of the station and you're plunged into North Laine's narrow streets – once teeming with slums and slaughterhouses, but now Brighton's altrnative heart. A colourful pick-and-mix of bijou boutiques, independent record shops, bookshops and cafés, it's the perfect place to get acquainted with the local counterculture, with an abundance of cafés offering a ringside view of the action. Three main shopping streets thread through its heart: Sydney Street, Kensington Gardens and Gardner Street – though forays into the terrace-lined backstreets can reap rich rewards.

Brightonians love a bric-a-brac fix, and tat and treasures abound in the famous Snooper's Paradise (*see p14*). Squeeze through the turnstile

Royal Pavilion

The Lanes

to browse its myriad stalls, crammed with everything from bags of buttons and Bakelite telephones to stylish 1960s lamps. Hidden away on a side street, North Laine Antique & Flea Market (5A Upper Gardner Street, 01273 600894) also offers rich pickings, whether you're in search of ceramics, costume jewellery or a statement chandelier. For vintage clothes, head for Sydney Street's To Be Worn Again (No.24A, 01273 680296) or the über-stylish Hope & Harlequin (*see right*).

If the allure of vintage pales, Abode (*see below*) stocks covetable contemporary homeware, while Tribeca (*see opposite*) has a beautifully edited selection of womenswear labels. For a more quintessential Brighton look, drop by Vegetarian Shoes (12 Gardner Street, 01273 685685, www.vegetarian-shoes.co.uk) or try a kitsch Mexican skull-print frock for size at Get Cutie (33 Kensington Gardens, 01273 687768, www.getcutie.co.uk). In a city so synonymous with dirty weekends, it also seems only right to drop by chic sex toy boutique Tickled (*see right*).

Café society is equally varied. Feast on creamy frozen yoghurt at Lick (*see opposite*) or ice-cream floats and syrup-drenched pancakes at the 1950s-style Off Beat Coffee Bar (37 Sydney Street, 01273 604206); for more substantial fare, fill up on hearty veggie cooking at Idyea (*see opposite*) or sample one of Pokeno's handsome pies (52 Gardner Street, 01273 684921).

Shopping

Abode
32 Kensington Gardens, BN1 4AL (01273 621116, www.abodeliving.co.uk).

Open 10.30am-5.30pm Mon-Fri; 10.30am-6pm Sat; 11.30am-4.30pm Sun.
Quirky wall stickers, elegant all-white ceramics and jewel-hued dessert bowls are among the covetable pieces at this beautiful homeware boutique. Look out too for local artist Rachel Eardley's idiosyncratic prints of Brighton, and the sumptuous scented candles (tomato and blackcurrant is glorious).

Hope & Harlequin
31 Sydney Street, BN1 4EP (01273 675222, www.hopeandharlequin.com). Open 10.30am-6pm Mon-Sat; noon-5pm Sun.
Specialising in top-quality vintage and in-depth style advice, Louise Hill's tiny boutique oozes old-school glamour: think cashmere jumpers, sweet 1950s lace frocks and lovely swing coats.

Snooper's Paradise
7-8 Kensington Gardens, BN1 4AL (01273 602558). Open 10am-6pm Mon-Sat; 11am-4pm Sun.
Paradise indeed: lose an afternoon amid Snooper's joyous jumble of retro coffee tables, royal memorabilia mugs, tarnished trumpets and 1950s 'Dainty but Daring' smutty slides, then emerge blinking into the light.

Tickled
59 Ship Street, BN1 1AE (01273 777822, www.tickledonline.co.uk). Open 10.30am-6pm Mon-Sat; noon-5pm Sun.
This female-friendly boutique sells cuffs, whips and sex toys of every description (and dimension). The saucier stock resides downstairs – which is off-limits to unaccompanied gents.

Tribeca
21 Bond Street, BN1 1RD (01273 673755).
Open 10am-6pm Mon-Sat; noon-5pm Sun.
Beautifully cut, understated pieces from
the likes of Isabel Marant, Vanessa Bruno,
Erotokritos and BiLaLi fill the rails – along
with iconic Spring Court sneakers and a
handful of hip jeans brands (Sass & Bide,
Acme and Earnest Sewn).

Eating & Drinking

Bill's Produce Store
100 North Road, BN1 1YE (01273 692894,
www.billsproducestore.co.uk). Open 8am-10pm
Mon-Sat; 9.30am-4pm Sun.
Buzzing with conversation and the convivial
clatter of knives and forks, Bill's serves huge
portions of home-cooked comfort food (cheddar
buck rarebit, eggs benedict, steak sarnies) amid
shelves of gleaming olive oil and chutneys and
piled-high organic produce.

Iydea
17 Kensington Gardens, BN1 4AL
(01273 667992, www.iydea.co.uk). Open
9.30am-5.30pm Mon-Fri; 9am-5.30pm Sat;
10am-5.30pm Sun.
This reasonably priced canteen-style café does
a roaring trade: once you've picked your main
course (chilli bean enchilada, say, or spinach
and mushroom lasagne), your plate is stacked
with seasonal salads and veg.

Lick
19 Gardner Street, BN1 1UP (mobile 07976
314707, www.lickbrighton.com). Open Summer
10am-10pm daily. Winter 11am-6pm daily.

Choose between a scoop or shake made from
creamy frozen yoghurt or ice-cream, then add
your toppings of choice – whether it be organic
fruit and honey or honeycomb and Oreo cookies.

THE LANES, WESTERN ROAD & THE SEAFRONT
Dividing North Laine and the Lanes,
North Street leads to Western Road – an
unprepossessing stretch where the major chains,
banished elsewhere in Brighton, congregate.
Still, two gems are worth noting for later in
the day: relaxed tapas joint Pinxto People (*see*
p16) and, for those taking a late train back to
London, cocktail bar Koba (*see p17*).

South of North Street lies the tangle of the
Lanes – Brighton's labyrinthine jewellery
quarter. As you'll invariably get lost anyway,
the wisest approach is to wander by the
glittering window displays with no fixed plan,
imagining the stories behind antique emerald-
set engagement rings and exquisite, diamond-
studded bracelets. On Meeting House Lane,
stop for oysters and champagne at Riddle &
Finns (No.12, 01273 323008, www.riddleand
finns.co.uk), a white-tiled temple to crustacea,
molluscs and sparklingly fresh seafood.

There's beautiful contemporary jewellery
to be oohed and aahed over at Goodman
& Morris (48 Market Street, 01273 738784,
www.goodmanmorris.com) and Rina Tairo
(13 Prince Albert Street, 01273 774288,
www.rinatairo.com), whose eponymous designer
conjures up gossamer-thin meshes of gold and
silver, dotted with precious stones. On Duke
Street, Jewel Thief (*see p16*) is one of the newest
and nicest additions to Brighton's jewellery
scene – and conveniently close to two heavenly

chocolate shops, Montezuma's (*see below*) and Choccywoccydoodah (No.24, 01273 329462, www.choccywoccydoodah.com).

In the South Lanes, East Street offers a cluster of mainstream names (LK Bennett, Cath Kidston, French Connection et al) and renowned vegetarian restaurant Terre à Terre (No.71, 01273 729051, www.terreaterre. co.uk) – although nearby Food for Friends (*see below*) is a worthy (and less pricey) alternative. Down on the seafront proper, under the Arches, browse the latest exhibition at Castor + Pollux (*see below*) or stroll by the Brighton Smokehouse (no phone) – a shipshape little establishment that's open on winter weekends and daily in summer: to find it, look for the black-painted smokehouse shed outside. Fresh anchovies with a squeeze of lemon, crab sandwiches or hot mackerel rolls make for a perfect picnic on the pebbles.

Shopping

Castor + Pollux
165 King's Road Arches, Lower Promenade, BN1 1NB (01273 773776, www.castorand pollux.co.uk). Open 10am-4.30pm daily.
Small linocuts start at around £36 at this superb little gallery, which showcases printmakers and illustrators – though prices climb for established names such as Rob Ryan. Alongside the changing exhibitions, a brilliant shop sells arty cards, books, jewellery, toys and ceramics.

Fidra
47 Meeting House Lane, BN1 1HB (01273 328348, www.fidra.com). Open 10am-5.30pm daily.
Fidra's Edwardian and Victorian treasures might range from a delicate gold necklace of seed pearl-studded swallows to a showstopping diamond and pearl brooch; heavy Whitby jet pieces are another speciality.

Jewel Thief
26 Dukes Lane, BN1 1BG (01273 771044, www.jewelthiefgallery.com). Open 10am-6pm Mon-Sat; 11am-5pm Sun.
Star turns here include Tina Lilienthal's luscious, resin-cast cherry necklaces (as seen in *Vogue*), Tufi Patah's chunky agate rings and Bena's laser-etched wooden initial brooches – the latter a steal at £20 a pop.

Montezumas
15 Duke Street, BN1 1AH (01273 324979, www.montezumas.co.uk). Open 9.30am-6pm Mon-Sat; 11am-5pm Sun.

Pintxo People

Chocolate purists adore the single-bean organic bars, adventurous types can opt for wasabi truffles or geranium thins, and serious addicts can invest in hefty one-kilo bars; free in-store samples make everyone happy.

Eating & Drinking

Food for Friends
17-18 Prince Albert Street, BN1 1HF (01273 202310, www.foodforfriends.com). Open noon-10pm Mon-Thur, Sun; noon-10.30pm Fri, Sat.
The vibe is laid-back and the globally influenced food excellent at Food for Friends. Share a plentiful meze plate, or take advantage of the express lunch offer – £11.95 for two courses.

Pintxo People
95 Western Road, BN1 2LB (01273 732323, www.pintxopeople.co.uk). Open 10am-1am Mon-Sat.
For casual dining, take your pick of the bite-sized pinxtos (Basque-style mini bruschette) and excellent tapas in the airy café, accompanied by a glass of sherry. Come the evening, head upstairs to the restaurant and glamorous cocktail bar, with impeccable renditions of all the classics and taster-sized 'canapé cocktails' to assist the indecisive.

Koba
135 Western Road, BN1 2LA (01273 720059, www.kobauk.com). Open 5pm-1am daily.
Hidden in the unlikeliest of locations, above an off-licence on Western Road, Koba is a chic cocktail-hour hangout with no fewer than ten different martinis on its menu. Expect traditional-with-a-twist offerings, including a fine sloe gin mojito.

KEMP TOWN
East of the Old Steine, Brighton's gay area is home to an enticing jumble of grand Regency crescents, antique shops and cosy pubs – as well as a naturist beach, discreetly shielded behind the shingle. Bar a couple of decent delis, the early stretch of its main drag, St James's Street, seems less than promising, with mobile phone shops, newsagents and a Starbucks. Do as any self-respecting Brightonian would do and cross the road to Red Roaster *(see right)* – one of the city's many independent coffee shops, and considered by some to be its finest. If it's time for afternoon tea, take a left on to George Street to find the irrepressibly camp Tea Cosy *(see right)*, complete with antique china and kitsch clutter of royal memorabilia.

The best shopping is along Upper St James's Street, where Brighton Flea Market's neon sign is a beacon for bargain-hunters. Antique and vintage shops cluster along the street: for furniture, lighting and ceramics, try In Retrospect (No.37, 01273 609374) or Metrodeco (No.38, mobile 07878 508719, www.metro-deco.com), where Kylie paid a visit when she was in town. For vintage clothes, check out the charming 30A *(see right)*. Here too are the diamanté collars of Doggie Fashion (No.44, 01273 695631), devoted to dog grooming and canine couture. A little further on, the street turns into St George's Road; at No.17, Andrew Fionda (mobile 07875 852926) is a polished vintage boutique. Run by one half of design duo Pearce Fionda, its stock is expensive but exquisite – with the odd bargain for keen-eyed collectors, and some beautiful bridal pieces.

By now you'll probably be in need of a rest: head back to the murky, much-loved Hand in Hand pub for a restorative pint of its own-brewed ale (33 Upper St James's Street, 01273 602521), or sink into a sofa at the friendly No Name café and bar *(see right)*. Locals also swear by the pick-me-up properties of a Rocky Six cocktail at Gin Gin (74 St James's Street, 01273 671119) – a strangely moreish concoction involving rocket, raspberries, black pepper, champagne and Tuaca liqueur.

Shopping

30A
30A Upper St James's Street, BN2 1JN (01273 681384). Open 11am-5.30pm Thur-Sat.
Brimming with treasures, Margaret Callagan's tiny vintage emporium is a favourite with fashion designers in search of inspiration. Fur hats perch precariously on drawers overflowing with dainty, paper-thin leather gloves, belts and doilies, while the rails are crammed with studded leather jackets, antique lace slips and floral 1940s utility frocks.

Brighton Flea Market
31A Upper St James's Street, BN2 1JN (01273 624006, www.flea-markets.co.uk). Open 10am-5pm Mon-Fri; 10.30am-5pm Sat, Sun.
There are some choice pieces to be found in this two-storey bric-a-brac emporium, ranging from resplendent carved bedsteads to pouty Brigitte Bardot film posters.

Eating & Drinking

No Name
82 St James's Street, BN2 1PA (01273 693216). Open 11am-11pm Mon-Thur, Sun; 11am-midnight Fri, Sat.
Chandeliers cast a warm glow over this welcoming café-restaurant, whose enormous windows overlook St James's Street. Splendid teas (from earl grey or peppermint to popcorn tea or rooibos crème caramel) are served in proper pots, and there's an inexpensive lunch menu.

Red Roaster
1D St James's Street, BN2 1RE (01273 686668, www.redroaster.co.uk). Open 7am-7pm Mon-Fri; 8am-7pm Sat; 9am-6.30pm Sun.
Red Roaster's loyal coterie of fans swear by its freshly roasted coffee and hot chocolate – notable for its deliciously gloopy, custard-like consistency.

Tea Cosy
3 George Street, BN2 1RH (no phone, www.theteacosy.co.uk). Open 11am-6pm Wed-Sun.
Tongue-in-cheek etiquette (no clanking of tea spoons or biscuit-dunking) applies at this diminutive tearoom, whose decor and menu are devoted to the royal family: think commemorative china and tea towels on the walls, and Charles & Camilla Elevenses or Princess Margaret and Diana Memorial Teas on the menu.

Discover that there is life outside London.

Advance fares from just **£9** one way. Boldly go to Bath, Bournemouth or the New Forest.

Call **0845 6000 650** or visit **southwesttrains.co.uk**

FIVE One-off shops

Kensington Rocking Horse Company
Reputed to be one of the best makers of rocking horses in the world; each horse is hand-carved to individual requirements and becomes an instant family heirloom. Opt for a delicate dapple grey on a swing, a rich mahogany steed with a deep rocker, or invest in a restored antique. And don't let the 'Business Centre' address put you off; the shop is set in converted farm buildings in rural Sussex, with grazing ponies and stables next door and rolling hills in the background. So if making a choice from the dozens on display proves challenging, you can always pop outside for a glimpse at the real things and find inspiration there.
Granary Rural Business Centre, Broad Farm, Hellingly, East Sussex BN27 4DU (08704 464687, www.kensington-rocking-horses. co.uk). Open by appointment.

Lincoln Whisky Shop
Close to the glorious cathedral in Lincoln (just under two hours from King's Cross), this shop has been specialising in whisky – and there are more than 1,000 varieties in stock – for the last 20 years. In addition to the 181 varieties of single malt and exotic blends from Japan and New Zealand is a huge range of other tipples, including Madeira, marsala and mead. Prices range from the affordable (there are 400 miniatures in stock) to the astronomical – a bottle of Macallan 1946 will set you back £3,000. Combine a visit with a wander round the historic city.
87 Bailgate, Lincoln, Lincolnshire LN1 3AR (01522 537834, www.lincolnwhisky shop.co.uk). Open 10am-5pm Mon-Sat.

The Model Shop
This little gem in Northampton (an hour by train from Euston) opened 72 years ago, before anyone had even flown a Lancaster bomber, let alone spent their pocket money on an Airfix model of one. It's still going strong, with a huge selection of radio controlled boats, aircraft and cars, as well as hardcore scratch-built model materials. And it's not all old boys' toys either; here you'll find a plastic kit featuring Wallace and Gromit with a bike, sidecar and plane, complete with all the paints you'll need, for just under £20, or an Airfix Dr Who set for less than £25 (add three AAA batteries to light up the Tardis).
230 Wellingborough Road, Northampton, Northamptonshire NN1 4EJ (01604 631227, www.modelshop-northants.com). Open 9am-5.30pm Mon-Sat.

Rennie's Seaside Modern
The cheerfully painted Edwardian shop exterior in aquamarine and orange gives a hint of the individuality of the stock, but it's still a surprise to walk in to find yourself surrounded by a range of 20th-century objects that spans everything from iconic Olympics posters to textiles, glass and furniture. So far, so Islington, but Rennie's strength lies in its careful sourcing and selection of ephemera that you'd be very hard-pressed to find outside a seaside town; silly things like pretty plastic masks at 50p a pop right through to 1940s sweetheart brooches. Owners Paul and Karen Rennie (who both worked in the auction rooms of Bonhams and Sotheby's before setting up shop here) obviously adore their work, their shop and their stock, and so will you.
47 The Old High Street, Folkestone, Kent CT20 1RN (01303 242427, www.rennart.co.uk). Open 11am-5.30pm Thur-Sun; by appointment Mon-Wed.

Southcoast Exotics
Forget bunnies and budgies, this is truly a pet shop for the brave, with lizards, snakes and chelonia (turtles to you) housed in over 100 vivariums. Staff are passionate and experienced – each one owns a menagerie of creepy crawlies themselves. There are stunning animals you're likely never to have seen before and will probably hope to never see again – the inky black and orange Halloween crab, for example. But spend enough time browsing and you might fall in love with a cuddly Egyptian Long-ear hedgehog, or even begin to consider taking a gorgeous gecko home – just don't call it Gordon.
109 London Road, Cowplain, Waterlooville, Portsmouth, Hampshire PO8 8XJ (023 9226 9362, www.southcoastexotics.com). Open 10am-5.30pm Mon-Thur; 10.30am-6pm Fri; 10am-4pm Sun.

Oxford

Join bookish dons and bright young things beneath the famous spires.

Everyone has their own idea and image of Oxford, and whether yours is drenched in sepia-hued Morse nostalgia, the Gothic creepiness of Harry Potter or the eccentric whimsy of Lewis Carroll, you won't be disappointed: this city of dreaming spires and extravagant architecture has been much mythologised for a reason. It also has a deceptive villagey feel. Yet to spend a day in the centre staring slack-jawed at its architectural wonders would only be skimming the surface of the myriad delights Oxford has to offer. To really get under the skin of this quintessentially English city you need to venture further.

Unlike other university towns, the town vs gown feud is redundant in Oxford. The university has won: it's the focal point for the whole city, and a nose around the beautiful college buildings should top any list of things to do here.

There are heaps of Oxford tours you can sign up to. Official tours are worth doing because they can often give you access to colleges otherwise closed to the public. Given the sheer quantity, some pre-visit research could be invaluable. A good starting point is the website www.visitoxford.org, with details of all official walks and tours, all bookable online. If these seem a little formal, then undergraduates occasionally put on more authentic, impromptu tours around the colleges. (A weekly *Brideshead Revisited* tour was taking place in 2008, led by a fey-looking guide with a teddy bear tucked under his arm.)

An unstructured wander is equally rewarding. Most of the university buildings lie at the southeastern end of Broad Street. Here you'll find the striking circular Radcliffe Camera building, the centrepiece of Radcliffe Square. Adjacent to it is the grand Bodleian Library (the 'Bod', if you're pretending to be a scholar), a vast Gothic building that houses more than eight million items and is connected underground to the Radcliffe by a network of tunnels and scurrying librarians. Both buildings are unfortunately off-limits to civilians, but you can have a nosy around the walled gardens and intricate architecture of the Schools Quadrangle and the tower that forms the main entrance to the library, the Tower of the Five Orders.

If you exit this courtyard to the right you come across the Venetian Bridge of Sighs, which joins two parts of Hertford College. Other must-see colleges are the 14th-century Christ Church College, the largest of the lot, with magnificent cloisters, a cathedral and beautiful memorial gardens that slope down to the river. Magdalen, off the high street, has a bewitching Gothic chapel, menacing gargoyle and stonework and vast grounds that include a rose garden and deer park. And the polychrome William Butterfield design of Keble College is worth seeking out not just for the striking architecture but also for an exploration of the chapel that contains William Holman Hunt's masterpiece *Light of the World*.

All 35 university colleges are open to visitors at varying times – and they all have their own distinctive characters and illustrious alumni, so stake out the college that appeals to you and book in advance. And if you fancy filling your head with more than just sights, don your trendiest tortoiseshell glasses and pretend to be an undergraduate yourself by attending one of the many open lectures at colleges around Oxford. (Check www.dailyinfo.co.uk for speakers and dates.)

The colleges empty of students and fill up with American tourists bussed in from the capital during the holidays, so if you want to avoid feeling like an extra in *National Lampoon's Vacation*, we recommend you hire a bike from one of the many hire shops and visit some of the city's less obvious attractions.

If you head south from the centre you'll hit Cowley Road – the 'real' Oxford and a bohemian's paradise, crammed full of vintage clothes shops, alfresco cafés, quirky delis, second-hand bike shops and street murals. There are some great cheap places to eat here – try the vibrant Café Coco (No. 23 Cowley Road, 01865 200232, www.cafe-coco.co.uk).

If it's a sunny day, there's no better way to spend it than picnicking, people-watching and pond-dipping in one of Oxford's parks and gardens. Christ Church Meadow borders the college and the River Isis, where college rowing

races are held. But easily the best spot to head for is Port Meadow on the outskirts of the town. Cycle east down the high street and north up St Giles, stopping off for an exquisite ice-cream at the cow-themed George & Davis' Ice Cream Café on Little Clarendon Street (No. 55, 01865 516652, www.gdcafe.com). Or stock up on some provisions from the delicious Greek deli Manos (105 Walton Street, 01865 311782).

Port Meadow lies at the bottom of this road, and is a vast expanse of untamed fields and manicured lawns bordered by the Thames. Several perfect waterside pubs beckon you in; the best is undoubtedly the Trout Inn at Wolvercote (195 Godstow Road, 01865 510930, www.thetroutoxford.co.uk). Despite having a generic-looking chain pub interior it has a fantastic beer garden with decking, peacocks and an unrivalled view of the Oxford spires in the near distance.

If messing about on the river is more your style, then hiring a punt and spending an afternoon drifting along the River Cherwell is a relaxing, if pricey, pursuit. For maximum fun and privacy we recommend commandeering one for yourself rather than going on a chauffeured excursion. Oxford Punting (Magdalen Bridge Boat House, Magdalen Bridge, 01865 202643, www.oxfordpunting.co.uk) offers both options, with the DIY version costing £14 an hour.

Museums can feel a bit redundant when you're surrounded by living history, yet unsurprisingly Oxford is crammed with them. You won't be able to visit many of them on a day-trip, but try to take in Modern Art Oxford (30 Pembroke Street, 01865 722733, www.modernartoxford. org.uk), which shows cutting-edge exhibitions from leftfield artists like Stella Vine, Mike Nelson and conceptual duo Janet Cardiff and George Bures Miller. The Pitt Rivers Museum (see p23) also merits a visit; part curiosity shop, part museum, it's exactly the sort of English oddity that prospers in Oxford.

From ground level, Oxford's spires are magnificent enough, but clamber up the 99 steps of the Carfax Tower (at the junction of St Aldgate's, Cornmarket Street and Queen Street, 01865 792653) and you'll discover a totally different view of the striking skyline and surrounding countryside. At any time of the year, the contrast between the spectacular man-made architecture and the bucolic scenery beyond it is worth seeing, but on a winter's day it can be up there with some of the loveliest sights in the country.

Winter is the season of both excessive consumption and spiritual reflection, and Oxford caters for both. With a biting chill in the air, twinkling Christmas lights and the waft of mulled wine, the city offers a more festive

Christmas shopping experience than anything the capital could offer, especially in the Covered Market off Cornmarket Street.

The high street has all the generic chain stores you could want to splurge in, but wander away from it towards Little Clarendon Street in the gentrified Jericho part of town and you'll find some fantastic independent shops, which are great for more unusual gifts. For womenswear, Lacy's (see p24) is well worth a look, as is Lizzie James and its separate occasions boutique Posh Frocks (Nos. 31 & 36, 01865 512936, www. lizziejames.com), specialising in slinky eveningwear by continental designers. At the end of the road, Sylvester (Nos. 22-24, 01865 847285, www.sylvesteroxford.com) is an antiquarian IKEA, stocking imaginative and inexpensive household furnishings – from wrought-iron book stands to fabulous Poole pottery. Make time to stop for lunch at one of the myriad resturants or wine bars on nearby Walton Street.

As you'd expect from a centre of academia, Oxford has some well-stocked second-hand bookshops, packed with treasures. Oxfam Bookstore (56 St Giles, 01865 310145), Arcadia (4 St Michael's Street, 01865 241757) and the gigantic branch of Blackwell's (48-51 Broad Street, 01865 792792, www.blackwell.co.uk) are all worth a gander; the latter's undergound Norrington Room stocks 160,000 volumes on over three miles of shelving, gaining it a place in the *Guinness Book of Records* for the world's largest display of books for sale in one room.

If you're on a serious shopping mission, then make sure you check out nearby Bicester Village (see p24), a mecca to designer consumerism at heavily discounted prices.

Diary Dates

FESTIVALS

Oxford Literary Festival
Various venues (01865 276152, www. sundaytimes-oxfordliteraryfestival.co.uk). Admission varies. Mar/Apr.
This annual book fest is now in its 13th year and attracts plenty of literary big hitters – last year Richard Dawkins, Philip Pullman and Hanif Kureishi gave lectures. A great place to feed your brain with like-minded literary souls.

May Day Celebration
Magdalen College, OX1 4AU (www.magd.ox.ac.uk). 6am 1 May
You'll need to get here bright and early for this one, but the Magdalen College Choir serenading the city from the Magdalen Tower while a sea of inebriated students – some 20,000 of them – toast the start of a new season is a magical historical tradition to take part in.

The Great Story Picnic Season
The University of Oxford Botanic Garden, Rose Lane, OX1 4AZ (01865 286690, www. botanic-garden.ox.ac.uk). Admission £3 adult, £2.50 reductions, free children. June.
This summer series of events brings storytelling sessions and musical performances to Oxford's leafy, lovely Botanic Garden, founded in 1621. Bring a picnic hamper and make a day of it.

Cowley Road Carnival
Cowley Road, OX4 (www.cowleyroadcarnival.co.uk). Early July.
It's not on the scale of the Notting Hill Carnival, but with some 25,000 visitors, three performance stages, sound stages, kids' activities and a parade, the Cowley Road Carnival can be just as much – if not more – fun than the sometimes overwhelming London version.

Oxford Shakespeare Company
Wadham College, Parks Road, OX1 3PN (0870 609 2231, www.oxfordshakespeare company.co.uk). Admission varies. Performances July, Aug.
Quality acting, thrilling material and a dramatic outdoor setting make this annual series of Shakespeare plays a winner.

Christmas at Christ Church
Christ Church, OX1 1DP (01865 276150, www.chch.ox.ac.uk). Various prices. Mid Nov onwards.
You can hear the Christ Church choir at any weekly evensong (Mon-Sat, 6pm), but from mid November until Christmas, activities are ramped up with a host of concerts and events. Special celebrity and religious guests give readings, while the cathedral choir performs a selection of seasonal hymns.

Eating & Drinking

Freud's
119 Walton Street, OX2 6AH (01865 311171).
Open 10.30am-11pm Mon-Thur, Sun; 10.30am-2am Fri, Sat.
This converted church makes an atmospheric drinking venue, with light streaming in through the stained-glass windows. It's also a centrepiece for the local community; gigs and art exhibitions are often held in its expansive interior, and the terrace is great for sipping a cocktail or cold beer in the summer. So we'll forgive the slightly shabby furnishings, unkempt toilets and average bar food.

Hi-Lo (Jamaican Eating House)
68-70 Cowley Road, OX4 1JB (01865 725984, www.hilojamaicaneatinghouse.co.uk). Open 10am-5pm, 7pm-2.30am daily.
This Caribbean restaurant is an unlikely Oxford institution, but the food is as good as anything you'd get in west or south London. The Jamaican proprietor is brilliantly acerbic, and you may have to wait for your order, but the place is full of charisma (you might well find yourself drinking cheap rum punch into the wee hours).

Luna Caprese
4 North Parade, OX2 6LX (01865 554812). Open noon-2pm, 6-10.30pm daily.
One of Oxford's best-kept secrets, Luna Caprese is busy every night of the week. The menu is no-nonsense, rustic Italian, with generous portions, tables piled with garlic bruschette and breadsticks and delicious desserts (try the 'flamed at the table' crème brûlée or indulgent special cassata Luna Caprese).

Old Bookbinders Ale House
17-18 Victor Street, OX2 6BT (01865 553549, www.oldbookbinders.co.uk). Open 5pm-midnight Mon-Thur; noon-midnight Fri, Sat; noon-11pm Sun.
This pub oozes authentic old-school charm, from the retro shabby decor to the brass ale pumps. It's refreshingly free from quaffing toffs, perhaps due to the extensive selection of Greene King and guest ales and the no-nonsense bar food. Most just tuck into the free barrel of monkey nuts, and chuck the shells on the floor. Quirky touches include double-handled doors that provide drunken amusement at closing time.

Peppers
84 Walton Street, OX2 6EA (01865 511592). Open noon-2pm, 5-11pm Mon-Fri, Sun; noon-2pm, 5pm-midnight Sat.
After a hiatus during which meat-starved devotees were forced back to kebab vans, Peppers has reopened. Thankfully, it still has the faded signage, idiosyncratic opening hours and the best burgers in town.

Shopping & Attractions

Bead Games Shop
40 Cowley Road, OX4 1HZ (01865 251620). Open 11am-6.30pm Mon-Sat; noon-5pm occasional Sun.
Run by local heroine Erika, this quirky shop stocks everything from fancy-dress staples to pashminas and joss sticks. Best of all are the old-school penny sweets, measured out and dispensed in little paper bags.

Bicester Village
50 Pingle Drive (off A41), Bicester, OX26 6WD (01865 323200, www.bicestervillage.com). Open 10am-6pm Mon-Wed, Sun; 10am-7pm Thur-Sat.
This slightly chintzy discount retail centre is a 20-minute drive to the north of the city. Ignore the twee surroundings and get stuck into the huge discounts at designer outlets from the likes of Ralph Lauren, Burberry, Donna Karan and Nicole Farhi. You'll also find high-street staples such as French Connection, Jigsaw, Diesel and the White Company.

Lacys
29 Little Clarendon Street, OX1 2HU (01865 552094). Open 10am-5.30pm Mon-Sat.
An upmarket boutique that stocks imaginative designer womenswear from labels as diverse as Joseph and Save the Queen.

Pitt Rivers Museum
South Parks Road, OX1 3PP (01865 270927, www.prm.ox.ac.uk). Open Phone for details.
Pitts Rivers is less museum, more what you'd imagine Indiana Jones's abode to look like: it's dimly lit and crammed full of weird colonial artefacts haphazardly balanced on teak dressers or secreted in butterfly drawers. The collection was bequeathed to Oxford in 1884 by General Pitt Rivers and is 'organised' typologically; there are Tahitian costumes next to Inuit clothing and trepanned skulls. An antidote to the generic modern museum, the place was undergoing a refurbishment as this guide went to press.

Reign
136 Cowley Road, OX4 1JJ (01865 250004). Open 11am-6.30pm Mon-Sat; noon-5pm Sun.
Oxford's best vintage shop stocks an enviable range of frocks and one-off jackets.

Bristol

Ship shape.

A clash of chocolate-box Georgian architecture, wide skies and urban grit, Bristol is Bath's larger, hipper and more cosmopolitan cousin – an extra ten minutes by train (from Paddington), but worlds apart where it counts.

In Bristol's busy town centre you'll find maritime history – the floating harbour, SS *Great Britain* (www.ssgreatbritain.org) – and modern excess – Cabot Circus's shiny new shopping centre, complete with miniature Harvey Nichols (www.harvey nichols.com). And you've definitely come to the right place if you're after quality museums (Explore, www.at-bristol.org.uk), waterside alfresco dining and an urban buzz. To get a feel for what really makes this city tick, though, you'll need to head a mile or so out of the centre to the neighbourhoods Bristolians know, love and love to hate.

Whether you make a beeline for swanky Clifton Village in the north-west of Bristol or head east to bohemian Montpelier and grungey Stokes Croft (and we suggest you visit both sides of the city), you'll find one fact remains – to get under Bristol's skin, you need to slow down. So stash that map in your back pocket, pull up a stool at the nearest bar and soak up the relaxed, creative vibe that makes Bristol a city where festival food stalls become hip restaurants and graffiti morphs into high-end art. This is a city of inventors, eco-warriors, foodies, artists and laid-back anarchists. It's a city where diversity is celebrated and new ideas grow and evolve (in their own good time). If you start the day with the best of intentions but lose half of it to a pub with good cider somewhere along the line, you've got the picture. And if it sounds easy, it's meant to – you're on Bristol time now.

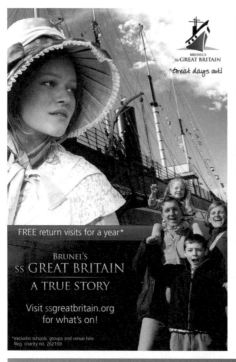

Classy, genteel and ever-so-slightly snooty, posh Clifton Village makes a picture-perfect escape from the daily grind. Before you get stuck into the bijou boutiques and delis, why not embrace Bristol's fondness for all things airborne (the International Balloon Fiesta, *see below*, is held here each year and Filton is the home of Airbus) by picking up a kite at the Kitestore (*see p30*) on Cotham Hill and heading to Clifton and Durdham Downs? This expansive green space (beside the Brunel Suspension Bridge and the dramatic chasm of the Avon Gorge) has a fabulously bucolic feel. It's ideal for perfecting a few stunts or just blasting away cobwebs with a bracing stroll.

Just downhill from here, Clifton Village itself is a fine place to lose a few hours browsing selections of artisan cheese (Chandos Deli), vintage furniture and collectibles (Focus on the Past) and everything from music to Mexicana in the appealingly twee Clifton Arcade (for all listings, *see p30*).

For a break from spending, Britain's longest Georgian crescent (the elegant Royal York Crescent) makes for a pleasant amble (wistful gazes into estate agents' windows afterwards are optional). You'll also find plenty of lovely local pubs, bars and cafés to sink into. For a leisurely afternoon's drinking and tremendous views head for the White Lion (*see p30*) at the Avon Gorge Hotel, Sunday lunches are spot on at both the Albion and Clifton Sausage (for both, *see p29*), and the Primrose Café (*see p30*) is great for brunch. Wherever your wanderings take you, make sure you don't leave Clifton without sampling cider so potent it has to be

Diary Dates

MARKETS

Bristol Farmers' Market
Corn Street, BS1 1JQ. Open 9.30am-2.30pm Wed.
No faddish new arrival, this weekly market has been here for decades, selling locally sourced fish, meat, artisanal cheese and organic produce.

Slow Food Market
Corn Street, BS1 1JQ (www.slowfood bristol.org). Open 10am-3pm 1st Sun of mth.
The first regular Slow Food market in the world has many stalls of meat, fish and veg, as well as more specialist items such as tea, chocolate and wheat-free cereal.

FESTIVALS

Slapstick Silent Comedy Festival
www.slapstick.org.uk. Jan.
In January each year, the Watershed, Arnolfini and even the Old Vic host comedians and silent movies with live accompaniment.

Love Food
www.lovefoodfestival.com. Mar.
An easy sell in this city: Love Food aims to get kids and their grown-ups out into the springtime countryside to watch and get involved in the production of food.

Bristol International Balloon Fiesta
www.bristolfiesta.co.uk. Aug.
You might not get to travel in one of the extraordinarily shaped hot-air balloons, but watching them fire up and take off at events like the Night Glow is a real summer treat. Weather permitting, there are 6am and 6pm launches throughout the festival.

Soil Association Organic Food Festival
www.soilassociation.org/festival. Sept.
The opening event for September's Organic Fortnight, this weekend festival on the Harbourside brings wellies, fine scoffing opportunities and cooking demonstrations, kids' activities and music together under the aegis of the Bristol-based farm certification body.

Bristol International Kite Festival
www.kite-festival.org.uk. Sept.
Another weekend of aerial antics: you can never have imagined how many different shapes, colours and sizes of kites there are. Come here for delicate artistic flyers and gut-wringing kite-riding stunts alike.

Bristol Festival
www.thebristolfestival.org. Sept.
This volunteer-run, city-centre festival puts local bands, DJs, actors, circus performers, food and booze in the same space for a weekend in mid September.

sold in half measures at the gloriously ramshackle (and locally adored) Cori Tap (Coronation Tap, *see below*).

Head east out of the city centre and the landscape couldn't be more different to the lofty green spaces of Clifton. The busy thoroughfare of Stokes Croft and bohemian neighbourhood of Montpelier have a buzzy – if rather grimy – appeal. Local group the People's Republic of Stokes Croft has declared the area 'Bristol's Cultural Quarter' and campaigns to encourage sustainable development and improvement (primarily through street art) in the area – it's always worth checking out the latest happenings at PRSC's gallery space (37 Jamaica Street, www.prsc.org.uk).

As Stokes Croft morphs into Cheltenham and then Gloucester Road, you'll find tiny but lovely gallery Friend & Co (set up by Tom Friend and Portishead's Geoff Barrow; *see p30*) showcasing the best local graffiti art. The latest venture from Guerrilla Galleries, which puts on regular pop-up shows, is always worth a look; check the website www.guerrillagalleries.com for the latest location.

You really don't need to step inside four walls to tap into Bristol's creative spirit, though – in these parts, the streets are the canvas. Make sure you clock Banksy's Mild Mild West as you walk through Stokes Croft (it's on a wall on the left as you walk towards the city centre). For some of the best work by female artists make a beeline for Montpelier (specifically the top of York Road, where Richmond Road joins Fairfield Road) to check out bright and bold work by Milk (www.321milk.com).

Eating is another local passion and this area has plenty of foodie appeal. Tuck into hearty fare at Zazu's (*see p30*) or fall in love with Bristol's finest pies at Pieminister (*see below*). Further afield but worth the short trek is child-paradise St Werburgh's City Farm (*see p30*) and its award-winning café. And should you find yourself in the neighbourhood later on in the day, Montpelier landmark the One Stop Thali Café (*see right*) serves tremendous curries. Bell's Diner (*see right*) is a more decadent neighbourhood stalwart and great for a classy dinner. If you've stayed this long – and well you might – join the locals for a pint in the Prince of Wales (*see p30*).

Eating & Drinking

Albion
Boyces Avenue, BS8 4AA (0117 973 3522, www.thealbionclifton.co.uk). Open 5pm-midnight Mon; noon-midnight Tue-Sat; noon-11pm Sun.

Classy and cosy in equal measure (think log fires, real ale, oysters and champagne), the Albion is a fine place to settle into for a hearty lunch (booking recommended, especially for the locally renowned Sunday menu) or afternoon tipple. There's a sunny beer garden out front, a slightly more formal restaurant area upstairs and a quality wine list.

Bell's Diner
1-3 York Road, BS6 5QB (0117 924 0357, www.bellsdiner.com). Open 7-10pm Mon; noon-2pm, 7-9.30pm Tue-Thur; noon-2pm, 7-10pm Fri; 7-10pm Sat.

This unexpectedly swanky neighbourhood restaurant offers decadent tasting menus and a low-key take on molecular gastronomy (think beef carpaccio with beetroot sorbet or coconut mousse with vindaloo ice-cream). The vibe is cosy, hip but undeniably slick.

Clifton Sausage
7-9 Portland Street, BS8 4JA (0117 973 1192, www.cliftonsausage.co.uk). Open 6pm-midnight Mon; noon-midnight Tue-Sun.

A stylish but informal restaurant and bar that's as suited to a boisterous weekend lunch as it is to sophisticated Friday night cocktails. Book for lunch (especially on Sundays) and tuck into top-notch sausage and mash, huge wedges of veggie quiche or crispy pork belly with all the trimmings.

Coronation Tap
8 Sion Place, BS8 4AX (0117 973 9617, www.coritap.co.uk). Open 5.30-11pm Mon-Fri; 7-11pm Sat; 2-11pm Sun.

A homely cider house with a reputation for fantastic live music, good vibes and nights no one can remember in the morning. Head straight for the bar for a Cori Tap Exhibition cider – and don't even think about asking for a pint (it's only served in halves for good reason). A splendid place to lose track of time completely.

One Stop Thali Café
12 York Road, BS6 5QE (0117 942 6687, www.onestopthali.co.uk). Open 6pm-midnight daily.

This fabulous vegetarian joint (check out the queues waiting to get their takeaway tiffin tins filled) started life as a festival food stall but now boasts several branches around town. This one is totally veggie (non-dairy options are available) and serves fantastic thalis with unusual chutneys.

Pieminister
24 Stokes Croft, BS1 3PR (0117 942 9500, www.pieminister.co.uk). Open 11am-8pm Mon-Sat; 10am-5pm Sun.

The ideal sustenance for a chilly wander around Stokes Croft. Pieminister's handmade meat and veggie pies (served with mushy peas, mash and gravy) are so good we doubt anyone's mother could compete. We recommend the chicken of aragon or 'wildshroom' and asparagus options.

Primrose Café
1 Clifton Arcade, Boyces Avenue, BS8 4AA (0117 946 6577, www.primrosecafe.co.uk). Open 9am-5pm Mon; 9am-5pm, 7-11pm Tue-Sat; 9.30am-3pm Sun.
Grab an outdoor seat for a lazy brunch (the eggs benedict is fantastic) and watch Clifton's yummy mummies and health-freaks stroll or jog past. The Primrose is also good for lunch and dinner, when it is transformed from a daytime café into a cosy, classy bistro.

Prince of Wales
5 Gloucester Road, BS7 8AA (0117 924 5552). Open noon-midnight daily.
This low-key and pretension-free boozer serves decent ales, good wine and sizeable portions of pub grub. There's a covered and heated beer garden out back for smokers.

White Lion
Avon Gorge Hotel, Sion Hill, BS8 4LD (0117 973 8955, www.theavongorge.com). Open noon-10pm Mon-Thur; noon-11pm Fri; 11am-11pm Sat, Sun.
It's all about the view and the beer garden here. Head straight outside on a sunny day (there are cosier places to drink in bad weather) and enjoy a breathtaking panorama of the Avon Gorge.

Zazu's
45 Jamaica Street, BS2 8JP (0117 923 2233, www.zazuskitchen.com). Open 8am-5.30pm Mon-Fri; 9am-5.30pm Sat; 9am-4.30pm Sun.
This charming café provides wonderful breakfasts (the unlimited DIY toast for £2.50 is a winner), healthy lunch options (chunky quiches, salads, huge plates of fish pie) and great coffee and cakes. There's free Wi-Fi and friendly service, with the place at once relaxed and refreshingly efficient.

Shopping & Attractions

Chandos Deli
6 Princess Victoria Street, BS8 4BP (0117 974 3275, www.chandosdeli.com). Open 9am-5pm Mon; 9am-7pm Tue-Fri; 9am-5.30pm Sat; 10am-4pm Sun.

Perfect for stocking up on picnic supplies before a stomp round the Downs. Pop in for a sandwich and emerge half an hour later with enough local cheese and olive bread to open your own branch.

Clifton Arcade
Boyces Avenue, BS8 4AA (www.cliftonarcade. co.uk). Open see website for individual shops.
Handy for a spot of browsing after lunch at the Albion. Check out antiques, jewellery, Mexican imports (Otomi), music (Clifton Arcade Music Shop), and cards and art prints (Soma).

Focus on the Past
25 Waterloo Street, BS8 4BT (0117 973 8080, www.focusonthepast.org). Open 9.30am-5.30pm Mon-Fri; 9.30am-6pm Sat; 11am-5pm Sun.
The first thing Londoners will notice here is the prices. On recent visits to this satisfyingly ramshackle vintage and antiques shop we've found bargain bentwood chairs, old cider barrels and farmhouse crockery, an amazing grey metal chandelier for £78 and a stone buddha for £18.

Friend & Co
8 The Promenade, Gloucester Road, BS7 8AL (www.friend-and-co.com). Open 11am-5pm Sat.
There's barely space to swing a magic marker – never mind a spray can – but this miniature gallery (set up by Tom Friend and Portishead's Geoff Barrow) displays some of the finest graffiti art in town. Recent shows have included works by 45RPM, Mr Jago and Horrors frontman Faris Badwan.

Kitestore
39A Cotham Hill, BS6 6JY (0117 974 5010, www.kitestore.co.uk). Open 9.30am-6pm Mon-Sat.
Kitestore stocks a fabulous array of stunt, beginners' and sport kites, with expert advice thrown in for nothing. Recommended entry-level kites include the single-line Super Rainbow Flyer (£6.99) for kids and, for newbie stunt pilots, the HQ Calypso 2 (£12), both ideal for making the most of the breeze on the Downs.

St Werburgh's City Farm & Café
Watercress Road, BS2 9YJ (0117 942 8241). Open café 10am-4pm Mon, Wed-Sun; farm 9am-4pm daily.
St Werburgh's is a bit of a trek from Stokes Croft, but worth the effort if you have kids in tow. The café dishes up huge portions of comforting staples (bangers and mash and the like) and has a great adventure playground outside. The farm itself is home to animals galore and there's even a pub next door.

Woodbridge

Go slow in Suffolk.

An ideal destination for city-dwellers yearning for a gentler pace of life, Woodbridge is a handsome market town offering a winsome mix of harbour views, riverside walks, cafés, shopping and general pottering about. And Sutton Hoo – the Anglo-Saxon burial site run by the National Trust – is just across the river. The town is prettily placed on the River Debden; if you arrive by train from Liverpool Street you're on the harbour side of town, and can immediately embark on a river walk (in either direction), going past working boatyards and into the very English countryside. If sitting down with a coffee and watching the boats go by is more your thing, then there are places to do that too, but do make sure you walk at least as far as the Tide Mill, a striking building and something of a symbol for the town.

Head away from the harbour, up Quay Street, and very soon you're in the centre of Woodbridge. Quay Street has a few shops and restaurants, including the well-thought-of Captain's Table (3 Quay Street, 01394 383145, www.captainstable.co.uk), but the main drag is the Thoroughfare, home to Browsers bookshop and café (*see below*) as well as plenty of idiosyncratic shops and eateries, such as the Georgian Coffeehouse (47A, 01394 387292, www.georgiancoffeehouse.co.uk).

Indeed, one of the joys of mooching around this town is that there are far fewer chain outlets than in many similar sized places. Another plus is that it's almost impossible to get lost – there are lots of attractive little streets off and around the Thoroughfare, but it really is a compact town. In fact, the furthest you need to stray for shopping opportunities is uphill to Market Hill (where the handsome Shire Hall is) and Church Street, where there's a collection of upmarket outlets such as contemporary crafts and vintage homeware shop Julie Phipps (17 Church Street, 01394 387115, www.juliephipps.com), plus the nicely sited Wild Strawberry Café (19A Market Hill, 01394 388881).

Walk a little further if you want to fully appreciate the rich architectural mix of the town: there are some lovely domestic buildings from a number of different eras. Have a look at the 15th-century St Mary (off Market Hill), an impressive church with a rare medieval Catholic Sacrament font and a beautiful graveyard, unusual in that it's lined on two sides by rows of houses.

Rainy day activities are limited: apart from the Tide Mill, there's just the Woodbridge Museum (5A Market Hill, 01394 380502) and the Suffolk Horse Museum (Shire Hall, Market Hill, 01394 380643), devoted to the Suffolk punch breed of heavy working horse; both are closed in the winter. There's not as much market action as you might expect either. The weekly town market is on Thursdays, so weekenders have to content themselves with a farmers' market every second and fourth Saturday of the month. There are monthly auctions (on Wednesdays, but with Saturday viewings) held at the Theatre Street Salerooms (see www.nsf.co.uk for details).

Good pubs are the other under-represented aspect of Woodbridge; your best bet is probably Ye Olde Bell & Steelyard (103 New Street, 01394 382933), a good-looking 16th-century inn under new ownership since April 2008.

Eating & Drinking

Browsers

60 The Thoroughfare, IP12 1AL (01394 388890, www.browsersbookshop.com). Open 9am-5.30pm Mon-Sat; 10am-4pm Sun.
An excellent independent bookshop and café. Stock is intelligently displayed and well chosen, and there's a good selection of local interest books; the café is known for its cakes and has plenty of outdoor tables in a leafy courtyard. Young Browsers, the stand-alone children's bookshop, is at no.33 (01394 382832).

Caravan Café

Quayside, Bass's Dock (no phone).
It may not look like much – it really is just a caravan kitted out with a handful of Formica tables – but this informal café does have a great location overlooking the harbour, and a fine line in bacon rolls and mugs of strong builders' tea. There are brightly painted benches and tables outside too. Cash only.

Tide Mill. See p31.

Waterfront Café
The Granary Building, Tide Mill Way, IP12 1BY (01394 610333, www.woodbridgefine foodcompany.co.uk). Open Summer 9.30am-5pm daily. Winter 10am-4pm daily.
The Waterfront Café is a lovely place to eat, all the more so if you manage to bag a table outside overlooking the harbour. The menu changes daily but fish is as fresh and as local as possible; in the autumn game makes an appearance. Children are welcome, staff are helpful and booking is advisable. The same owners also run the Woodbridge Fine

Food Company in the centre of town (2A New Street, 01394 610000), if you'd prefer to buy picnic supplies.

Whistlestop Café
Station Road, IP12 4AU (01394 389320). Open Summer 7.30am-5pm Mon-Fri; 9am-5pm Sat, Sun. Winter 7.30am-4pm Mon-Fri; 9am-4pm Sat, Sun.
A sweet little café in Woodbridge's old station building, the Whistlestop Café serves straightforward but decent breakfasts, light meals and teas and coffees.

Rye

Cobbles and quaintness rule the roost in Rye.

Rye has it all: a well-preserved, attractive centre that's a joy to walk around, lots of shops, pubs and cafés, plus a fetching harbour area – and, of course, just along the coast at Camber (*see p69*), the best beach for miles. Although much of the place is given over to genteel tourism, it remains a working town, with enough real stores and down-to-earth pubs – and a commercial fishing fleet – to prevent there being a theme park atmosphere. It's easy to get to by rail as the walk from the station to the heart of town takes about a minute.

The place has history galore – it became a Cinque port in the 13th century but declined in importance as access to the sea changed over the years; by the 18th century smuggling played a big role in the town's economy. Soak up the atmosphere and architecture by investigating cobbled streets such as West Street, Mermaid Street and also Church Square. From here there are wonderful views, especially if you make the climb to the top of 900-year-old St Mary's church.

Henry James lived in Rye for years, at Lamb House on West Street; later residents include novelists EF Benson and Rumer Godden. It's owned by the National Trust and has limited opening times, but these do include Saturday afternoons, late March-late October (see www.nationaltrust.org.uk for details).

Pottering round the shops is a favourite pastime in Rye. Food shops in general punch above their weight: there's Ashbee & Son (100 High Street, 01797 223303), a butcher's with especially good sausages, and Rye Delicatessen (28B High Street, 01797 226521), an excellent source of picnic fare. For fish sold fresh off the boat, try Market Fisheries (Unit 1, Simmons Quay, Rock Channel East, 01797 225175) but note that it's only open until 2pm on Saturdays. There's a farmers' market every Wednesday morning at Strand Quay, but sadly nothing at weekends. And take a butchers at Britchers & Rivers (109 High Street, 01797 227152), an old-fashioned sweetshop that often has a queue coming out of it on Saturdays – try its hardcore sour sweets.

There are plenty of antique and bric-a-brac shops too, from specialists such as Glass etc (*see p34*) and Jane Wicks Kitchenalia (vintage kitchen equipment and crockery, Strand Quay, 01424 713635) to the retro treasure trove New 2 You (Cinque Ports Street, 01797 226379), right next door to modern antiques shop Bidgoods (*see p34*). Also of interest to day-trippers who like to rummage are the second-hand bookshops and charity shops dotted around town, and for vinyl junkies, Grammar School Records (Old Grammar School, High Street, 01797 222752), which has more than 20,000 records in stock.

Finding somewhere to eat in Rye is easy – the streets are lined with decent options from cheap and cheerful eateries such as Anatolian Kebab (16A Landgate, 01797 226868), Kettle o' Fish (*see p34*) and Simply Italian (The Strand, 01797 226024) to destination restaurants such as the Fish Café (*see p34*), the George (*see p34*) or the Landgate Bistro (*see p34*) – and you're never far away from a teashop. There's a good array of pubs too: have a drink in the Mermaid Inn (Mermaid Street, 01797 223065, www.mermaidinn.com) for its olde worlde charm and collection of signed photographs, or soak up the view in the beer garden at the Ypres Castle Inn (Gun Gardens, 01797 223248) with a pint of Timothy Taylor; we also like the Standard Inn (High Street, 01797 225996, www.standardinn.co.uk), a friendly pub with a roaring fire and local cider.

Diary Dates

FESTIVALS

Rye Arts Festival
www.ryeartsfestival.co.uk. September.
Two weeks of classical concerts (expect lots of Haydn and Mendelssohn in an anniversary year for both composers), literary leanings and stand-ups galore.

Eating & Drinking

The Fish Café
*17 Tower Street, TN31 7AT (01797 222226,
www.thefishcafe.com). Open noon-2.30pm,
6-8.30pm Mon-Sat; noon-2.30pm, 6-9.30pm
Sat, Sun.*
Some of the best seafood in the area – grilled
fillet of Rye Bay plaice, served with crayfish
and chive sauce, for example. But there are also
decent steaks and the odd veggie option, all
served in a sleek, smart setting.

The George
*98 High Street, TN31 7JT (01797 222114,
www.thegeorgeinrye.com). Open 11am-11pm
daily.*
A revamped coaching inn, where ex-Moro chef
Rod Grossmann cooks up a storm. Expect the
likes of pan-fried calf's liver with cumin and
seasoned yoghurt, followed by classic puds.
There's still a tap room, where real ales are
served. A crackling fire adds to the cosiness.

Kettle o' Fish
*25 Wish Street, TN31 7DA (01797 223684).
Open 11am-9.30pm daily.*
It may look a bit utilitarian, but the Kettle is a
good bet for fish and chips, eat-in or takeaway,
and has the space to deal with large groups.

Landgate Bistro
*5-6 Landgate, TN31 7LH (01797 222829,
www.landgatebistro.co.uk). Open 7pm-late Wed-
Fri; noon-3pm, 7pm-late Sat; noon-3pm Sun.*
A small restaurant in two interconnecting
Georgian cottages, where the emphasis is firmly
on local produce, such as potted wild rabbit or
Romney Marsh lamb with gratin potatoes.

Shopping

Bidgoods
*52 Cinque Ports Street, TN31 7AN (01797
225700, www.bidgoods.co.uk). Open 11am-
4.30pm Wed-Fri; 10.30am-5pm Sat; noon-
4pm Sun.*
Bidgoods has a small but always tempting
collection of 19th- and 20th-century furniture
and pottery.

Glass etc
*18-22 Rope Walk, TN31 7NA (01797 226600,
www.decanterman.com). Open 10.30am-5pm
Mon-Fri; 10.30am-6pm Sat; noon-5pm Sun.*
An unpompous antique and 20th-century glass
shop, run by Andy McConnell, one of Britain's
leading authorities on glassware.

Lewes

Crafty devils abound in a town famous for its Bonfire Night celebrations.

An hour away from London by train, and a world apart, Lewes is a handsome county town set amid the South Downs. Stepping off the train you're greeted by elegant Regency architecture and the manicured lawns of a bygone era. But behind this well-heeled veneer there's a definite edge, with remnants of Lewes's anarchic past and independent spirit in evidence everywhere – from the quirky bookshops steeped in local history to the conspiratorial pubs and right-on artist co-operatives.

The town is so independently minded, in fact, that in September 2008 retailers introduced their own currency, the 'Lewes pound', with the aim of encouraging people to spend locally. (Local 17th-century agitator and revolutionary Thomas Paine is the figurehead on the notes.) The town's behind-doors revolutionary spirit – you feel that locals would happily embrace a republic of Lewes – spills out on to the street once a year for the infamous Lewes Fireworks Night; a bacchanalian celebration that draws thousands of revellers, some from across the Channel. For those seeking a more sedate day out, we recommend a visit in late summer or autumn, when you will be able to explore this eccentric spot at a more civilised pace.

Bill's Produce Store & Café. See p37.

TOWNS & CITIES

The hub of Lewes is its high street, a joy to those seeking a refuge from the anodyne British chain store, and a great source of original Christmas presents. Start out at the Needlemakers, an arty, crafty shopping emporium. Then head up Market Street to the High Street – perhaps stopping for a swift half and a ploughmans in much-fêted local pub the Lewes Arms.

Lewes has the middle-class foodie market sussed; there's something for most tastes, from upmarket confectioners (Bonne Bouche, Bruditz chocolatiers) to specialist fromagerie Cheese Please (46 High Street, 01273 481048, www.cheesepleaseonline.co.uk) and the beguiling Bill's Produce Store & Café (56 Cliffe High Street, 01273 476918, www.billsproducestore.co.uk), stacked with colourful fruit and veg displays and rows of own-made condiments. There are also some great antique shops, with eclectic curios and art deco lamps at Southdown Antiques (48 Cliffe High Street, 01273 472439), and more fashionable, reclaimed salvage pieces at Cliffe Antiques Centre (47 Cliffe High Street, 01273 473266).

May's General Store (49 Cliffe High Street, 01273 473787) is also worth a nose around, but stick to the herbs, handmade soaps and health foods at the front – the back room is crammed with random gift items, from felt rainbow hats to Ganesha smoking pipes, that often crosses the line between idiosyncratic and plain tat. For beautifully packaged and expensive-looking gifts (such as the gorgeous bath soaks), try Wickle (Old Needlemakers, West Street, 01273 474925) instead. It's not worth lingering on the other side of the bridge over the River Ouse, but well worth a visit for a spot of alternative local culture is Harvey's Brewery (see p38) and Shop (the Brewery Shop, 6 Cliffe High Street, 01273 480217, www.harveys.org.uk).

West up the high street from the war memorial, the architecture is particularly picturesque, especially if you go off-piste for a stroll in the twittens (Sussex alleyways). Head north and you'll come across antique bookshops, craft shops (such as Tash Tori Arts & Crafts) and a wealth of artists' studios and galleries (Hop Gallery on Castle Ditch Lane and the artist-run Chalk Gallery collective on North Street deserve further exploration).

Reflecting the rich musical and craft heritage of the town, there are several bespoke guitarmakers in residence. Local flamenco guitarist Pablo Requena (1 Castle Ditch Lane, 01273 487919, www.spanishguitar.org.uk) handcrafts Spanish guitars from rosewood and German spruce, while luthier Richard Osborne specialises in mandolins and bouzoukis

(www.osborneguitars.co.uk). Proper guitar enthusiasts have headed here in past Julys for the week-long Lewes Guitar Festival; however, the festival was cancelled in 2008 and 2009, so it remains to be seen if it will re-emerge in 2010.

A stroll up the tiny Pipe Passage, off the high street, brings you to a bijou, nameless bookshop run by the affable David Jarman. It houses a fine selection of second-hand art books and fiction ranging from 50p to £100 (for a hardback complete set of Sir Walter Scott). For collectable children's books, try the labyrinthine Fifteenth Century Bookshop (99-100 High Street, 01273 474160, www.oldenyoungbooks.co.uk).

If you're visiting in winter, stop off for some restorative mulled wine and mince pies at the delightful Pelham House Hotel (St Andrews Lane, 01273 488600, www.pelhamhouse.com), tucked away behind the high street. In warm, sunny weather, buy a Winkle tartan picnic blanket, stock up on provisions at Bill's (see above) and head south down Keere Street to the postcard-perfect Southover area of Lewes. The Anne of Cleves Museum, occupying a 15th-century townhouse, is best admired from the

Diary Dates

FESTIVALS

World Pea Throwing Championship
Lewes Arms (see p38). Oct.
This annual event, run by the Friends of the Lewes Arms for over ten years, is a local, idiosyncratic fave. The size, weight and outer skin of the peas are strictly invigilated. If you want to start training for it, bear in mind that the current record is 127 feet.

Lewes Bonfire Night
www.lewesbonfirecouncil.org.uk. 5 Nov.
Lewes's famously riotous Bonfire Night commemorates not just the Gunpowder Plot, but the burning of 17 Lewes Protestant martyrs at the stake. From 4pm the town shuts down and the streets are crammed with street vendors peddling upmarket veggie burgers and real ale. The climax of the night is the Grand Union Procession, where seven different bonfire societies make their way through the streets brandishing flaming torches and donning outlandish fancy dress. Hedonistic parties go on to the early hours.

outside, while lazing in the lush, romantic surroundings of the Southover Grange Gardens (Southover House, Southover Road, 01273 484999).

The striking 11th-century stone motte-and-bailey castle is the centrepiece of the town, and a perfect setting at sunset, when a hike to the top of the tower rewards you with breathtaking panoramic views across the steep sweep of the Downs stretching out to the coast. To the right of the castle is a beautifully preserved Georgian townhouse, Bartholomew House, clad in polished black tiles, which now sells antiques by appointment. If you duck under the adjacent dovecote, the cobbled walkway plateaus out on to a bowling green overlooking the verdant east of the town. There is something heady about being on the cusp of such stunning countryside while only five minutes from a latte. It's why many day-trippers choose to stay longer, the numerous estate agent offices along the high street enticing them to become a more permanent part of this animated community.

Eating & Drinking

Gardeners Arms
46 Cliffe High Street, BN7 2AN (01273 474808). Open 11am-11pm Mon-Sat; noon-10.30pm Sun.
This minuscule boozer has all the bonhomie of a village pub: many of the original regulars from the Lewes Arms (*see below*) have relocated here, and it's often a struggle to get a seat. The decor is functional, with beer mats stuck to the bar and a slightly grubby carpet, but that's why you come here – to escape the focaccia-munching, latte-quaffing hordes. There's a superb choice of real ale and cider, with Harvey's bitter on tap and five guest beers – Dark Star, Archers, Squirrel, Hepworths and Hogs Back at the time of writing, and the fruity Moles Black Rat Cider. A range of no-frills bar food – pasties and pies from the local butcher – will give you change from a fiver.

Lewes Arms
1 Mount Place, BN7 1YH (01273 473152). Open 11am-11pm Mon-Thur, Sun; 11am-midnight Fri, Sat.
There have been revisions afoot at this much-loved local following a change of hands. Luckily, they haven't been too drastic, though. The family room still has the real fireplace, the main bar its shelves of fiction, and the cosy panelled bar in the hub of the three rooms remains intact. While there have been some rumblings about the change of menu to more gastro-led fare, most

locals are happy to see the mobile phone ban lifted and nicotine stains removed. A great selection of real ale includes local Harvey's bitter and seasonal ales, with a special malt of the month at £1.45 a pop. There's a small balcony area for the summer.

Pelham House
St Andrews Lane, BN7 1UW (01273 488600, www.pelhamhouse.com). Lunch served noon-2.30pm Mon-Sat; noon-3pm Sun. Dinner served 6.30-9.30pm Mon-Sat; 6.30-8.30pm Sun.
This converted 16th-century manorhouse is now a 31-bedroom boutique hotel, and long may it remain. With its tasteful decoration, period features, airy spaces and attentive service, Pelham is as artful and discreet as any private members' club. Stop here for lunch in the impressive Garden Room, with its eau de nil walls and magnificent views across the gardens, or for afternoon tea on the terrace or dinner in the ornate Panelled Room. Head chef Peter Winn has created a simple but appealing menu; try the pan-fried scallops and chorizo, or chicken liver parfait for starters, the rib-eye steak or glazed organic salmon for mains, and make sure you leave room for utterly delicious desserts: first prize goes to the butterscotch parkin pudding.

Real Eating Company
18 Cliffe High Street, BN7 2AJ (01273 402650, www.real-eating.co.uk). Open 9.30am-11pm Mon-Sat; 9.30am-4pm Sun.
The Real Eating Company is a slick operation, serving well-sourced, supremely fresh dishes. Whether you opt for breakfast, lunch or dinner, you are guaranteed a good meal, but the place is probably at its absolute best for brunch, when you can enjoy an imaginative vegetarian breakfast with spinach and hash browns or an egg royale/egg florentine mix. Another highlight is that the menus and specials constantly rotate, reflecting the organic, locally sourced credentials. The wide, light-filled space, stripped wooden floors and friendly staff make this a welcoming space.

Shopping & Attractions

Harvey's Brewery
The Bridge Wharf Brewery, 6 Cliffe High Street, BN7 2AH (01273 480209, www.harveys.org.uk).
Independent regional brewers are an endangered species, but Harvey's has survived thanks to a mixture of pluck, guile and innovation. Besides the signature rich ales it also produces a range of seasonal draft brews, such as the dark

Christmas Ale (at a jolly 8% strength) and the more mellow honey-malted Harvey's Kiss on Valentine's Day. If you can stand the smell of hops, then a trip round the brewery is a fascinating introduction not just to the brewing process but to the heritage of Lewes itself. Make sure you book in advance and note that tours only take place on weekdays and between June and November. If you miss out on the tour, make sure you pop in for a pint at the adjacent John Harvey Tavern, or check out the range of merchandise in the shop on Cliffe High Street.

Needlemakers
West Street, BN7 2NZ
(020 7700 4114, www.needlemakers.co.uk).
Open 9am-5.30pm Mon-Sat; 11am-4.30pm Sun.
This cavernous ex-candle factory is home to 20 independent shopping outlets. Upstairs, Sky Lark sells a fine selection of world music, brilliant music 'zines and hippie gifts, from dream catchers to handknitted Peruvian finger puppets (£2.30 a pop). Dawdlers can sup Fairtrade coffee and gluten-free cake in the café, get their hair done at the organic hairdressers Jamayda, or browse the buzzing Patchwork Dog & Basket haberdashery

shop, crammed full of ladies who lunch working on their quilts. The real Aladdin's cave is downstairs, however, where you could easily while away a day sifting through the vast array of bric-a-brac and vintage ephemera. The Box Room does a great line in 1950s stoles, antique hatpins and rare books, comics and annuals.

Sussex Guild Shop
The North Wing, Southover Grange,
Southover Road, BN7 1UF (01273 479565,
www.thesussexguild.co.uk). Open 10am-
5pm daily.
Housed in the lovely Grange manor house, the Guild shop looks like a rather dull art museum, with products marooned on white surfaces and hidden away in glass cabinets. But don't let that put you off; there's some great stuff in here. Of particular note are the beautifully crafted natural edged bowls of local wood turner John Plater (www.johnplater.co.uk) and the original pewter work of Fleur Grenier – look out for her sculptural compasses and original desk clocks. There are also some fantastic original ceramics and textiles; we love the Liberty prints of Louise Bell.

Harvey's Brewery

www.treesforcities.org

Trees for Cities
Charity registration number 1032154

Travelling creates so
many lasting memories.

Make your trip mean
something for years to
come - not just for you
but for the environment
and for people living in
deprived urban areas.

Anyone can offset their
flights, but when you
plant trees with Trees for
Cities, you'll help create
a green space for an
urban community that
really needs it.

Leave
Your
Mark
Create a green future for cities.

FIVE Shopping extravaganzas

Bath

What do Bath and Florence have in common? Beautiful bridges with shops on them, of course. Robert Adam's Pulteney Bridge, built in 1773 is, along with the Ponte Vecchio in Florence, one of only two bridges in the world with shops incorporated into the original design. And it's an absolute delight, stuffed with tiny shops selling antiques, souvenirs, fashions and, in the Dolls House Miniatures of Bath (nos.15-16, 01225 426161, www.dollshouse miniaturesofbath.com), thousands of teeny things for dolls' houses, including miniature plants, flowers, bicycles and bathrooms; there's even a too-cute thimble-sized Jack Russell terrier with a food bowl.

Bath is shopping heaven – particularly if you're after high-end, individual gift shops and posh clothing chains. The setting lends itself to handsome shopfronts, and you won't be disappointed by the likes of the Guildhall Market (High Street, open 9.30am-5.30pm Mon-Sat), located in a Grade II-listed building built in 1891 and housing around 30 traders selling a wide variety of goods, including food (Nibbles cheese stall, Bath bakery, a delicatessen and Bath humbug shop should sort you out with everything you need for a grand picnic lunch), household goods, books, antiques and some crafts.

Another fine covered shopping space is the Green Park Station (Green Park Road, 01225 787910, ww.greenparkstation.co.uk), a lovely former Victorian railway station that now houses a variety of shops, a twice-weekly general market and a farmers' market on Saturdays, selling everything from antiques and collectibles to clothing, books and crafts. But, of course, when it comes to markets, the pièce de résistance has to be the city's famed Christmas market: 123 traditional wooden chalet stalls selling handicrafts, original gifts, cards, decorations, holiday food and drink, all in a suitably festive setting tucked between Bath Abbey and the Roman Baths.

Broadstairs

Broadstairs excels at quaint independents, complete with gloriously woeful names. A clutch of characterful shops is gathered around the compact centre that stretches south down from the station towards the

Canterbury. See p42.

promenade. Miss Ritzy at Ritzy Retro (4 York Street, 01843 600737) has been collecting vintage clothes for some 20 years to which her fine collection of 1950s pencil skirts, '40s tea dresses and '60s circle skirts bears witness. Close by on Charlotte Street is the Bottle Neck (nos.7-9, 01843 861095, www.thebottleneck.co.uk), a carefully sourced collection of Australian and New Zealand wines. A few streets away on Harbour Street, the Herbal Apothecary (no.2, 01843 863096, www.herbal apothecary.co.uk) is stuffed with organic beauty brands, including Burt's Bees, Lavera and the hard-to-find A'Kin. Qualified herbalist Patina Blakeney is also on hand with a stash of natural remedies.

You can park the kids in the well-stocked play area at children's shop Ziggy Pickles by the Sea (53 High Street, 01843 861662) on the high street while you shop for Petit Bateau and Noukie, then drop in for a tea-and-cake pitstop at the Oscar Road Tea Rooms (15 Oscar Road, 01843 872442, www.oscarroadbroadstairs.com). Colourful retro beach accessories are sold in the adjoining store. Equally cute is the Bee Antique & Teddy Market, where you can buy vintage teddy bears or even have your own restored in the teddy hospital. Once you've browsed for second-hand gems at the Albion bookshop and stocked up on traditional sweets at Sweet Yesterday on the high street, there's just time for a sundae at Morelli's old-fashioned ice-cream parlour (*see also p72*).

Canterbury

For a scenic shopping experience, stroll down the historic streets of Canterbury's 'King's Mile' (www.thekingsmile.com), comprising Northgate, the Borough and Palace Street, where you can find a great range of little shops selling everything from dolls' houses to vintage cameras. Chris and Les Harper's Siesta (1 Palace Street, 01227 464614, www.siestacrafts.co.uk) started in 1983 as a market stall selling handicrafts from Mexico and Guatemala. Now it imports from all over the world, and specialises in ethnic musical instruments. The somewhat whimsically named Bohemia arts market (fourth Saturday of the month) is also worth a look. Baby Love (54 Palace Street, 01227 451801, www.babylove online.co.uk) is a beautiful baby shop selling organic, ethical clothing for newborns to kids of up to seven years, as well as handmade and vintage toys. Further along is Armoire (40 Palace Street, 01227 764754, www.armoireonline.co.uk), where, if you dig deep, you'll find a variety of well-priced casual and evening clothes.

For bag upon bag of old-fashioned sweets, head to the Sugar Boy (31 Palace Street, 01227 769374, www.sugarboy.co.uk), which sells half a tonne of the stuff each week. Just around the corner on Burgate is Hawkin's Bazaar (no.34, 0844 573 4508, www.hawkin.com), filled to the rafters with great kids' (and grown-up kids') toys, such as a Make-your-own-Morph set and a spud gun. Stop by the excellent farmers' market inside the Goods Shed (Station Road West, 01227 459153, www.thegoodsshed.net), a converted engine shed right beside Canterbury West station; here you'll find plenty of pastries and deli goods, as well as specialist cheeses, fruit and veg, meat, fish, breads, preserves, and a good selection of local wine and apple juice.

Guildford

Guildford might not immediately call to mind a shopping mecca, but the compact centre has everything a discerning retail fan could want. Here are the likes of Jo Malone, Cath Kidston and Jack Wills bang in the middle of the pretty Surrey town centre. Radiating out from here is a network of medieval sidestreets stuffed with independent fashion, accessories and homeware boutiques, not to mention plenty of cosy cafés. Should rain or cold dictate a desire for warmth and shelter, there are some decent shopping centres – we like White Lion Walk (High Street, 01483 506877), which links North Street and High Street and features a good range of indies, such as gift shop Apache Tears, in a small, intimate mall; and Tunsgate Square (the entrance is halfway up the cobbled high street opposite the lovely Guildhall clock) – a surprisingly pleasant centre that's home to an imaginative range of shops, including a Heal's and independents such as Jon Dibben. Fans of Lakeland Plastics should know that the brand has a branch on Swan Lane (nos. 7-11, 01483 440626, www.lakeland.co.uk).

And if markets are your passion, Guildford boasts three: a farmers' market on the high street (first Tuesday of the month, *see p217*), a traditional market on North Street (every Friday and Saturday), and the Guildford Town Bridge craft market (every Saturday and Sunday).

Southwold

Southwold's terrific pier never fails to amuse the little ones (or those of us who still hanker after the wittily inventive genius of Tim Hunkin), but in its well-stocked and spacious gift shop it's also got lots to offer grown-ups looking for unusual presents. Deservedly voted Best Tourism Experience in the east of England's six counties in 2008, the family-run, privately owned pier is open from 10am every day of the year (except Christmas Day). Everything from stocking-fillers to delicate jewellery and gorgeous tableware is attractively displayed alongside colourful woollen accessories and an imaginative range of preserves and food gifts in tempting packaging.

Back in town, two bookshops, Bookthrift (10 Market Place, 01502 724999) and Orwell Book Shop (64 High Street, 01502 724370), traditional sweet shop the Tuck Shop (Main Street, 01502 723025) and department-store style boutique Collen & Clare (25 Market Place, 01502 724823, www.collenandclare.co.uk) offer additional gift items, as does the Amber Shop (15 Market Place, 01502 723394, www.amber shop.co.uk) and the Cellar & Kitchen Store (4 Drayman Square, 01502 727244), which sources wines from independent growers. Denny of Southwold's (11 Market Place, 01502 722372) fab selection of scarves, gloves, hats and socks makes for superior standby presents.

Dicing for Bibles

Throwing dice on an alter at Pentecost to determine which 12 local children get a bunch of free bibles might sound like something out of *Monty Python*, but this centuries-old custom still takes place in All Saint's Church every Whit Tuesday. It began in 1698 at the bequest of Robert Wilde, an eccentric poet and Puritan clergyman who set aside money in his will to buy the bibles. The village is reportedly running out of children who actually want bibles, free or otherwise, and they've moved the gambling bit off the alter and on to a table in the church, all of which suggests it's only a matter of time before the whole thing dies out. Catch it while you can, and, while you're here, check out the Chapel of St Ledger, a sweet little construction in the middle of the town's bridge. Built as a chapel in the early 15th century, it's also served as a toll house, inn and a private residence (when two extra floors were added). Along with the bridge, it's now a Grade I-listed ancient monument.
St Ives, Cambridgeshire (www.stives-town.info). Whit Tuesday.

Firing the Fenny Poppers

This event, whose history stretches back some 300 years, celebrates the life of Thomas Willis, the founder of the science of neurology. Six ceremonial cannons resembling large iron beer mugs are fired at noon, 2pm and 4pm, the gunpowder touched by a 12-foot metal rod made red-hot in the church furnace. This gives the church with which the event is associated, St Martin's, the dubious distinction of being the only one in the whole of England to hold a gunpowder licence allowing the cannons to be fired. Occasionally, the mighty guns are discharged to mark other events – In 1901, 81 salutes were fired to mourn the death of Queen Victoria, while on 1 January 2000 a volley of cannon fire marked the beginning of the second millennium. The cannons are also fired during the town's new Fenny Poppers summer festival (see www.fennyfestival. org.uk), but the main event remains the November firing, when the day's festivities culminate in a boozy turkey dinner at the ancient Bull tavern.
Fenny Stratford, Buckinghamshire (www. stmartinmk.co.uk/events.htm). 11 Nov.

Kichel throwing

Food figures large in many English village activities, and no more so than in Harwich, Essex. At noon on the appointed day, the mayor throws kichels (specially baked torpedo-shaped currant buns), from an open window of the council chamber to the assembled – and hopefully hungry – throng below. What's the significance of a bun-throwing mayor? Nobody knows, but we'll bet religion and politics have something to do with it.
Harwich, Essex (www.harwich.net). Third Thur, May.

Rochester Sweeps' Festival

Rumours of the death of Morris dancing have been wildly exaggerated – at least if Rochester's five-day May Day festival is anything to go by. Home to the biggest Morris dancing knees-up of the year, the festival also incorporates a rather more unusual tradition, in the shape of chimney sweeps 'awakening' the Jack-in-the-Green (a seven-foot character, covered in foliage from head to foot) at dawn. Once Jack's awake, there follows a sweeps' parade and ball, attended by real chimney sweeps and suitably soot-daubed children.
Rochester, Kent (www.medway.gov.uk/ sweepsfestival). May Day.

Weighing the Mayor

An annual ceremony in High Wycombe sees the mayor and various other officials publicly weighed (and raucously booed if they've put on a few pounds since the previous year) on a gloriously over-the-top weighing machine. The weighing is carried out by a macebearer and his assistants, attired in tricorne hats and white gloves. Behind the silliness lies a reminder of the public accountability owed by elected officials to their constituents, and the townsfolk claim the tradition can be traced back to medieval times.
High Wycombe, Buckinghamshire (www.mayorofwycombe.co.uk). Late May.

TOWNS & CITIES

Country

Grantchester 46
White Horse Hill 48
TEN Perfect country pubs 53
Ashwell 55
Henley-on-Thames 58

Grantchester

A stroll replete with cultural leanings – and a freed jailbird.

Sylvia Plath 'declaimed Chaucer/To a field of cows', Ted Hughes wrote in *The Birthday Letters*, describing how her 'voice went over the fields towards Grantchester'. You aren't going to bump into the departed Ted or Sylvia on this bucolic stroll from Cambridge (itself 45 minutes by train from King's Cross) to the well-fed village of Grantchester, but the cows are still here, should one of the *Canterbury Tales* spring to mind as you wander through the water meadows.

COUNTRY

Those arriving in Cambridge by coach or park-and-ride are decanted near Emmanuel College, heading from here to the river along Downing Street, where unreconstructed drivers can join the route from the Corn Exchange Street car park. Cross Trumpington Street and keep walking to the pub at the end of Mill Lane. The walk proper starts opposite, in Sheeps Green, where the river widens and divides. Follow the paths around the right-hand side of the green, cross the road (Fen Causeway) and keep an eye out for a bridge just after the large, rectangular paddling pool on the far bank. From the train station, follow your nose to Hills Road, then jink right along it, before turning left on to Bateman Road. The end of Bateman Road – also the

entrance to the lovely Cambridge University Botanic Garden (1 Brookside, 01223 336265, www.botanic.cam.ac.uk) – is almost opposite Coe Fen. A clear path veers right after the hawthorns to cross two bridges; the second is the one near that paddling pool.

Cross the bridge on to Lammas Land and follow the hedge-lined back road to a junction. Turn left down Grantchester Street, take a diagonal right along Eltisley Avenue (no.55 was Hughes and Plath's first marital home) and find yourself at the end of civilisation – or rather Skaters' Meadow, a fenced-off Wildlife Trust reserve with pollarded willows and a central lamp-post that remains from when the field used to be flooded for ice skating. In April, expect yellow marsh marigolds and pink ragged robin; by summer, there are orchids and dragonflies. Snipe often fly in for winter.

Once you've had enough of leaning here like a yokel, take the narrow paved path between hedge and fence until you see the river again. This is Grantchester Meadows, as idealised in the loping 1969 Pink Floyd song. Beside willows and rushes, the path mimics the river's sluggish turns as you climb stiles through hawthorn and cross little bridges. Crows caw over the hedges, joined by warblers in summer. In spring, keep an eye out for the flash of electric blue that indicates a kingfisher. Depending on the time of day and the season, you might be accompanied by punters or canoeists, by moon-struck lovers or dour anglers, and the river also offers surprisingly pleasant swimming. The riverpath is most fun, but if there's been rain it's also a slapstick combination of slipperiness and claggy mud. In those conditions, you can opt for the paved, straight path along the top of the field, where the only hazard is silent cyclists.

Before too long, there's a weighty decision to be made: pub or tearoom? For the pub, keep an eye out for a building at the top of the field. When you see it, strike up the field for the path into Grantchester village. Turn right on the main road and you're soon at the Green Man (59 High Street, 01223 841178). The low beams, dark wood and fireplaces in the main bar room (grab a slouchy sofa to the right of the counter) tick all the boxes for classic country pub, in contrast to the brighter and less atmospheric dining room. The hearty, Frenchified food may be a touch overambitious, but there are great ales and decent wine.

For the tearoom, stay with the river path until your way is blocked by a fence. The little yellow arrow on it suggests a public right of way, but a friendly local dogwalker advised us there was nothing beyond but the home of Tory peer, multi-million-selling novelist and former jailbird Jeffrey Archer. Head instead to the stile at the non-river end of the fence, through which you clamber into the grounds of the Orchard Tea Garden (45-47 Mill Way, 01223 845788, www.orchard-grantchester.com). The green wooden tea pavilion here is a boon for inclement weather, but the real pleasure is sipping a restorative brew under apple blossom in one of the striped deckchairs, as 'Varsity men' have been doing since 1897. The self-service counter indoors offers at least a dozen types of cake, as well as lunches.

The roster of famous writers and intellectuals who have had tea here is extraordinary, among them Ted and Sylvia of course, but also Crick and Watson, John Cleese and all the spies

who made up the 'Cambridge Five'. But it was those who gathered around charismatic poet Rupert Brooke – novelists EM Forster and Virginia Woolf, philosophers Bertrand Russell and Ludwig Wittgenstein, economist Maynard Keynes, painter Augustus John – who became known as the Grantchester Group. Brooke famously wrote of 'some corner of a foreign field/That is forever England'; nowadays, a corner of the Orchard's car park is a free, single-room museum dedicated to the poet. It contains a few artefacts (Tahitian sunglasses, war binoculars), books, postcards, poems and a great deal of biography.

Once you're ready to move on again, stretch your legs downhill past Grantchester's church (Brooke's name is on the war memorial). Through the village, a bit further than the road entrance to the Orchard, you'll find the Old Vicarage, identifiable by an odd statue of Brooke outside; the poet used to rent a room, but it now belongs to the Archers. Take the path that cuts between high walls to the right of the Old Vicarage and you'll come out on placid Mill Pond.

Rejoin the road behind Mill House (where Russell wrote fearsome tomes of philosophical logic) and cross the two bridges – the Cam has again divided. Immediately after the second bridge, turn right into the woods. This thoroughly charming sliver of trees is in the process of becoming the Wildlife Trust-managed Trumpington Meadows Country Park. It's a quiet area and, especially in a misty twilight, delightfully spooky. This is where you'll find Byron's Pool, a wonderfully situated but otherwise disappointing modern concrete dam and weir at the meeting of four river channels. It is said that Romantic poet and man-of-action Lord Byron used to swim here; certainly Brooke and Virginia Woolf came skinny dipping – as, on a separate occasion, did Wittgenstein. Brooke's poem 'The Old Vicarage, Grantchester' gives at least as much attention to the river as that dreary church clock stopped at ten to three: we recommend you read it here rather than joining any verse-junkies in the churchyard. Those sick of poets altogether can watch for other wild things: springtime tadpoles in the ponds or drumming woodpeckers, in summer the butterflies. During winter, sweetly drab little grebes can be seen.

For a truly classic Varsity adventure, hire a punt from Scudamore's at the end of Mill Lane (01223 359750, www.scudamores.com) and pole your way upriver. Just be warned: punting is harder than it looks and that champers won't make it any easier.

White Horse Hill

Uffington's prehistoric chalk figure rewards in unexpected ways.

Glorious hills and dipping dales dotted with fluffy white sheep, thoroughbred horses and contented cows are the setting for the focus of this day out: a piece of ancient English history that lies just two hours' drive from London. Just off the B4507, halfway between Wantage and Swindon, the White Horse of Uffington in Oxfordshire is a 374-foot hill carving thought to date back to the Bronze Age. Although it can only be seen in its entirety from a high altitude, attempting to catch a glimpse of the horse from the ground is part of the fun of a visit here, and creates an interesting way of exploring the surrounding scenery.

The strange thing about the White Horse of Uffington – and actually no one's quite sure whether it's a horse or a dragon – is that you could spend the whole day exploring the area on which the hill figure is drawn without actually being able to see it for what it is. This is exactly why a trip here is such fun: toiling up Dragon's Hill, following the ramparts of the long-gone Uffington Castle, tramping down the ancient-looking folds of the valley known as the Manger, all the while trying to catch a glimpse of the frustratingly elusive figure in your midst, is an exhilarating way to spend a day in the countryside… and what countryside!

Approaching from the M4 via Lambourn allows you to admire the gentle downs. Some 2,000 racehorses are bred and trained here each year – the area is known as the Valley of the Racehorse – and the rolling fields are criss-crossed with white racing fences. As you climb up towards White Horse Hill and the Ridgeway National Path, the land spreads out like a green carpet. (It's the springiness of the turf, created by easy drainage into the underlying chalk, that makes it so well suited to racehorse training.) Soon you reach the land just below White Horse Hill, the eerily beautiful Manger Valley.

Looking ancient and faintly menacing, the Manger Valley's unusual vertical folds create a mesmerising landscape and a fitting approach to the horse itself. Indeed, the two are linked by more than geology: the Manger takes its name from folklore, which has it that the White Horse came down the valley to feed on moonlit nights. At the height of summer, the whole thing looks as if it's been covered, Christo and Jeanne-Claude-style, by a huge blanket of green; in the shimmering frost of a winter's day, the grassy tufts look like brooding rock, making it hard to imagine ancient Britons carousing across them and rolling cheese down the slopes, as they did during a festival held here until the 19th century.

The Manger forces you to take a circuitous route to White Horse Hill, such that when you finally reach the National Trust car park it's possible that you'll have completely lost your bearings. But the signposts and the hordes of sturdily shod families, couples and walkers starting out on one of the many trails around the hill make it hard to get lost.

The beautifully stylised White Horse may be some 3,000 years old, but with its expressive abstract lines and stark white form, the long figure looks far more modern – more like a Matisse than a prehistoric carving. It's as elegant as its real-life counterparts grazing in nearby Lambourn, and as you head to the top of the ridge you'll catch sight of it stretching down the hill – yet only in tantalising fragments. In fact, it would be easy to miss them altogether and assume the stark white lines cut in the hillside were paths, were it not for signs asking you to keep off. Take a climb alongside the horse down a steep path (of sorts) to Dragon's Hill, a natural chalk hill with an artificial flat top on which, legend has it, St George slew the dragon. The dragon's blood left a bare white patch where nothing grows. Again there's a mythical link with the white figure above it, which is supposed to represent either St George's horse or the slain dragon. From here, the view of the Manger is breathtaking.

Back at the top of the ridge, a meandering path that offers wonderful views (including the cooling towers of Didcot power station, nearly 20 miles away) leads to the remains of Uffington Castle, a Neolithic hill fort that's little more than a round lawn with raised sides. Again the views are terrific and the grazing sheep on the lawn make a great photo opportunity; a sense of peace and calm prevails.

Uffington itself, just a mile and a half away, is, with its row of thatched cottages, a lovely village to explore; the large, thatched Clock House is particularly (ahem) striking. Apart from popping into St Mary's Church (see p50) or Tom Brown's School Museum (see p51), however, there's not actually that much to do, so you should have time to make another stop; heading for nearby Fernham will give you another opportunity to chase that elusive view. Once there, head into the Woodman Inn (see p50), where you can ponder on the images you've seen of the White Horse. The fact that it's almost impossible to see the whole image, unless from the air, gave rise to the theory about it being created as a signal to aliens. After a sometimes frustrating but delightful day of chasing the dragon, it might not sound quite so barmy.

Eating & Drinking

Fox & Hounds
High Street, Uffington, SN7 7RP (01367 820680, www.foxandhoundsuffington.co.uk). Open Summer noon-midnight daily. Winter noon-3pm, 5pm-midnight daily.
Uffington's only pub has little to recommend it in winter, since the interior lacks character and both the tiny dining rooms are far too cold for comfort during the long wait for lunch. Fortunately, the food is worth waiting for; a short specials board (always a good sign)

features the likes of home-made faggots and mash or ham, eggs and chips, particularly good when washed down with the local Butts ale. In summer it's an entirely different prospect, as the gorgeous setting comes into its own and the cheerful big gardens provide some of the area's best views of the Ridgeway and the White Horse.

Woodman Inn & Restaurant
Fernham, near Faringdon, SN7 7NX (01367 820643, www.thewoodmaninn.net). Open 11am-11pm daily.
The pretty exterior and a house-high pile of logs outside enticed us into this free house – and we weren't disappointed. Inside this lovely 400-year-old country pub, a hearth big enough to roast at least two hogs blazed gloriously in an atmospheric space that also featured a smaller

log fire. Coffee and hot chocolate were sufficient to warm our cold fingers on this occasion, but the selection of real ales, wide-ranging bar snacks and good menu (pork with spring onion mash and apple red wine gravy, for example) were all tempting.

Attractions

St Mary's Church
Broad Street, Uffington, SN7 7RD (01367 820363/820230, www.uffington.net).
Dating back to the 13th century, the 'Cathedral of the Vale' is visible as you climb down into the valley from White Horse Hill and, while it lacks any stand-out features, it's a terrific example of a medieval cruciform construction. Some lovely stone carvings and inscriptions can be found in

the interior and on the gravestones of the pretty churchyard, and there's a literary connection too: Sir John Betjeman was a church warden here during the 1930s.

Tom Brown's School Museum
Broad Street, Uffington, SN7 7RA (www.museum.uffington.net). Open Easter-Oct 2-5pm Sat, Sun & bank holiday Mon.
Housed in the nearly four-century-old schoolroom that was the inspiration and setting for Thomas Hughes's book *Tom Brown's School Days*, Uffington's local museum is Tardis-like in its ability to pack a lot into what, from the outside, looks like a tiny space. Jostling for room are displays of local history and archaeology, as well as mementoes relating to Hughes (including 136 different editions of his book).

Wayland's Smithy
160ft north of the Ridgeway National Trail, signposted from White Horse Hill (www.nationaltrail.co.uk).
If you want to extend your walk on White Horse Hill, head for nearby Wayland's Smithy. Named after the Saxon god of metalwork and set in a pretty beech grove, this impressive and chillingly atmospheric Neolithic burial chamber (technically a chambered long barrow) dates back almost 6,000 years. Of the first phase of building there's no visible evidence, but the site retains from the second phase the Saracen slabs that edged the burial mound, and part of an elaborate entrance façade. This gives way to a stone-lined passage, with two chambers off it forming the shape of a cross. The place looks like giant's teeth, and is decidedly spooky in the right light.

TEN Perfect country pubs

Black Horse

Big on portions, service and cosy nooks, the Black Horse is the kind of pub you pop into for a swift one but can't bear to leave before closing time. Summer lunches in the courtyard are suitably idyllic, but the seasonally changing menu (great salads, grills and deli boards) is a goer whatever the weather. In short, a pleasingly pretension-free zone.
1 Bedford Street, Woburn, Bedfordshire MK17 9QB (01525 290210, www.blackhorse woburn.co.uk). Open 11am-11pm Mon-Thur; 11am-midnight Fri, Sat; 11am-10.30pm Sun.

Duke of Cumberland Arms

An idyllic little pub, surrounded by several acres of garden dotted with trout ponds, the Duke of Cumberland feels hidden away, but its reputation (very agreeable atmosphere and friendly service, as well as excellent food and real ales) means that booking is essential if you want a table for a weekend lunch, either in one of the snug whitewashed rooms or outside under the large green umbrellas.
Henley, Fernhurst, West Sussex GU27 3HQ (01428 652280). Open noon-3pm, 5-11pm Tue-Sat; noon-3pm, 5-10.30pm Sun; (bar only) noon-3pm, 5-11pm Mon.

Falkland Arms

A leafy 16th-century exterior, wonky interior and sun-trap gardens secure the Falkland's perfect country pub status in an instant. And that's before you've tucked into the deliciously fuss-free food (roasts, sausage and mash, huge ploughman's platters) and decent ales, or contemplated staying put for the Sunday night folk session.
Great Tew, Chipping Norton, Oxfordshire OX7 4DB (01608 683653, www.falkland arms.org.uk). Open 11am-3pm, 6-11pm Mon-Fri; 11.30am-midnight Sat; noon-10.30am Sun.

King's Head

What this pub might lack in fancy gastro menus and artfully distressed interiors, it more than makes up for with its expansive gardens and riverside setting – you can even arrive by boat, if you so desire, making use of the free mooring. Find a patch of grass, sample a pint of local ale and forget your cares.
Church Street, Wadenhoe, Northamptonshire PE8 5ST (01832 720024, www.kingshead wadenhoe.co.uk). Open 11am-11pm Mon-Sat; noon-5pm Sun.

Lickfold Inn

Roaring fires in winter and plenty of outside seating for summer make this a popular choice for lazy weekend lunching. Join the converted for such crowd-pleasing classics as haddock with fat chips and massive burgers washed down with pints of Hogs Back TEA, and feel good in the knowledge that owner Chris Evans gives half the profits to charity. The traditional interior ups the country-escape factor brilliantly.
Lickfold, Petworth, West Sussex GU28 9EY (01798 861285, www.evanspubs.co.uk). Open noon-11pm Mon-Sat; noon-5pm Sun.

Noah's Ark Inn

For a picture-perfect village setting, complete with green, look no further than the Noah's Ark. This charming 16th-century inn ticks every bucolic box – and serves heartily satisfying roasts to boot. A fine place to forget about city living and watch the afternoon disappear through the bottom of a pint glass, and equally appealing in winter (log fires, leather sofas) and summer (masses of outdoor seating).
The Green, Lurgashall, West Sussex GU28 9ET (01428 707346, www.noahsarkinn.co.uk). Open 11am-11pm Mon-Sat; noon-4pm Sun.

Ram Inn

A 17th-century inn just a few miles from the coast that's much loved by locals and walkers for the unfussy interior, log fires and big garden. Firle itself is a very pretty village and there are lovely walks from Firle Beacon. Pints of Harveys Best, guest ales and ciders, and hearty dishes (a chargrilled 10oz steak with big chips, say) are further pluses.
The Street, Firle, Lewes, East Sussex BN8 6NS (01273 858222, www.theram-inn.com). Open 11.30am-11.30pm Mon-Sat; noon-10.30pm Sun.

Sportsman

Located on the old coastal road between oyster mecca Whitstable and Faversham, the Sportsman has a reputation – and,

COUNTRY

since 2008, a Michelin star – for excellent food. Ingredients for the chalked-up, daily changing menu are locally sourced and might include the likes of pork belly with apple sauce or delicately flavoured roast red mullet. Gluttons will want to get their mouths around the imaginative tasting menu (£55; needs to be pre-ordered). The sea is just a few yards away – though you can't see it from the pub – so a brisk walk along the shore is a must before heading home. Book at weekends to avoid being turned away.

Faversham Road, Seasalter, Whitstable, Kent CT5 4BP (01227 273370, www.thesportsman seasalter.co.uk). Open noon-3pm, 6-11pm Tue-Sat; noon-10.30pm Sun; (bar only) noon-3pm, 6-10pm Mon.

Three Chimneys

Find yourself a corner tucked beneath the beams of this traditional pub and soak up some serious Kentish charm. Food is locally sourced where possible and there's a fantastic terrace for a spot of classy alfresco drinking. Beautiful gardens, packed with herbs and lavender, make a summer visit decidedly fragrant, and there are open fires for winter huddling.

Hareplain Road, Biddenden, Kent TN27 8LW (01580 291472, www.thethreechimneys.co.uk). Open 11.30am-3pm, 5.30-11pm Mon-Fri; 11.30am-4pm, 5.30-11pm Sat; noon-4pm, 6-10.30pm Sun.

Vine Tree

A tiny, welcoming 18th-century mill house-turned-freehouse serving very good food with a strong emphasis on local produce (the roast beef comes from the farm next door and game from local estates, for example). Wine and beer (Tinners ale from St Austell, Butcombe bitter from Bristol) are given proper attention too. Flagstone floors and a big fire are interior attractions, while outside there's a smart sun terrace. Note that opening times do vary, especially in winter, when the pub is sometimes closed in the afternoon, so phone to check times if you're making a special journey.

Foxley Road, Norton, nr Malmesbury, Wiltshire SN16 0JP (01666 837654, www.thevine tree.co.uk). Open noon-11pm Mon-Sat; noon-10.30pm Sun.

Vine Tree

Ashwell

A village that seems as pleased to see you as you will be to see it.

Mummified rats, medieval graffiti, serene springs and some great walking combine to make the north Hertfordshire village of Ashwell a perfect spring-day outing. And that's before you begin to explore the delights of the picture-postcard pubs and houses steeped in centuries of history. Lots of English villages have an air of self-satisfaction about them that can make them feel less than welcoming to outsiders. You can recognise such places by the suspicious looks from locals as you attempt to park in the tiny high street or the tight-lipped, smiling 'Can I help you?' issued as soon as you open the door to the local gallery and crafts shop. At first glance the village of Ashwell, nestling in the chalk hills east of the A1, might appear to be one of these, but once you're wandering about, you'll find yourself seduced by an ancient settlement that has an abundance of quiet charms.

Set firmly in the commuter belt, modern-day Ashwell is used to outsiders coming and going. It's had residents for far longer: human habitation here goes back 4,000 years, the first written reference to the village appears in 990, and the Domesday Book recorded the village as a wealthy, flourishing market town. Those heady days of commerce are long gone, but that's a huge part of the village's appeal. This is an everyday English village, one that has no second homes, no holiday cottages and no gourmet delis for tourists and townies. It has the kind of shops that serve the immediate needs of the community – post office, general store, butcher, baker and pharmacy… as well as the near-obligatory gallery and florist.

What Ashwell does have, though, is a wealth of lovely buildings, each of them a pleasure to gawp at as you wander about, some of them open to the public for exploration within. For immediate orientation and to help you get the most from this lovely hamlet, your first stop should be the local museum (*see p57*). Now housed in a Tudor market shop, the collection was established by local schoolboys Albert Sheldrick and John Bray in the 1920s, before settling in here in 1930. It claims to be the oldest village museum in Britain; we can certainly confirm that it's one of the best we've visited. Like a mini version of the V&A, the two-storey building is a hymn to British arts and crafts through the centuries, as well as home to a fascinating hoard of ephemera dating back to Roman times. It's here that you'll find those mummified rats (black ones, their demise brought about by having been trapped in a chimneypiece), and also lovely

fragments of late Tudor frescoes, delicate examples of embroidery and samplers, jewellery – dating back to the late Roman period – from a shrine to the goddess Senuna, a gorgeous Womens' Institute quilt depicting village buildings, and one-time school caretaker Alan Picking's collection of Ashwell model buildings – his re-creation of local butcher MV Crump is a perfect scaled-down version of the real thing just across the road from where it is displayed. There are also more esoteric delights: our favourite was the 'garden gleanings', a vitrine stuffed with hundreds of things dug up in one man's garden – clay pipes, animal bones, marbles and shells feature prominently. This kind of dedication to recording and preserving an illustrious past lies at the heart of Ashwell, as you'll discover once you're back outside, armed with the 'Ashwell Village Walk' map bought for 20p from the museum shop.

You don't need a map, of course – just as well: the museum is only open on Sunday and bank holiday Monday afternoons, although there are more maps and walks at the post office, which is open daily. However, your pleasure in the village's stunning houses, farmhouses and one-time commercial buildings will definitely be enhanced by being guided. Not to be missed are the high street's 14th- and 15th-century Foresters' Cottages, the quaint 16th-century timber-framed cottages at the junction of Mill Street and Rollys Lane, the grand 19th-century country house known as the Bury (it was designed by Edwin Lutyens, with a garden by his frequent collaborator Gertrude Jekyll), Ducklake Farm at Spring Head and, back on the high street,

COUNTRY

the Guildhouse with its ornate and slightly sinister first-storey plasterwork, dated 1681.

Pottering around these lovely buildings and gardens will give hours of pleasure, but all the while you'll be aware of one other building that demands attention. With its 170-foot spire (the tallest in the county), the gorgeous medieval church of St Mary's (*see opposite*) dominates the village, but without overwhelming it. Have a sit-down in the cemetery, or head inside to scratch your head over the famous medieval graffiti. Outside, look for the nearby lychgate, whose purpose was to shelter a corpse on its bier until it was time to take it to the funeral.

There are more pleasures in the village in the shape of three excellent pubs: the Three Tuns, the Rose & Crown and, opposite the church, the oddly named Bushel & Strike (for all, *see opposite*). All of them serve decent food. But make sure you leave enough time to explore Ashwell's namesake. Easily reached by the footpath from Hodwell or stairs from the high street, the 1,000-year-old Ashwell Springs, one of the sources of the River Cam (also known as the Rhee), form the centrepoint of a small wooded recreational area that is perfect for pootling about, jumping the stones back and forth across the spring, sitting on one of the benches or making a little picnic area in one of many copses. It's the perfect way to round off a lovely day.

Ashwell is situated about three miles east of the A1 at Junction 10, and roughly the same distance north of the A505 (Baldock Road). A particularly pleasant approach off the A1 is via the village of Newnham, the slight incline crested by a picture-postcard view of Ashwell. In winter, the brilliantly lit steeple of St Mary's is visible for miles, making the drive along the unlit, deserted Northfield Road eerily atmospheric. If you don't have a designated driver and you fancy spending some time in one of those pubs, regular trains run from King's Cross to Ashwell or Morden, two miles away.

Rose & Crown
69 High Street, SG7 5NP (01462 742420).
Open 11.30am-3pm, 5.30-11pm Mon-Fri;
noon-11pm Sat; noon-10.30pm Sun.
Ashwell's oldest public house dates from the 17th
century. You'll find wooden beams, open fires,
hearty Sunday roasts and decent handpumps.
For the weekend of the summer solstice (nearest
to 21 June), this pub hosts the Ashwell Summer
Solstice Festival, a music and real ale jamboree.

Three Tuns
6 High Street, SG7 5NL (01462 742107,
www.tuns.co.uk). Open 11am-11.30pm
Mon-Sat; noon-11pm Sun.
Ashwell's only Queen Anne building is also
a fine country hotel, pub and restaurant, with
a fireplace you could roast a large hog in and
well-behaved tortoiseshell and tabby cats
swishing about like watchful landlords. The
food's excellent and available all day, and both
bars are comforting enough to make when to
leave the hardest decision during the winter.

Shopping & Attractions

Ashwell Gallery
Dixies Barns, High Street, SG7 5NT (01462
743366, www.ashwellgallery.com). Open
10.30am-5.30pm Wed-Fri; 11am-4pm Sat.
This little gallery holds exhibitions of painting,
pottery, prints and sculpture by local artists.
The shop stocks a nice range of gift cards.

Ashwell Village Museum
Swan Street, SG7 5NY (01462 742956,
www.ashwell.gov.uk/museum.htm). Open 2.30-
5.30pm Sun & bank hols. Admission £1.50.
This two-storey museum, packed to the rafters
with historical artefacts related to village life,
is a delight. Trades and craftsmanship spanning
centuries are well represented, and the higgledy-
piggledy feel to the collection makes it lively and
fun, rather than dry and boring.

St Mary's Church
Mill Street, SG7 5QQ (01462 742601, www.st
marysashwell.org.uk). Open 8am-dusk daily.
From any direction, St Mary's is postcard
perfection, its lovely cemetery – with extensive
paths – one of the village's nicest places to sit.
A free guide maps points of interest, including
medieval graffiti. The best examples are in the
tower, where you'll find delicate outlines of Old
St Paul's (the London cathedral destroyed in the
Great Fire and replaced by the current Wren
version) and an account of the great plague of
1348 and a brutal St Maur's Day storm in 1361.

Eating & Drinking

Bushel & Strike
Mill Street, SG7 5LY (01462 742394).
Open noon-11pm Mon-Sat; noon-7pm Sun.
A pint from the great range of real ales – among
them Wells Eagle IPA and Bombardier, Courage
Directors, Young's IPA and regular guests –
supped in the pretty garden opposite the church
is a perfect way to spend a summer afternoon
in Ashwell. Move indoors to the cosy bars in
winter, or fill up at the Sunday carvery in the
surprisingly airy and modern dining room.

Day's of Ashwell Bakery
61 High Street, SG7 5NP (01462 742202).
Open 7.30am-4pm Mon-Fri; 7.30am-2pm Sat.
Hertfordshire has eight branches of Day's, but
this is the original – and it's still going strong
in a pretty, centuries-old building. There's no
indoor seating, but take your cakes and pastries
to the Springs or Swan Street's Ashwell Cottage
Garden to enjoy them at your leisure.

Henley-on-Thames

Messing about on the river.

The main attraction at Henley, a pretty medieval market settlement just an hour west of Paddington by rail or road, is its annual rowing regatta (*see p60*), a huge international tournament held over five days in July. Running since 1839, it has come to be associated with a particular social mentality; expect to find heaving riverbanks of people wearing striped blazers and getting very excited at the sight of a plastic shell travelling at 12 miles per hour. If you're after a more relaxing escape from London, come at any other time of the year to enjoy Henley's small, peaceful centre, dotted with independent art galleries, antiquarian shops and endless good pubs – and use the town to launch into a number of serene Thameside walks (*see p58*).

That said, even non-rowers will enjoy the River & Rowing Museum (*see p60*) and appreciate the history of the somewhat older Leander Club (01491 575782, www.leander.co.uk), founded in 1818; Sir Steve Redgrave's alma mater, Leander has won more Olympic gold medals than any other sporting club in the world. Both institutions contribute to the sense that this is safe, conservative Britain: charming, 'native' and old-fashioned; picnic baskets, Pimm's and pedigrees.

This kind of ambience has its advantages, of course. Wander the compact centre between New Street, King's Road, Friday Street and the riverside itself and you'll find a cluster of interesting one-offs. Jonkers Rare Books (24 Hart Street, 01491 576427, www.jonkers. co.uk) and Richard Way Antiquarian Books (54 Friday Street, 01491 576663) are inspiring stops for bibliophiles. Lovers of other ancient items can easily wander between the Ferret antiques shop (5 Friday Street, 01491 574104) and its carpet-specialist neighbour Knight's Antiques (01491 414124), which both deserve a rummage; wood-beamed Tudor House Antiques (49 Duke Street, 01491 573680), meanwhile, is situated in the loveliest premises.

Modern aesthetes will be equally satisfied strolling between contemporary art spaces, such as the Lemongrove Gallery (10 Duke Street, 01491 577215, www.thelemongrove gallery. co.uk), Bohun Gallery (15 Reading Road, 01491 576228, www.bohungallery.co.uk) and Barry Keene Gallery (12 Thameside, 01491 577119, www.barrykeenegallery.co.uk).

Venture outside the town itself to explore local country mansions like Greys Court (01491 628529, www.nationaltrust.org.uk) – a beautiful Tudor building with a walled garden, to the west of Henley. Nuffield Place (01491 641224, www.nuffield-place.com), former home of 1930s car-designer William Morris (aka Lord Nuffield), is popular with motor vehicle enthusiasts, and has attractive gardens. Perhaps the most pleasant of Henley's environs is Stonor (01491 638587, www.stonor. com), a medieval house five miles to the north, crammed with period artwork and Catholic history. Check in advance for seasonal closures at all these destinations.

WALKS AROUND HENLEY
You could ignore Henley altogether, and simply indulge in the tranquillity of the Chilterns. Turn right out of the train station, then right again when you hit the river, and you'll soon find yourself among meadows, barges and fishermen. Alternatively, follow the river left: either cross the bridge and take

the Thames Path beyond Temple Island towards Hambledon, or veer westwards up to Stonor (*see p59*) and Pishill. Three Henley walks are fully detailed in volumes one and two of Time Out's *Country Walks Near London*. Staff at the local tourist information office (King's Arms Barn, Kings Road, 01491 578034, www.visithenley-on-thames.co.uk) can also point you in the right direction.

Eating & Drinking

Angel on the Bridge
Thameside, RG9 1BH (01491 410678, www.theangelhenley.com). Open 11am-midnight Mon-Sat; 11am-11pm Sun.
This unmissable 1728 building perches right over the Thames and prides itself as being the only pub in Henley to do so. Needless to say it

---

Diary Dates

MARKETS
01189 404318, www.southoxon.gov.uk.
As well as a weekly food market, held along Market Place every Thursday, a farmers' market comes to town every fourth Thursday.

FESTIVALS

Henley Food Festival
www.henleyfoodfestival.co.uk.
Two days in May.
One everyone should enjoy; a riot of produce and catering stands, cookery demonstrations, cook-off challenges and entertainment... not to mention a food retail area. Yummm.

Henley Royal Regatta
www.hrr.co.uk. First week of July.
It's ten years since a royal was in attendance at this five-day boatathon, but it's still pretty highfalutin'; bring your old school blazer to enjoy a spiffing day out with the crème de la crème.

Henley Festival of Music & Arts
www.henley-festival.co.uk.
Second week of July.
Five starry evenings of arts celebration on the banks of the Thames (as well as on floating stages and rafts), from folk and opera to comedy and film, plus lots of fringe events during the day.

---

is inordinately rammed come regatta season – but catch it on a quiet day and you'll have the river terrace to yourself. There's even a mooring for those arriving by boat.

Crooked Billet
Newlands Lane, Stoke Row, RG9 5PU (01491 681048, www.thecrookedbillet.co.uk). Open noon-2.30pm, 7-10.30pm Mon-Sat; noon-10.30pm Sun.
This may not be the most easily accessible restaurant in Oxfordshire, but it's quite possibly the best. Paul Clarehugh has picked up consistent critical accolades for his fine food, and the restaurant has become something of a destination in itself for food-loving Londoners. The 1642 premises segue from a delightful fireside spot to a more formal dining space; the generous menu includes much local meat (beef and sheep from Paul's own smallholding) – indeed, the owners often swap lunch with produce from the locals – and prices are utterly reasonable for this quality. Be sure to ring (or check the website) for directions.

Shopping & Attractions

Gorvett & Stone
28 Duke Street, RG9 1UP (01491 414485, www.gorvettandstone.co.uk). Open 9.30am-5.30pm Mon-Sat.
This justly lauded chocolate shop sells a delicious selection of handmade treats, always tantalisingly presented. Wedding favours, hot chocolate and fondues, and even a bespoke 'design your own' service are all on offer.

Hobbs of Henley
Station Road, RG9 1AZ (01491 572035, www.hobbs-of-henley.com).
If you want to enjoy the Henley Regatta or Festival from the river, or just a boat trip along the Thames, Hobbs offers a nice range of options, including self-drive motorboats and rowing boats for hire, sightseeing trips and chauffer-driven boats, and private charters.

River & Rowing Museum
Mill Meadows, RG9 1BF (01491 415600, www.rrm.co.uk). Open Summer 10am-5.30pm daily. Winter 10am-5pm daily. Admission £7.
It's the upstairs room that takes the gold medal here, offering an insight into the rowing mentality and the sport's equipment: the ceiling is dominated by several large boats. Downstairs, a permanent *Wind in the Willows* exhibition that brings the story to life (with the help of 3D models) will enthral children.

Coast

West Wittering 65
Camber Sands 69
FIVE Ice-cream parlours 72
Dungeness 73
Botany Bay 76
Littlehampton 79
FIVE Retro resorts 81
Whitstable 82
TEN Beach activities 85
Leigh-on-Sea 86
Mersea Island 87

West Wittering

Feel the sand between your toes in this tranquil Sussex haven.

The prospect of a day at the beach for Londoners doesn't always conjure up idyllic images. Southend, the closest strand, is more about cheesy fun on the Pleasure Pier than getting away from it all. Brighton, the other obvious choice (*see p13*), is stylish and sexy, but its nickname is London-by-the-Sea – and its pebbly beach isn't exactly barefoot luxury. But look beyond the usual suspects, and you'll discover that near-paradise can be found. West Wittering (www.westwitteringbeach.co.uk), a tranquil beauty on the coast of West Sussex, has pristine sandy shores, grassy dunes and clean Blue Flag waters. With gently shelving sands and shallow, sun-warmed tidal pools, it offers Londoners a proper day at the beach.

West Wittering is certainly a good bathing spot, especially for families. It's less exposed than Camber Sands, and, sheltered by the Isle of Wight and the rolling swell of the South Downs, it enjoys its own benign microclimate, earning it the sobriquet 'God's pocket' among locals. Even on blustery days, there's a chance the sun will still be shining down here – and if not, cups of hot chocolate from the beach café and old-fashioned British stoicism fortify the faithful and their wetsuit-clad offspring. Yet inviting as its clean sands and calm waters may be, that's only half the story. At the western end of the beach, East Head's shifting sand dunes and salt marshes possess a desolate, otherworldly beauty – a haven for wildlife and those in search of solitude.

The best way to get to the beach (and bypass the snaking queue for the car park that builds up on summer weekends) is to cycle down from Chichester (90 minutes from Victoria station) on the Salterns Way Cycle Path (01243 775888, www.conservancy.co.uk/out/cycling.asp). Eleven miles long, it runs past sleek, gleaming boats at Chichester Marina, across sun-dappled fields, along lily-covered waterways and through cool, dim copses before finally emerging in West Wittering village, a charming slice of nostalgia with its Sussex flint-studded cottages and tiny, peaceful church. If you're travelling on four wheels, take the A286 south from Chichester for seven miles; if you're coming by train but don't want to cycle, go to Chichester and catch the 53 bus.

The sandy beach is tranquility itself: no jagged cliffs or pounding breakers here. Bathers potter in the shallows at the edge of the sea: a vast, shimmering expanse, broken only by the white yacht sails that dot the Solent. Further out rises the green-grey outline of the Isle of Wight.

The inland vista is equally idyllic. There are no crazy golf courses and amusement arcades to distract the kids from sandcastle-building; no naff bungalows and caravan parks to encroach on the landscape's pristine beauty. Instead, the wide, sloping sands are backed by a tall tamarisk hedge, a row of weathered beach huts and a 20-acre swathe of grassland, occupied by butterflies, picnicking families and pleasingly wonky lines of parked cars. Beyond, the gently undulating South Downs form a picture-perfect backdrop.

Simple pleasures are the order of the day here. At low tide, a quarter of a mile of fine, softly sloping sand emerges, along with shallow tidal pools and a sandbar-sheltered lagoon. Children paddle and drift on dinghies in the smaller pools (note: there are lifeguards from May to September). The bigger tidal lagoon, meanwhile, is perfect for a sedate swim, and a mecca for kitesurfers and windsurfers – its calm waters are ideal for showing off (the old hands) or falling off (the novices).

If you want to spend all day frolicking in the sea, you can rent a wind surfer (Wittering Surf Shop, 13 Shore Road, East Wittering, 01243 672292, www.witteringsurfshop.com) or go for a sail (www.wwsc.co.uk). The firm sands are also conducive to kite buggying (www.west witteringsbuggyclub.co.uk) and horseriding (Cakeham Equestrian Club, Cakeham Road, 01243 672194).

Aside from the windsurfing shop, the beach's sole concession to commercialism is a low block housing a beach shop, a café and two takeaway hatches. Most beachgoers bring a picnic or spark

COAST

up a barbecue: come midday, the heady smell of browning sausages wafts across the dunes, and sandcastles are momentarily forgotten.

At the western end of the beach, East Head, a lovely sand and shingle spit, marks the entrance to Chichester Harbour. On its seaward side, the sandy strand is narrower than the main beach, but infinitely quieter. Here, the sea deposits treasures: pearl-lined slipper limpet shells, razor clams, cockles and whelks.

The northernmost tip is the busiest spot, as passing yachts drop anchor for lunch and a dip, and day-trippers sprawl on the sand. Off-season, their place is taken by a colony of harper seals, who swim across from Thorney Island to bask in the winter sunshine and solitude. But even at the height of summer, there's peace and quiet to be found. Venture away from the shoreline, into the giant sand dunes, and you're suddenly in glorious isolation. Skylarks flit overhead, singing out warning of an intruder, while tiny lizards dart away, leaving narrow trails criss-crossing the sand.

The spiky marram grass also forms and reforms in new patterns according to the wind and the shifting sands. Roped-off areas protect ringed-plover nesting sites and dunes where rare silver spiny digger wasps burrow – one of the reasons this is a designated Site of Special Scientific Interest (SSSI), protected by the National Trust (*see p68*).

Spread a picnic blanket amid the dunes and delicate sea bindweed flowers, and you could be the last person on earth – until an intrepid small child appears on the horizon, playing hide and seek.

On the landward side, the salt marshes are bleakly beautiful at any time of year, and transformed in early summer into a meadow of purple sea lavender. Where East Head meets the mainland, a footpath meanders around the harbour to the sailing village of Itchenor. Along the way is the green triangle of Snow Hill Common and the diminutive, white-painted row of old coastguard's cottages, built to deter 18th-century smugglers, who used Snow Hill Creek to transport contraband.

Here too is the crabbing pool, where small children (and competitive fathers) gaze with rapt attention into the murky depths, trying to entice its scuttling, suspicious inhabitants with bacon-baited lines. At Itchenor, summer boat

trips explore the harbour, and the footpath stretches onwards to Chichester Marina and beyond. But the handsome, red-brick Ship Inn beckons, with its outdoor tables, locally brewed real ales and gargantuan portions of fish and chips.

With the day drawing to an end and small fry's bedtimes fast approaching, the beach at West Wittering slowly empties. Follow the meandering footpath back, find a vantage point on the dunes and drink in the view. As the sun sets over the glittering Solent, God's pocket truly does seem blessed.

Eating & Drinking

Locals are unanimous that the best fish and chips on the peninsula are to be found at the Boathouse in East Wittering (10 Shore Road, PO20 8DZ, 01243 673386).

If you're prepared to venture a little further afield, the East Beach Café (*see p80*) in Littlehampton, a 30-minute drive away, might tempt you with its jaw-dropping Thomas Heatherwick-designed architecture and superb dishes made with local ingredients.

Beach House
Rookwood Road, West Wittering, PO20 8LT (01243 514800, www.beachhse.co.uk). Open Summer 8am-10pm Tue-Sun. Winter 8am-3pm Wed, Thur, Sun; 8am-10pm Fri, Sat.
This bright and breezy B&B is also known for its restaurant. Claim a table on the wooden veranda and enjoy some sterling local seafood: Sussex smokies, whole tail scampi or beer-battered fish and chips. Off-season, it's only open Friday and Saturday evenings for dinner.

Comme Ça
67 Broyle Road, Chichester, PO19 6BD (01243 788724, www.commeca.co.uk). Open 5.30-10.30pm Tue; noon-3pm, 5.30-10.30pm Wed-Sat; noon-3pm Sun.
This Chichester fixture has a discernible French connection. With a chef from Normandy, the food is authentically Gallic – expect the likes of fish soup, moules marinières, confit of Barbary duck, foie gras, and chateaubriand – but British flavours creep in: Stilton soufflé, say, or Scottish smoked salmon. Finish off with a medley of French cheeses. In the summer, the garden room and patio come into their own.

Crab & Lobster

Mill Lane, Sidlesham, PO20 7NB (01243 641233, www.crab-lobster.co.uk). Open noon-2.30pm, 6-9.30pm Mon-Fri; noon-2.30pm, 6-10pm Sat; noon-2.30pm, 6-9pm Sun.

Perched by Pagham nature reserve, the Crab & Lobster has a romantic setting – the patio overlooks the marshes – and lots of character (the building is 350 years old). Locally caught seafood is the culinary forte – specifically crabs, which turn up as a Selsey crab and crayfish sandwich, crab risotto with diver-caught Scottish scallops and a crab and lobster fish pie, among others. If you don't like seafood, English comfort food is available in a variety of guises.

Field & Fork

Pallant House Gallery, 9 North Pallant (entrance on East Pallant), Chichester, PO19 1TJ (01243 816579, www.fieldandfork.co.uk). Open 10am-4pm Tue; 10am-4pm, 6-10pm Wed-Sat; 11.30am-4pm Sun.

A small restaurant with a big reputation, Field & Fork now has a new home in the Pallant House Gallery, to complement the cosy lunch spot on Baffins Court (Baffins Lane, PO19 1UA, 01243 784890). Sam Mahoney upped sticks from London's chi chi Kensington Place to run his own show here, and his Modern British menu relies heavily on seasonal and local ingredients – stuffed loin of Sussex pork, say, or red mullet from the Channel – but also spans the globe in flavours.

Old House at Home

Cakeham Road, West Wittering, PO20 8AD (01243 511234, www.oldhousepub.co.uk). Open Summer 8am-11pm Mon-Sat; 8am-10.30pm Sun. Winter 8am-9pm Tue-Fri; noon-10.30pm Sat; noon-5pm Sun.

West Wittering's only pub is a good one. Its menu offers hearty pub classics (sausage and mash, scampi and chips, game casserole) made with local produce. Inside, three log fires keep things warm in winter; in the summer, the deck patio and garden are a good place to soak up the sea breeze.

Ship Inn

The Street, West Itchenor, Chichester, PO20 7AH (01243 512284). Open 11am-11pm Mon-Sat; noon-10.30pm Sun.

This traditional English pub is perched near the shores of Chichester Harbour. Much of the menu comprises immaculately fresh, locally caught fish – plaice, mackerel, crab and lobster – complemented by locally brewed real ales (the pub is recommended by CAMRA).

Nearby Attractions

Bognor Regis

www.bognor-regis.org.

If West Wittering is resolutely uncommercial, Bognor Regis, just east, is a shameless people-pleaser. Its safe bathing and five-mile stretch of sand and shingle have been drawing the crowds for decades, though these days its modesty-protecting bathing machines and genteel boarding houses have given way to a giddy whirl of seaside pleasures: amusements galore, chippies, a miniature train, trampolines and crazy golf.

Chichester

Tourist office, 29A South Street (01243 775888, www.visitchichester.org). The historic city of Chichester exudes a peacefully quaint market-town charm, but as the mournful cry of seagulls will remind you, the water is not far away. It was founded in AD 70 by the Romans, and history still oozes from its streets, most notably in the Georgian architecture and Chichester Cathedral. Known for its soaring medieval spire – it's the only cathedral that can be seen from the sea – it blends Norman and Gothic styles and is graced with a Marc Chagall stained-glass window (for info, call 01243 782595, www.chichester cathedral.org.uk). Chichester's other cultural highlight is the Pallant House Gallery (9 North Pallant, 01243 774557, www.pallant.org.uk), which hosts an outstanding collection of 20th-century British art that takes in works by Henry Moore, Peter Blake, Bridget Riley, Lucian Freud and Barbara Hepworth.

East Head

07799 072593, www.nationaltrust.org.uk. East Head, a beachy nature reserve at the end of West Wittering, is an SSSI (a Site of Special Scientific Interest), an SPA (Special Protection Area) and an SAC (Special Area of Conservation). What's all the fuss about then? The fragile, ever-eroding sand and shingle spit is home to some buxom sand dunes, and botanists go wild for its maritime plants, from sea holly to maram grass. Birders have lots to ogle too: migrant wildfowl includes sanderling, redshank, curlew and godwits. Chichester Harbour, which East Head faces, is also something of an avian hotspot during the winter, and there are regular nature walks and boat trips run by Chichester Harbour Conservancy (01243 512301, www.conservancy. co.uk). You can access East Head from West Wittering village, or from the car park at the main beach.

Camber Sands

Delight in the dunes on England's south coast.

A great day at the beach always starts with that first magical glimpse. There are beaches that spread out before you as you approach them, laying their features out like a market stallholder displaying sparkling gewgaws. There are beaches that tempt from a distance, coming into focus as you descend from the hills. And there are beaches that hide their majestic landscapes behind high dunes, rewarding you at the last minute with surprising views; sometimes leaden, slate-grey skies and black seas, sometimes crashing waves, sometimes the sea so far out that it's barely there and the sky stretching on forever, and sometimes – those perfect times – bright blue seas, glorious blue skies and golden sand.

Such a beach is Camber Sands (reached by car via the A259 from Hastings/Rye towards Hythe, then via the B2075), which withholds its beauty until the last second. Hidden behind a mountain of dunes, it's an awesome spectacle: a vast, windswept expanse of soft, sandy beach, seven miles long and, at low tide, a staggering half a mile wide. Situated west of Dungeness and east of Rye, Camber lacks the character of the former and the classiness of the latter, but, in terms of pure, unadulterated beach, this is arguably the best strand on the south coast.

Camber Sands' immensity also breeds versatility. Here are families hunkering down in their sturdy windbreak bunkers (you'll need them, and they're available for hire) and building huge sandcastles, or paddling and swimming in the clean seas. At the water's edge are couples walking dogs and riders gently cantering through the surf on horseback (01797 225207 for information). Kiteboarders and windsurfers, for whom Camber is a huge destination, career across the sand and through the waves (for info on watersports, contact 01797 321885, www.actionwatersports.co.uk or 01797 225238, www.ryewatersports.co.uk). Back in the dunes, nature-lovers watch the wildlife.

The sand dunes are an anomaly along the pebbly Sussex coast. No piddly little mounds these, but towering peaks and broad valleys that give you some idea of what walking in a desert must be like. In fact, the dunes have stood in for deserts in a number of film shoots – notably acting as the Sahara in the 1967 film *Carry On... Follow That Camel*. To act out your Lawrence of Arabia fantasies, walk away from the village to the west end of the beach. Here, the dunes are at their biggest and the sands are secluded.

Not only are the dunes rare for these parts, they're also a Site of Special Scientific Interest. They host wildlife (hen harriers, short-eared owls and snow bunting all spend winters here) and have an interesting geological story to tell: they have gradually formed over the last 350 years and are growing by about 300,000 square

COAST

feet every year. The mounds take shape when sand blows inland and builds up around plants and fences – in Camber's case, pretty, traditional chestnut fences, erected to help stabilise the dunes. Mother nature contributes too: marram grass, which fringes the beach, has a deep root system that holds the sand in place.

If not for these defences, both natural and man-made, the village of Camber would be swallowed up by the sea or buried under the sand. For some people, this wouldn't be such a bad thing. Bordered by a 3,000-capacity car park and a Pontin's Holiday Camp, Camber village is not exactly synonymous with classiness in the popular imagination. In fact, it was once determinedly downmarket and downright unappealing.

But the area is subtly changing, particularly at the western end. Though the western car park has a nasty-looking café (think cheap burgers and plastic beach tat), it has recently been overshadowed by a spiffy new neighbour. In fact, the scene calls to mind a hoary old John Wayne in a frontier town, facing off the young brash sheriff across the road – in this case, the Place (*see p72*), a brasserie and boutique hotel. Opened in 2003, the Place kickstarted the gentrification of Camber, generating acres of

FIVE Retro ice-cream parlours

Fusciardi's
Portraits of knickerbocker glories hang on the walls, while locals sit on the chrome and red Formica chairs in this family gelateria. Try the pear and amaretto Moonraker or the Mintnight Express.
30 Marine Parade, Eastbourne, East Sussex BN22 7AY (01323 722128). Open Summer 9am-10.30pm daily. Winter 9am-5pm daily.

Rossi's
A recent refurb stripped this Southend institution of its Lloyd Loom wicker chairs and marble-topped tables; delicious artisan ice-cream a retro logo and wistful views more than compensate, however.
12-14 Western Esplanade, Southend-On-Sea, Essex SS1 1EE (01702 348376, www.rossiicecream.com). Open Summer 8.30am-8pm daily. Winter 8.30am-5pm daily.

Morelli's
Few places can match the character of this popular doo-wop era diner. With an outpost in Harrods and flavours including Pimm's sorbetto and cucumber gelato, it has some of the finest ice-cream in the UK.
14 Victoria Parade, Broadstairs, Kent CT10 1QS (01843 862500, www.morellisgelato.com). Open Summer 8am-10pm daily. Winter 8am-5pm daily.

Macari's
On the bustling promenade next to the Edwardian Dome cinema, flavours here change daily but mainstay specialities include Cointreau and orange, turkish delight and twists on classics.
24-25 Marine Parade, Worthing, West Sussex BN11 3PT (01903 532753, www.macarisrestaurant.co.uk). Open July, Aug 9am-11pm daily. Sept-June 9am-5pm Mon-Fri; 9am-5.45pm Sat, Sun.

Ives Ice Cream Parlour
Serving locally sourced organic churn and Swiss-imported ices, this tiny parlour attracts snake-like queues in the summer; the tequila sunrise flavour is a winner.
160 High Street, Aldeburgh, Suffolk IP15 5AQ (01728 452264). Open Mar-Nov 11am-5pm daily. Dec-Feb 11am-5pm Sat, Sun.

press coverage. It was converted from a 1960s motel, and now architecturally interesting buildings are springing up in the nearby village.

Back on the beach, the Kit Kat café (*see below*), fenced off from the sands with posts made from driftwood, is a characterful spot. While away an hour on the deck, eating ice-cream, watching the world at play or listening to the wind whistle. Against a constant sea breeze, the grass on the dunes looks as if it's being brushed with an invisible hand. And it is this soothing scene, rather than the plastic tat and holiday camps, that leaves the biggest impression. That, and the first memorable glimpse that awaits you at the top of the dunes.

If you want to venture beyond Camber, a few miles west is Winchelsea Beach (www.winchelseabeach.org.uk). This is a typical south coast shingle beach whose dilapidated groynes and mirror-like rock pools give it an ethereal beauty – great for long walks and atmospheric photographs, particularly at low tide. If the shingle proves too tricky, there's a promenade, so you can keep your eye on the sky without wobbling around on the ground.

Eating & Drinking

With the exception of the Place, Camber is a bit of a culinary wasteland; foodies are better off venturing into nearby Rye (*see p33*).

Green Owl
11 Old Lydd Road, TN31 7RE (01797 225284, www.thegreenowl.co.uk). Open lunch noon-2.30pm daily, dinner 6pm-late.
The Green Owl pub has got a great location – a short distance away from the beach. It serves the usual pub grub, if a picnic in the sand doesn't hold any appeal.

Kit Kat Café
Old Lydd Road, TN31 7RH (01797 222413).
A basic caff serving basic grub: all-day breakfasts, bacon butties, tea and cakes.

The Place at Camber Sands
New Lydd Road, TN31 7RB (01797 225057, www.theplacecambersands.co.uk).
A minimalist boutique hotel near the best part of the beach, the Place opened in 2003 and made it OK to go to Camber again. The brasserie has been garnering lots of press: it serves locally sourced produce (including wines) and seafood from sustainably fished sources. The chic decor – all glass and blonde wood – is a far cry from the nearby holiday camps, and marks the new face of Camber Sands.

Dungeness

Kent's alternative beach resort.

Dungeness is not the typical setting for a day at the beach. A picnic in the sand? A paddle in the shallows? Kiss me quick? Not here. This lonely strip of hard, unyielding shingle doesn't just look different to the average Kent beach – the entire promontory barely looks like England at all. The sky stretches wide over flat marshland; a scattering of fishing shacks looks small and vulnerable against the eerie, light-filled expanse; the steep pebbly banks are constantly reshaped by the relentless sea.

And yet all this isolation and strangeness has its advantages: on fine days, when the English Channel turns a rich, deep blue, the beach remains sparsely populated. And when the weather's not so clement, Dungeness comes into its own, allowing you to believe that you're the only person left on this cramped island, with only the roiling grey water and the hum of Dungeness power station for company.

Dungeness is most easily reached by car (take the M20 to Ashford, the A2070 towards Brenzett and the A259 towards New Romney, followed by the B2075 towards Lydd); alternatively, take the train to Rye (*see p33*) and then hop on the 711 bus to nearby Lydd from where it's a short taxi ride.

In a landscape where there are many unusual features, the imposing hulk of a nuclear power plant is the most unexpected. But the biggest danger to day-trippers is not a nuclear explosion – touch wood – but the treacherous waters. Where the shingle meets the sea, there's no gentle lapping and no possibility of cooling off up to the knee. Waves rise to the edge of the banks, smash down and then suck the shingle mercilessly. If paddling is hazardous, swimming would be suicide.

No wonder anglers are a more common sight here than families. Apart from solitary walkers, Dungeness's bread and butter consists of those hoping to ensnare a fish. In fact, the same conditions that make for lousy swimming ensure wonderful fishing: thanks to the steep shelving, the water is so deep that it's possible to fish off the edge of the beach just as you might from the banks of a deep reservoir. Local diehards eat the fish caught here, despite any possible deleterious effect from the power station's warm, chlorinated waste waters.

If dangerous to swimmers, the currents are no more forgiving to boats; there is still an RNLI station here, and the coast is littered with wrecks. Maps framed in the Old Lighthouse pinpoint the lost vessels.

Built in 1904, this lighthouse is now defunct (there is a new, black-and-white striped one, built in 1961), but is still open to the public (you can even get married here). Squeeze yourself on to the viewing platform to really understand the

lie of this odd land. From the highest vantage point, dark railway tracks slash through the sparse and scrubby earth below; Dungeness is the end of the line – physically and spiritually – for the Romney, Hythe & Dymchurch Light Railway (www.rhdr.org.uk, *see p232*). From above, the bleakness of this landscape is magnified; featureless to the average eye, it soon becomes apparent why Dungeness has been deemed Britain's only desert.

Bizarrely, the natural environment seems to have benefited from the industrial detritus (gravel pits, nuclear power station). Dungeness is a breeding ground for unusual and rare forms of flora and fauna. There are some 600 species of plants, many of them rare. Fluttering above, the rare Sussex emerald moth appears in July. The old gravel pits harbour the protected great crested newt and the medicinal leech. Spiders are in their element too: there are 302 species (arachnophobes beware).

Twitchers will have a field day: there is an RSPB nature reserve with hides for viewing species such as the Slavonian grebe, the smew and bittern.

From birders to beatniks, this moody corner of Kent has never been short of fans, who have found a singular charm in its bleak ambience. The film director Derek Jarman lived here, in Prospect Cottage (*see also p152* Five Works of art), where his garden of beachcombings, driftwood and weird sculptural plants still draws curious visitors, years after his passing.

COAST

Jarman's experimental style has set a trend. Just as visually unique is the RIBA award-winning Vista house, built by architect Simon Conder: here, the bones of a 1930s wooden fishing hut have been shrink-wrapped in matt black rubber. Nearby, other buildings have been improvised out of old railway coaches.

The wonderfully twisted result looks something akin to a frontier community; a far cry from the neatly turned-out bungalows of nearby Lydd. But it's worth taking these roads less travelled. Just don't expect seaside jollity. Dungeness is a defiantly alien place, and one that seems proud to be flouting the normal rules of the British seaside.

Eating & Drinking

Britannia
Dungeness Road, TN29 9ND (01797 321959). Open Summer 11am-11pm daily. Winter 11am-2.30pm, 6-9pm daily.
Dungeness's Britannia is a basic pub that serves generous portions of fish and chips and Shepherd Neame, the local ale.

Light Railway Café
Dungeness Station, Dungeness Road, TN29 9NB (01797 320221). Open Summer 10am-6pm daily. Winter 10am-3pm Sat, Sun.
The Light Railway Café serves fish and chips and numerous cups of tea, as well as Sunday roasts. It's open every day that the miniature railway is running, and at weekends during the winter.

Pilot
Dungeness Road, TN29 9NJ (01797 320314, www.thepilot.uk.com). Open Summer 11am-11pm daily. Winter 11am-3pm, 6-10pm Mon-Fri; 11am-10pm Sat; 11am-9pm Sun.
The Pilot is the most popular local eaterie, perhaps by default, as there's not much choice around here. It's nothing special: the atmosphere is jovial enough, but the only culinary highlight is the fish and chips.

Romney Bay House Hotel
Coast Road, Littlestone, New Romney, TN28 8QY (01797 364747).
This small hotel has a glamorous past. Designed and built in the 1920s for the doyenne of gossip columnists, Hedda Hopper, it's the creation of Sir Clough Williams-Ellis, who built Portmeirion, the Welsh village made famous by *The Prisoner*. Today, it's noted for its quietly classy restaurant, run by Ritz-trained chef Clinton Lovell. Expect modern Anglo-French food prepared with fresh, local ingredients and matched by an excellent wine list. Cream teas hit the spot, rain or shine.

Shopping & Attractions

Dungeness Gallery
Caithness, TN29 9ND (01797 320497, www.dungenessgallery.co.uk). Open 10am-5pm daily (times & days may vary).
Housed in three Edwardian railway carriages, this gallery is not short on atmosphere. The art, a mix of photography and watercolours, focuses mostly on local scenes.

Old Lighthouse
Dungeness Road, TN29 9NB (01797 321300, www.dungenesslighthouse.com). Open Mar, Apr, Oct 10.30am-4.30pm Sat, Sun. May, June, Sept 10am-4.30pm Thur-Sun. July, Aug 10.30am-4.30pm daily. Admission £3.
Opened in 1904, the old lighthouse was a guiding light for sailors in the English Channel for 56 years. It is no longer operational, but you can climb the 169 steps and soak in the stellar view.

Romney, Hythe & Dymchurch Railway
New Romney Station, New Romney, TN28 8PL (01797 362353, www.rhdr.org.uk).
As the world's smallest public railway, this sweet little train adds some fun to melancholy Dungeness. For 13 miles, it chugs merrily from Dungeness Point to Hythe, stopping at the small beach towns along the coast. In addition to the flat, bleak scenery, it seems to sweep through several back gardens along the way.

Romney Sands
www.greatstone.net.
Romney Sands is notable for two reasons. It's a sandy beach – rare for these parts – and has an interesting military twist. Nearby, at Greatstone, are the 'listening ears'. These aeroplane-detecting sound mirrors were constructed for World War II, but their usefulness was ultimately eclipsed by the arrival of radar. The massive concrete structures have an eerie beauty that suits the landscape, and could double as modern art installations by some radical South Coast artist.

RSPB Dungeness Nature Reserve
Dungeness Road, TN29 9PN (01797 320588, www.rspb.org.uk). Open 9am-dusk daily. Admission £3.
The strange landscape at Dungeness is as alluring to birds as it is to humans. Through a picture window at the Visitor Centre, you can watch an avian spectacular unfold in the large gravel pit. Hides are dotted around the nature trails; during the winter, keep your eyes peeled for bitterns and bearded tits.

Botany Bay

A proper sandy beach with a dramatic backdrop.

A secret treasure, Botany Bay is, remarkably, less than two hours from London. 'People say it reminds them of Portugal,' says Kevin Dunmore, the kiosk man at this hidden cove on the eastern tip of the Kent coast, as he wistfully gazes out into the grey seas of the Dover Strait.

This is certainly the prettiest of the seven little bays that dot this shoreline. All are characterised by their chalk cliffs – the longest continuous stretch of them in Britain – but Botany Bay wins the postcard prize for its much-photographed chalk stacks. It's this signature geological feature (rather than the weather, light or summer temperatures) that tends to bring to mind the Algarve.

Despite being halfway between the resorts of Margate and Ramsgate, Botany Bay is not well known. The approach is through quiet suburban streets (from Broadstairs follow the B2052, then turn off down Percy Avenue, Kingsgate Avenue or Botany Road; trains run to Broadstairs from London's Charing Cross and Victoria stations). There are no fairground waltzers, no donkey rides, no chippies, no amusement arcades, no candyfloss, no doughnut dispensers... This is an old-fashioned beach, where you make your own entertainment. And that's its charm.

That, and the cliffs. They dominate this diminutive strand (it's only 600 feet long), sweeping round the sandy cove and framing the sea. Indeed, with the tide in, the bluffs make Botany Bay feel safe and sheltered. But as the water recedes, the beach opens up and the horizons broaden. Time it right and you can walk along the shore to Broadstairs in an hour, clambering over rocks along the way.

Botany Bay may be well hidden, but it has a cult following. Even on an unseasonably chilly Saturday in July, for instance, the soft sandy beach is colonised by hardy families determined to have A Good Day Out. A series of temporary encampments springs up, demarcated by striped windbreaks (available for hire from the kiosk) and small children frantically digging. Sandwiches and crisps are unpacked, beachmats unfurled, newspapers opened and ball games initiated, but leave the dogs at home (from 15 May to 15 September, they're banned during the daytime). Children (who, it seems, never feel the cold) pull on their swimming costumes and head, squealing, into the sea, while parents paddle more tentatively or watch from the windbreaks. In the centre of the beach is the sporty Surf Rescue team – tanned young things in red cagoules. If you are feeling particularly active, you can hire body boards from nearby Joss Bay Surf School (07812 991195, www.jossbay.co.uk).

Botany Bay is a social place, and the kiosk, a small, blue wooden building at the foot of the steps, is the hub. 'The variety of people is great,' says Dunmore, who ran the business for four summers in a row. 'Grandparents, families, dogwalkers, school trips, Jo Brand... no two days are the same.' Some customers linger at the kiosk's café tables scoffing snacks, ice-cream and tea. Dads pitch up to hire body boards for their kids, or buy coloured nets for rock-pooling.

Indeed, rocks are a distinguishing feature of the landscape here. When the tide goes out, the sea reveals an extensive chalk reef – deemed to be the best in Britain – that makes geologists weak at the knees. Pretty chalk pebbles wash up along the tideline, smoothed into ovals, sometimes with worn holes that make odd little faces. 'Rock Doc' walks are organised by the Thanet Coast Project (www.thanetcoast.org.uk), along with Summer Seashore Safaris, where even amateur rock-poolers can turn up starfish, crabs, piddocks and cuttlefish eggs.

Botany Bay's rocky terrain and cliffs endeared it to smugglers, who plied a lucrative trade in the area during the 18th century. Establishments such as the popular chain pub the Captain Digby Inn (above Joss Bay) revel in this unscrupulous past. The landscape shows signs of it too: hidden around the chalk stacks and headland in nearby Kingsgate Bay, smugglers' holes are carved into the cliffs. Natural caves, eroded by the waves, were useful for stashing booty too.

The smugglers may be gone, but this curious corner of the South-east is still a bit of a law unto

itself. Pushing into the sea at the foot of the Thames Estuary, the peninsula likes to think of itself as removed from Kent. Once cut off by the Channel, it maintains its 'Isle of Thanet' moniker despite being attached to the mainland for a century. It boasts of being closer to France than to its county town of Maidstone, though culturally it feels closer to 1978.

The busy shipping traffic prevents the sense of remoteness you find on the west coast, but the sands are still pristine, owing to a particularly fastidious beach cleaner.

Eating & Drinking

Botany Bay is not a foodie favourite – the only place on the beach that provides any kind of sustenance is the Kiosk (no phone, www.the beachkioskatbotanybaykent.co.uk); Broadstairs, however, is great. As well as the places listed below, the town is home to the retro ice-cream parlour Morelli's (*see p72*).

Neptune's Hall
1-5 Harbour Street, Broadstairs, Kent CT10 1ET (01843 861400). Open noon-11pm Mon-Fri; noon-nidnight Sat, Sun.
When visiting Kent, it's imperative to drink the ales by Shepherd Neame, the county's biggest brewer. The friendly Neptune's Hall pub offers a good selection, complemented by seasonal guest ales, bar food and tapas, and a beer garden.

Chiappini's
1 The Parade, Broadstairs, Kent CT10 1NB (01843 865051). Open Summer 9am-5.30pm daily. Winter 9am-4pm daily. (Closing times may vary.)
Serving cappuccinos since long before the Starbucks generation was born, this vintage Italian coffee bar is a delicious slice of 1960s nostalgia. Grab a table on the promenade, and watch the world go by, or serve yourself some lunch: freshly made pasta or salads. Top it off with an obligatory ice-cream: choose from a

range of Italian flavours, or order something fancy in a tall glass with a long spoon and a cherry on top.

Osteria Pizzeria Posillipo
14 Albion Street, Broadstairs, Kent CT10 1LU (01843 601133, www.posillipo.co.uk). Open noon-10pm daily.
A big and bustling, much-lauded pizzeria. Order an impeccable pizza from the wood-fired oven and eat it on the terrace overlooking Viking Bay. Booking is recommended.

Royal Albion
6-12 Albion Street, Broadstairs, Kent CT10 1AN (01843 868071, www.albion broadstairs.co.uk). Open 11am-11pm daily.
This 1760 hotel was once a favourite watering hole of Charles Dickens. Today, it's still a good drinking spot: it carries Shepherd Neame, the much-loved local Kentish ale. The menu leans towards local seafood. Make the most of the seafront location and grab a seat on the terrace.

Shopping & Attractions

Broadstairs
Broadstairs, a short drive from Botany Bay, is the quintessential faded English seaside town. It's got the cockles and whelks and the candyfloss. But the tiny streets are brimming with Victorian and Edwardian architecture and quaint shops (*see p41* Five Shopping extravaganzas); and it's not all twee either – retro 1950s Italian coffee shops are a forte here. The old-fashioned credentials come from a rich maritime history and a Dickensian air (the author used to spend his summers here, and every June it holds a Dickens festival: www.broadstairsdickensfestival.co.uk). Children can let off steam on trampolines at Viking Bay, where there is still a traditional Punch and Judy show in the summer – you can't get more nostalgic than that. If it rains, take shelter at a screening in the dinky Palace Cinema (Harbour Street, 01843 865726, www.palacebroadstairs.co.uk).

Bleak House
Fort Road, CT10 1EY (01843 861400, www.bleakhouse.info).
Dickens had a soft spot for Broadstairs. He spent a month here every summer, and wrote *David Copperfield* and *The Old Curiosity Shop* here. This castle-like house was his summer home at the height of his fame. Perched grandly on the top of a cliff, it overlooks Viking Bay. Called Fort House in his day, the building was renamed

Bleak House, after the book which he planned in his study here. Once a museum, the building is now privately owned, but its splendid crenellated features and majestic position still make an impression.

Dickens House Museum
2 Victoria Parade, CT10 1QS (01843 861232). Open 2-5pm Wed-Sat. Admission £2.70 adults, £1.50 children.
Dickens House, now a small museum, was once the residence of a Miss Mary Pearson, who inspired the character of Miss Betsey Trotwood, David Copperfield's aunt (in the book, this house was moved to Dover, to avoid embarrassment). This Tudor building is filled with Dickens memorabilia, from prints by HK Browne (one of Dickens's illustrators) to letters written by Dickens about Broadstairs (which he refers to as 'Our English Watering Place'). See also www.broadstairsdickensfestival.co.uk.

Joss Bay
Kent may not be synonymous with surfing, but Joss Bay (two bays round from Botany) is the choice of the south-east boarders, on account of its decent groundswell. Surfing is at its best here from September to April (lessons and hire can be arranged via www.jossbay.co.uk). Sheltered by white chalky cliffs, the bay was named after notorious 18th-century smuggler Joss Snelling, a local legend who managed to evade the noose and live till the age of 96. For his efforts, he was presented to the future Queen Victoria as 'the famous Broadstairs smuggler'. Overlooking the beach, the North Foreland Lighthouse marks the southern entrance to the Thames. Nearby, Minnis Bay is is great for rock-pooling and kids. Sailing, windsurfing and seal trips are offered.

Margate
www.visitthanet.co.uk.
Best known for binge-drinking and Tracey Emin, Margate has evolved into an arty enclave. But there's still old-school seaside fun: candyfloss, waltzers and donkey rides, plus Margate Caves (lessons and hire can curious Shell Grotto (www.shellgrotto.co.uk), covered with 4.6 million shells, and a museum of smuggling.

Viking Coastal Trail
The Viking Coastal Trail, a 27-mile cycle route around the Thanet coastline, covers beaches galore, plus smugglers' haunts, dramatic clifftops, historic churches, nature reserves and Dickens' memorabilia. (www.vikingcoastaltrail.co.uk).

Littlehampton

A traditional seaside resort washed in its first wave of gentrification.

Vogue may have hailed Littlehampton the 'coolest British seaside resort' in 2007, but many who visit may struggle to believe the hype; the place still has some way to go before it becomes Sussex's equivalent of Kent's Whitstable. Yet, herein lies the appeal for many; with its pretty coastline, faded promenade, colourful beach huts and old-school fairground, the place still has a ramshackle charm. And, with a pair of architecturally striking, and, in the case of the East Beach Café, gastronomically lauded, seafront eateries – as well as retro chippies – it has also become something of a destination for foodies.

It may be a little hard to imagine the place as it used to be – the holiday destination of artists and bohemians such as Byron, Constable and a young Graham Greene, but Littlehampton is a good place to head to if you're after the simple pleasures of a British seaside resort – and it's less than two hours by train from Victoria. Visit on a bright summer's day, head straight for the seafront and you may well fall for its low-key charms.

Framed by brightly coloured beach huts at one end, and a grand Regency crescent on the other, the East Beach has views across sweeping manicured lawns to the sea. The landscape is somewhat blighted, however, by a Harvester restaurant and rows of scruffy shops off the promenade, along with a fairground with miniature log flume and bumper cars. There's fun to be had hooking a duck, gambling pennies in the arcade or bingeing on candyfloss, but what most come here for is the East Beach Café (*see p80*), the gastronomic venue that put Littlehampton on the map. Nestled on the beach like washed-up driftwood, it draws diners from Brighton and beyond, and is the most apparent sign of the gentrification that might eventually see Littlehampton, with its old-school marina, quirky rusty red bridge and art deco apartment blocks, becoming Sussex's equivalent of Kent's Whitstable. For now, though, the town remains resolutely unpretentious, and free from the latte-quaffing crowds you get further up the coast.

That picnicking on the beach, lounging in hired deckchairs and building sandcastles are all favourite summer activities here means that the spot is still every bit the British seaside resort. The 'Blue Flag' East Beach is even good for swimming – particularly if you head eastward past the groynes. Best of all the shingle fades into sand so you don't stub your feet in the shallows.

The West Beach is more rugged, with wild dunes to the rear, perfect for a spot of secluded sunbathing or sheltering from the wind on blustery days. For natural beach lovers, this is seaside nirvana – with a long stretch of unadulterated sand, free from neon clutter, and a horizon that seems to stretch on forever. Pack a picnic blanket and a hamper, or better still grab some gourmet fish and chips and own-made ice-cream from the West Beach Café (*see p80*). You can also handily hire binoculars for £1, providing light-hearted amusement for birdwatchers and nosey-parkers alike.

It's Littlehampton's low-key ambience, as well as its strong winds and busy tides, that have seen it become a popular destination for windsurfing and kitesurfing; even surfers have been heading here in recent years. In summer, there are watersports schools on both the East and West beaches, (see www.littlehampton kitesurfing.co.uk for details). Littlehampton also hosts the Kitesurfing Championships in midsummer, which provides high-octane spectacle by day and beach-party entertainment at night. You can also try out more unusual seabound pursuits by chartering a boat for a spot of wreck-diving or invigorating sea-fishing; we recommend family-run outfit Michelle Mary, run by the chirpy, boat-obsessive Ivan (www.michellemary.co.uk)

Eating & Drinking

East Beach Café
Sea Road, BN17 5GB (01903 731903, www.eastbeachcafe.co.uk). Open Summer 10am-5pm, 6.30-9pm daily. Winter 10am-2.30pm Mon-Wed, Sun; 10.30am-2.30pm, 6.30-8.30pm Thur-Sat.

COAST

Designed by visionary architect Thomas Heatherwick, of *Sitooterie* fame (*see p151*), this monocoque café is fresh and functional. From the outside it looks like a giant brown clam shell, with its organic, sculptural form, while the interior feels more like a boutique restaurant than a beachside café, with its quirky curved white ceiling, smart navy decking and floor-to-ceiling windows with dramatic sea views. The menu runs from simple classics such as beer-battered fish to imaginative seafood dishes such as mussel, gurnard and salmon saffron chowder under the eye of Ritz-trained head chef David Whiteside. Service is friendly and efficient and with its buzzing ambience East Beach Café is worth the day-trip from London alone. The restaurant seats 60 and is available for private hire. Book in advance.

West Beach Café
Rope Walk, BN17 5DL (01903 718153, www.eastbeachcafe.co.uk). Open Summer 10am-6pm Mon-Wed; 10am-7.30pm Thur-Sun. Winter 10am-4pm Sat, Sun.
Distinctly less showy than its East Beach sister, this place is still a cut above your usual beach-side café – it's also architect-designed, for a start (this is Asif Khan's first building). The boxy structure is dominated by light, which pours in through the floor-to-ceiling windows and also comes from the clever use of overhanging lamps inside. In summer the doors open out on to the patio next to the beach. West Beach sells simple fare such as fish cakes, scampi, toasted sandwiches and very good fish and chips with minty mushy peas. It's licensed but also does a nice line in big hot mugs of tea.

FIVE Retro resorts

Broadstairs
Charles Dickens loved Broadstairs, and it's easy to see why. In this sweet Kent seaside town everything has an old-world charm and toy-town appeal, from the dinky Palace cinema (01843 865726, www.palacebroadstairs.co.uk) to the tiny streets criss-crossing the town, wee fishermen's cottages and seven pretty beaches. Stop in on the front for ice-cream at Morelli's, a seaside caff and ice-cream parlour (*see p72*) built in 1932. *See also p76* Botany Bay and *p41* Five Shopping extravaganzas.

Cliftonville (Margate)
Just a few minutes' walk along the coast from Margate is genteel Cliftonville, a determinedly traditional bucket and spade suburb of the Victorian seaside town. Its chief delights are its beautifully manicured lawns backing on to the parade, some great art deco houses, a beautiful Lido tower and, the showstopper, a terrific Arnold Palmer-designed miniature golf course. Fore!

Eastbourne
Parp Parp! Head straight to the pretty 1930s bandstand for some traditional brass band music on the traditional seaside promenade, admiring the lovingly tended gardens – geraniums lined up with military precision – en route. Then hop on a Dotto train named after famous lovers or risk a tooth on a stick of rock in the camera obscura on the Victorian pier. And end with a climb to the top of Beachy Head, of course.

Hastings
Take the thrilling West Hill Cliff Railway funicular (Britain's steepest) up the cliffs to the ruins of Hastings Castle and site of John Logie Baird's first radar experiments and admire the looming black double-decker fishermen's huts down below, or enjoy the old-school promenade pleasures of this West Sussex town, including crazy and mini-golf, a bingo hall and an amusement park. Explore the narrow streets leading away from the front for antique and vintage clothing shops, and Judges, an organic bakery and deli (51 High Street, 01424 722588). Hastings Country Park has plenty of walking trails and amazing clifftop views.

Thorpeness
This seaside oddity lies in the shadow of Sizewell B nuclear power station, and just along the Suffolk coast from Southwold (*see p42*). It was a fishing hamlet until bought in 1910 by a Scottish landowner, who built a model village. There's a boating lake (the meare), mock Tudor houses galore, a windmill and 'the house in the clouds' (a cunningly disguised water tower) – and of course, the delights of the (pebbled) beach.

COAST

Whitstable

Shellfish, a shingle beach and beautiful sunsets.

A coastal town that revels in its quirkiness, Whitstable is still, for all its charm and diversity, predominantly famous for two things: oysters and Peter Cushing. Yet it has far more to offer the rat-race weary Londoner than aphrodisiac shellfish and Hammer Horror. Despite substantial modernisation, the town has successfully retained a sense of historical allure and, at less than an hour and a half from London's Victoria station by train, makes for an easy day out from the capital.

Whitstable still has a working harbour, so you can observe fishermen going about their daily rituals as you soak up the local ambience. Upon return from the treacherous seas, fishermen of yore would have retreated to the quaint weatherboard cottages that still line the town's narrow streets. You can appreciate some excellent examples of these still-inhabited houses with a walk down Sea Wall and Island Wall, where the small dwellings sit on quiet roads. The only noise that's likely to disturb you on your stroll is the gentle lapping of the waves on the nearby seafront, or the unmistakeable crunch of stone against stone from walkers on the adjacent pebble beach.

It takes only a minuscule shift of the imagination to envisage what Whitstable would have been like in the past, with exhausted fishermen trudging wearily home and flinging off their boots. And today, with its squawking seagulls and sea-breeze aromas, it pulls off relaxed coastal style with aplomb.

During the summer months, the town is especially beautiful. Make the most of good weather by joining the locals in some hearty indulgence – namely traditional, paper-wrapped fish and chips messily devoured on the beach: VC Jones is the favourite local chippy (25 Harbour Street, 01227 272703). The easily guilt-laden might then want to burn off the excess calories with a short stroll along the sea wall to Peter Cushing's former residence – a pretty but inconspicuous house identified only by a modestly sized plaque.

From the seafront it's only a short walk to Whitstable Castle. This well-preserved building with its colourful and ornate gardens is closed for renovation until 2010, but if you make your way to the top of the hill you'll come out just opposite Tower Hill Tea Gardens (Tower Hill, 07780 662543), an idyllic and seldom-packed location that combines quaint, bucolic charm with invigorating sea air and coastal vistas. If you haven't eaten already, or if you've been patient enough to save your fish and chips, then the Tea Gardens makes a brilliant picnic spot. Another summer favourite is the Whitstable Oyster Festival (*see p84* Diary Dates, and *p224*, Five Seasonal food events).

Whatever the time of year, though, a leisurely stroll down Harbour Street is a must, as it's the best showcase of Whitstable's diversity. Stop off for excellent tapas at the distinctly un-Spanish-sounding Williams & Brown (48 Harbour Street, 01227 273373), or have an inventive and superior seafood dish such as mussels and potato soup or deep-fried bream with chillies at local favourite Birdies (41 Harbour Street, 01227 265337).

Oysters are, of course, Whitstable's celebrated delicacy, and there's no better place to sample both native and Scottish Rock ones than Wheelers Oyster Bar (*see p84*). Unsurpassed when it comes to fresh, locally sourced fish, seafood fans will not be disappointed – unless they've failed to book well in advance. In which case two stalwart and consistently good alternatives are the excellent Whitstable Oyster Fisheries Company (*see p84*) or the equally fab East Quay Shellfish (East Quay Harbour, 01227 262003) – a self-service restaurant and café bar housed in a series of buildings (originally an 18th-century oyster grading house) that celebrate the fruits of the sea by means of a little exhibition on the town's oyster dredging history, which should keep you busy while you wait for the food – the fish in beer batter and chips is excellent.

Pub-restaurants the Pearson's Arms (*see p84*) and the Sportsman (*see p53* Ten Perfect country pubs) also serve quality fish dishes, with the former offering spectacular sea views and the latter, slightly further afield in Seasalter, boasting a Michelin star. For the best alfresco afternoon pint, head for the Old Neptune (Marine Terrace, 01227 272262, www.neppy. co.uk). Set right in the middle of the beach, you can sit at one of the many benches that look out to sea, with stunning sunsets and views of the Isle of Sheppey providing a sensational backdrop to your tipple. The Whitstable Brewery Bar (*see p84*) also offers dramatic views of the Thames Estuary and distant wind farms.

Another impressive natural feature of Whitstable is the Street, a spit of land that extends out to sea, from which you can look back at the town for a break from sea views. Of course, you can only reach the spot at low tide, but it's popular with beachfront wanderers and curious amblers. Ensure that you're familiar with the tides beforehand, though, as it can be a potentially dangerous venture otherwise.

COAST

Diary Dates

MARKETS

Whitstable Harbour Market
South Quay, CT5 1AB (01227 262433, www.whitstableharbourvillage.co.uk). Open 10am-5pm Sat, Sun (weekdays during high season).
Local products from independent local suppliers selling produce, clothing, plants and homeware.

FESTIVALS

Whitstable Oyster Festival
Various locations in town (01227 862048, www.whitstableoysterfestival.co.uk). Dates Mid-late July.
It may be a bad time to eat oysters (there being no R in the month), but this summer festival nonetheless attracts thousands of visitors. Expect fine food, local wares, community events and live music in abundance.

Whitstable Regatta
Tankerton Slopes (01227 378100). Dates Early Aug.
An offshoot of the Oyster Festival, this sailing and watersports celebration originally consisted of yawl races, rowing races and swimming. Today, the last Oyster Yawl can be viewed at Island Wall, where once were shipyards, sailmakers' sheds and forges.

If you fancy getting out on to the water itself, you'll find ample off-shore coastal tours on offer from March to October, courtesy of Bayblast (01227 373372, www.bayblast.co.uk) or the sailing boat *Greta* (01795 534541, www.thames barges.co.uk). You can visit the Wind Farm at Kentish Flats, as well as the eerie Red Sand forts that were part of the East Coast defences during World War II, and housed pirate radio stations in the 1960s, such as Radio Invicta, Radio Sutch and Radio Essex. You can also venture out to the Barrow Sands, a popular destination with both grey and common seals.

Whether you visit Whitstable during the summer or more sedate winter period, this coastal retreat makes for an appealing day out from the city, one that will leave you feeling you've experienced a rare sense of old-world charm and simplicity.

Eating & Drinking

Pearson's Arms
The Horsebridge, Sea Wall, CT5 1BT (01227 276125). Open noon-11pm daily.
As well as offering an excellent shellfish- and seafood-led menu upstairs (with impressive views to match), the Pearson's Arms has an informal, affordable bar menu downstairs to accompany a quiet pint or two.

Wheelers
8 High Street, CT5 1BQ (01227 273311, www.whitstable-shellfish.co.uk). Open 1-7.30pm Mon, Tue, Thur-Sat; 1-7pm Sun.
Ask a local where to go for a decent plate of seafood and they'll almost certainly point you in the direction of Wheelers. The original of the long-gone London version was always the best, and still holds its own among the strong local competition. Relatively simple food – a bowl of eels with bread, whole bay octopus, snapper, roasted cod, steak, ale and oyster pie or, of course, just the oysters – are served in a tiny Victorian parlour behind a small pink and blue shopfront featuring a chilled and loaded display of shellfish. Bring your own wine or beer (there's a Threshers across the road) and you won't even be charged corkage.

Whitstable Brewery Bar
East Quay, CT5 2BP (01227 772157). Open noon-11pm daily.
This tucked-away local fave is best appreciated during the summer. When the sun's shining, it's a hub of activity, beer-drinking and general merriment, and it's just across from the habitually busy south quay.

Whitstable Oyster Fishery Company
Horsebridge, CT5 1BU (01227 276856, www.oysterfishery.co.uk). Open noon-2.30pm, 6.30-9pm Tue-Thur; noon-2.30pm, 6.30-9.30pm Fri; 8.30am-2.30pm, 6.30-9.30pm Sat; 8.30am-3.30pm, 6.30-8.30pm Sun.
Once home to the Royal Native Oyster Stores, the Oyster Fishery Restuarant is renowned for excellent seafood. To start, you can go native with Whitstable oysters, pay half as much for non-natives or opt for squid, clams, moules or sardines. Mains include top-notch organic salmon, sea bass, cod and lobster, and the dessert list offers the likes of treacle tart, sticky toffee pudding or chocolate torte. You can have a drink in the bar upstairs while you wait for your table (booking is essential). The Whitstable Brewery beer is worth a try, though there's a decent wine list if you prefer grape to grain.

COAST

TEN Beach activities

Beachcombing
Herne Bay East in Kent is the place to find fossilised sharks' teeth, ancient coins or perhaps even a mammoth tusk – but be prepared to get grubby in the muddy bay as you search. Look for ancient sharks' teeth around the foreshore – jet-black, around an inch in length and therefore easily differentiated from the shingle.

Birdwatching and shellfish hunting
Backed by dunes, then salt marsh, East Head beach at West Wittering in West Sussex (see p65) is the perfect terrain for birds. On the beach itself, look out for razor clams, slipper limpet shells, cockles and whelks. In Suffolk, Walberswick is another twitcher's paradise, with more than 280 species recorded at its National Nature Reserve.

Dog-walking
Whitstable in Kent (see p82) not only welcomes two-legged visitors, but also dogs. They're allowed to take a turn along the shingle beach, then accompany their masters to the Old Neptune, an excellent beachside pub.

Fishing
Dunwich in Suffolk (see right) has bass scavenging in the surf in summer, and cod hungry for bait in winter. Dungeness (see p73) in Kent is a good bet too; the steeply banking pebbles mean it's usually just you, the odd angler and the fish.

Fossil-finding
Walton-on-the-Naze in Essex is home to prehistoric turtle fossils, bird fossils and extra-large sharks' teeth, in red clay cliffs thought to be two million years old. Look around the base of the cliffs or along the foreshore, particularly following a storm. Bracklesham Bay in West Sussex also offers rich pickings after a storm, when sea-polished sharks' teeth and fossilised shells reward sharp-eyed fossil fanatics.

Getting your kit off
After 30 years of nakedness, Britain's first official nudist beach is still going strong. Shielded from voyeurs and the idly curious by a bank of pebbles and located at the far end of Brighton seafront (opposite Duke's Mound, just before the Brighton Marina), Black Rock Beach is the place to come for an all-over tan. Don't forget a blow-up lilo if you want to protect your tender bits from those pebbles.

Kitesurfing and horseriding
Camber Sands (see p69) is pretty much the perfect beach for any activity; on any given day, from summer's golden hazes through to wonderful wintery seaside scenes, kitesurfers and horses co-exist peacefully among the dog-walkers, castle-building families and couples walking along the seashore.

Photography and painting
The pictureque groynes and silvery, shimmering pools at Kent's Winchelsea beach (near Rye) create a beach that's perfect for playing with your exposures and apertures. And if Suffolk's Dunwich beach was good enough to be painted by Turner and Constable, it's surely worth getting the watercolours out for, isn't it?

Rock-pooling and crab-catching
Samphire Hoe in Kent is a rock-pooler's dream, with seven species of crab, prawns and shrimp, lovely mermaid's purses and even ham-eating anemones. West Wittering in West Sussex (see p65) has a dedicated crabbing pool, while at Hope Gap in East Sussex you can see pretty strawberry anemones and velvet swimming crabs with red eyes. Botany Bay's Thanet Beach in Kent (see p76) is good for starfish and all sorts of crustaceans. Serious crabbers head to the British Open Crabbing Championship in Walberswick, Suffolk.

Traditional entertainments
Dymchurch in Kent (between Dungeness to the east and Hythe to the west, and best reached by the terrifically fun Romney, Hythe and Dymchurch Light Railway, see p73) is a step back in time. There's a teeny amusement park that's unlikely to amuse anyone over the age of five, along with proper rock and candyfloss for small fry and martello towers for the grown-ups.

COAST

Leigh-on-Sea

Estuary views, cockle sheds and proper pubs make for a very English day out.

It's only 45 minutes on the train from Fenchurch Street, but surprisingly few Londoners know about seaside gem Leigh-on-Sea. Perhaps it's because it adjoins Southend-on-Sea, a town known for having the longest pleasure pier in the world but not a lot else, or perhaps it's because it's in easily mocked Essex, rather than classy Kent (though with its picturesque seafront strand, estuary views and villagey feel, Leigh does call to mind Whitstable). Either way, their loss. Tiny, sweet and quintessentially English, Leigh is essence of seaside, with a proper life of its own once the day-trippers have departed.

Old Leigh is a pretty cliff walk away from Southend and a short but steep climb down the ridge from its modern counterpart. The main street is flanked by cheerful cafés, various marine businesses, an art gallery, a couple of restaurants and a happily disproportionate number of pubs. The sea is on the doorstep, behind beer gardens, wharves and cockle sheds, a shingly strip home to working boats and the occasional rowing crew. At the west end, there's a tiny sandy beach, sandy, at least, until the tide goes out and reveals a muddy gulch hugely enjoyed by children – slightly less perhaps by the parents who have to clean them up. For 'sea' might be nominally correct, but this is equal parts estuary, with views to Kent that, with their hazy horizons, passing tankers and industrial landmarks, are fascinating as much as beautiful, though the light is always lovely.

There's not a whole pile to do here, but it's important to do it in the right order. Leaving Leigh-on-Sea station or car park, walk east and pick up a cup of bargain seafood from the Osborne Bros Seafood Merchants (Billet Wharf, High Street, 01702 477233, www.osbornebros. co.uk). Spear your cockles as you amble onwards along the high street, earmarking your drinking options for later. Now install yourself on the beach, lunching on fish and chips served by a nameless café just back on the high street, or, if you want to skip to dessert, an ice-cream. When you've enjoyed sufficient idleness, start the not-so-long walk back, fortifying yourself at a couple of the pubs en route. We like the Crooked Billet (51 High Street, 01702 480289), with its creamy frontage, outdoor loos and real ales. Its two rooms are so small that you'll likely need to take advantage of the waterfront beer garden. For dinner, Simply Seafood (1 The Cockle Shed, High Street, 01702 716645) is a recent arrival, with a smarter menu and decor than its name might imply.

Diary Dates

FESTIVALS

Leigh Folk Festival
www.leighfolkfestival.co.uk. Late June.
Several stages host a very respectable roster of acts.

Mummers' Play & Sea Shanties
Billet Wharf (01702 349847). Boxing Day.
The Thameside Mummers have been performing a Christmas play on Billet Wharf every Boxing Day for more than three decades, followed by several hours of singing in the Crooked Billet pub.

Mersea Island

Where time, tides and a seafood lunch wait for no man.

For some 20 hours a day, the road linking Colchester to Mersea Island is simply a half-mile stretch of the B1025. But as high tide rises across the mud of the Colne and Blackwater estuaries, the road becomes dramatically submerged – becoming the 'Strood' causeway and turning Mersea into England's most easterly island.

There can be few places within 50 miles of London where planning a day-trip involves a map and a tide timetable. If your aim is lunch at the Company Shed, then miscalculation can mean a seriously rumbling tummy. But even if you're kept waiting until the water subsides, it's still worth heading on to Mersea's most famous eaterie. You won't have lost your booking, as there aren't any – if you're not there early, you simply join the queue. And don't worry about smart attire, since the weatherbeaten, slatboard shack is no place for airs and graces.

COAST

Richard Haward (01206 383284, www.richard hawardsoysters.co.uk) produces some of the country's finest farmed flat oysters, as his family has done since William Haward first sailed to Billingsgate in 1792; Richard's wife Heather runs the 'shed' (she won't allow it to be called a restaurant) on Coast Road (01206 382700). Beyond the wet fish counter, where everything is sourced daily from local boats, stand a dozen ramshackle tables with plastic covers, and a shelf of ill-assorted wine and beer glasses. You bring your own bread and drink, grab a seat – taking care not to trip over the trolley-load of crabs being wheeled through to the filtration tanks – and prepare for a feast so fresh it's almost wriggling.

There's a small selection of hot specials, such as seared scallops or mussels topped with gruyère, and the offer of a side salad – a token nod to greenery. What almost everyone comes for, though, are the local oysters. Gigas 'rocks' come from the edges of nearby Salcott Creek, while gourmet Colchester Natives (available only from September to April) are dredged from deeper waters, where they've lain for four years or more, before being placed in warmer, shallower stretches of the creek during spring to plump up.

This ideal fattening ground was known to the Romans 2,000 years ago, when they declared that oysters were 'the only good thing to come out of Britain'. Tucking in to a seafood platter – just £8.50 per head for half a crab, cockles, mussels, smoked mackerel, prawns and smoked salmon – the denizens of the Company Shed would beg to disagree.

Step back outside and the sound of masts clanking in the wind serves as an immediate reminder that this is both a working port and a popular haven for pleasure-boating. Indeed, Mersea's population of 7,000 increases rapidly during the summer months, as the caravan parks and campsites fill up with visitors keen to take advantage of the clean, gently shelving sand and shingle beaches or enjoy the annual regatta (www.mersearegatta.org.uk). Held every August since 1838, the week of sailing and rowing culminates in a 'round the island' race in which boats are lifted over the Strood by hand. Hardier souls take a Boxing Day dip in aid of the local lifeboat station.

A short walk from the oyster farms and boatyards is the small town of West Mersea. The council office in Melrose Road has a selection of useful leaflets and guides. At its heart is the delightful 11th-century parish church of St Peter & St Paul, with colourful kneelers depicting local seafaring scenes and a stunning stained-glass window installed in 2005 as a memorial to the island's fishermen and oystermen. The Mersea Museum (01206 385191, www.merseamuseum.org.uk) next door has interesting displays on the area's marine and natural history. If you're in need of refreshment, the Art Café (01206 385820, www.islandart cafe.co.uk) opposite serves light meals and an excellent fry-up, as well as selling attractive local artwork. And if you want quality meat as well as fish to take home with you, Arthur Cock & Sons (01206 382111) sells lamb reared on the saltmarshes a few miles away.

Mersea Island was thus described by a local bod in 1880: 'A more desolate region can scarce be conceived, and yet it is not without beauty'. As you drive out of West Mersea along the only main road towards the opposite end of the five-mile-long island, things seem to have changed little in the intervening years. All that spoils the view is the hulk of Bradwell Power Station, currently being

Company Shed

decommissioned, on the south-westerly horizon at the mouth of the River Blackwater.

The highest point of Mersea Island is only 75 feet above sea level. Low tide exposes wide expanses of alluvial mud around the shoreline, and the flatness accentuates the big skies characteristic of the east coast. East Mersea itself is nothing more than a village store, post office and pub serving the permanent residents and summer holiday parks, while the road peters out at the entrance to Cudmore Country Park (www.essexcc.gov.uk/countryparks).

This is a paradise for birdwatchers and nature-lovers, and there's an observation hide for visitors to use. Cormorant, grebe and merganser arrive from Siberia and Scandinavia to spend the winter along the Colne estuary, the rich mudflats support countless types of wader, and spring brings migrant birds such as warbler, wheatear and whinchat. On summer days, up to 15 types of butterfly can be seen around the meadows and hedgerows, while common seals have been spotted in the estuary.

A stroll along the cliff edge shows the erosive power of the sea, with 300,000-year-old animal bones revealed in the soft sands and gravels. The mud flats are criss-crossed by the remnants of brushwood fences, installed in an earlier attempt to reduce the impact of the tides. The remains of two searchlight batteries confirm that this was a strategic

site during World War II; nor was it any less important 300 years before that. Earth banks provide evidence of a blockhouse fort built to defend the mouth of the River Colne in the 17th century. A few hundred feet north, East Mersea Stone is a stopping point for the 12-person foot ferry (01206 302200) between Brightlingsea and St Osyth.

Mersea stages a food and drink festival in May, with the liquid element supplied by the island's own vineyard and brewery (01206 385900, www.merseawine.com). Ten acres are under cultivation, with five grape varieties producing around 20,000 bottles each year of dry and medium-dry whites and rosé, plus a characterful sparkler. Bottle-conditioned beers include the oaty Island Oyster, with local molluscs included in the recipe – eight per cask. There's an on-site shop.

During the summer months, Mersea Island exudes an air of working-class jollity. Like the resorts of Clacton, Jaywick, Frinton and Walton further along the so-called 'Essex Sunshine Coast', it has long attracted Londoners in search of an affordable break. Visit out of season, though, when the car parks are empty, the wind is howling and the beach huts look forlorn, and you can't help but feel you're perched on the very edge of England.

For more details, check out www.west-mersea.co.uk and www.mersea-island.com.

Nature

Burnham Beeches 92
Salcey Forest 95
TEN Gardens 97
RHS Wisley 101
Westonbirt Arboretum 104
Conservation Volunteering 106
The Stour Estuary 108
TEN Natural encounters 109
Surrey Hills Llama Trek 112

Burnham Beeches

Autumn in technicolour.

Buckinghamshire's Burnham Beeches – 540 acres of ancient woodland, open space and walking paths – is a remarkable area of natural beauty that attracts some half a million visitors annually. The beech trees for which it's named make it a natural marvel in themselves, but the National Nature Reserve is also rich in wildlife, and home to over 60 rare or endangered species.

Many of the beech trees are hundreds of years old, partly the result of centuries of regular 'pollarding' (pruning to above head height), which dramatically increases their lifespan. This method of preservation has continued since the landscape was bought by the City of London in 1879. The trees provide the area's famously clean, untainted air and, in autumn – the most popular time to visit – their myriad beautiful hues make for a reviving and stimulating day out from the capital.

Burnham itself (a 30-minute train journey from Paddington) is a charming, sleepy little village with opulent houses tucked away down quaint sidestreets; it's a complete contrast to the nearby town of Slough – home of the famous trading estate, and butt of countless jokes and satirical documentaries.

Setting foot in Burnham Beeches feels like stepping into a world of mythical creatures, a place where you might expect a character from Maurice Sendak's *Where the Wild Things Are* to suddenly emerge from the undergrowth. It's unsurprising that the woodland has been used as a set for numerous films. (It appears in *Harry Potter and the Order of the Phoenix*, *First Knight*, *Goldfinger*, *Ivanhoe*, *The Crying Game*, *A Town Like Alice* and *The Princess Bride*.) This is a place that marries real-world beauty with a magical quality.

The woodland is busiest in autumn, when dark reds, warm oranges and earthy yellows permeate the forest. Dewdrops on the trees and the satisfying crunch of dry leaves under foot make this a breathtaking time to visit.

Summer, on the other hand, is the best time to appreciate much of the wood's varied wildlife and flora. The Top Pond is home to the yellow iris, white-flowered bog-bean, and dragon- and damselflies during the warmer months, while the Middle Pond is known for its water horsetail and moorhens.

The pollard beeches themselves are immediately recognisable by their distinctive shapes, with gnarled branches and sprawling compositions that give them an unusual and unique character. Many are some 450 years old or more. Druid's Oak, set apart from the others, is the oldest living tree in the woodland; having notched up some 800 years of history, the respected elder now needs the help of cables to support it. The trees provide habitats to numerous insects, plants and fungi, including toadstools and bracket fungi. In fact, Burnham Beeches is one of the most important European beech woodlands in terms of rare species of fungi, which add yet more colour and idiosyncrasy to the kaleidoscope of vibrant and striking foliage.

Beetles, reptiles, amphibians and larger animals, such as ponies, sheep and cows, can be found throughout the woods. To enter the habitat of some of the smaller animals without disturbing their surroundings, take a stroll along the Boardwalk through the mire, a narrow wooden pathway that weaves through the animal-rich marshland. If you're lucky, you can expect to see common toads, adders, grass snakes, slow worms, red-veined darters, common centaury and bog pimpernel as you wind your way along the path. The Boardwalk is located just off Sir Henry Peek's Drive, and is only a short walk from the main car park.

If you fancy embarking on a set walk, the Downy Emerald Trail is a good choice for families with young children. This mile-long trek is named for the eponymous dragonfly, which is found in woodland ponds. The walk takes you on a gentle mosey around the area known as Lord Mayor's Drive, and alongside

► Salcey Forest (*see p95*) and Westonbirt Arboretum (*see p104*) are also must-visits for tree lovers.

FIVE Autumn hotspots

Epping Forest

Epping Forest is one of the larger areas (6,000 acres) of ancient woodland around London. As well as numerous trees, which take on distinct russet tones during the autumn, there are also rivers, ponds and grassland. Also known as the People's Forest, Epping is more than able to cater for those Londoners in search of some vivacious splashes of autumn colour. *High Beach, Loughton, Essex IG10 4AF (020 8508 0028, www.cityoflondon.gov. uk/openspaces).*

Savernake Forest

Part of the Marlborough Woodlands, Savernake Forest is an excellent place to appreciate some of autumn's inimitable charm. With its mixture of ancient trees and small saplings, oak trees and beech trees, plus a smattering of other deciduous trees, Savernake makes for a beautiful and varied woodland. *Marlborough, Wiltshire SN8 3HP (01672 810302, www.savernakeestate.co.uk).*

Thetford Forest Park

Thetford Forest Park is guaranteed to impress with its golden autumnal hues. Ishbeth Woods, Santon Downham and Lynford Arboretum are all located in the forest and are fine spots to appreciate some vibrant foliage. The Arboretum is also home to some unusual tree species, including the Sitka spruce and Douglas fir. *Thetford Road, Santon Downham, Brandon, Suffolk IP27 0AF (01842 816020, www.forestry.gov.uk/thetfordforestpark).*

Wendover Woods

With its beech, ash, oak and larch trees, Wendover Woods is a great place to appreciate the changing seasons. The variable golden hues of the trees are particularly striking as they're interspersed with verdant evergreen conifers. For stunning vistas, follow the all-ability trail for panoramic views of the woods and adjacent Hale Wood across the vale. *Wendover, Buckinghamshire HP22 5NQ (01420 520212, www.forestry.gov.uk).*

Whipsnade Tree Cathedral

At a diminutive 9.5 acres, Whipsnade is a little less sprawling than other woodlands near London. Still, the garden is quaint and charming, and the trees are, as its odd-sounding name suggests, arranged roughly in the shape of a cathedral, with grass areas demarcating a nave, chancel and cloisters. The gardens were originally planted to commemorate Edmond K Blyth's memories of World War I. *Whipsnade, Dunstable, Bedfordshire LU6 2LL (01582 872406, www.national trust.org.uk).*

---

both the Top Pond and Middle Pond, where you'll see mandarin as well as mallard ducks, and a wide variety of fauna, flora and fungi.

For a slightly longer stroll, try the Green Woodpecker Trail, which, at two and a half miles, takes up to an hour and a half to complete. Although a little more arduous than the Downy Emerald Trail, it's still suitable for families. Seasoned walkers looking for a bit more of a challenge might prefer to try the Historical Trail, a calf-stretching five-mile walk that takes you past an Iron Age fort.

One of the greatest joys of a visit to Burnham Beeches is a meander off the main footpath into the forest's heart. There are assorted routes throughout the woods and the danger of getting hopelessly lost is virtually non-existent. Take a walk over the Nile, a small stream that replaces its namesake's magnitude, potency and majesty with diminutive charm

and gentle trickling. Not far beyond, you'll arrive at Egypt Woods, another example of seemingly incongruous African nomenclature. Egypt is also a hamlet to the north of Farnham Common.

There are guided walks throughout the year, where you can learn about the trees themselves, visit the famous film locations or even glean some fascinating insights into Burnham Beeches' role during World War II. Walks last at least an hour and are generally undertaken at a gentle pace. There are also events such as Build a Nest Box and the Easter Treasure Hunt, aimed at young families.

Burnham Beeches Office
Hawthorn Lane, Farnham Common, Buckinghamshire SL2 3TE (01753 647358, www.cityoflondon.gov.uk/openspaces). Open 8am-5pm Mon-Fri.

Salcey Forest

Go down to the woods today.

The resolute urbanism of Milton Keynes makes an odd welcome mat for one of the largest ancient woodlands in Britain. Salcey Forest – just a 30-minute train ride from Euston – is a former medieval hunting ground that's home to over 1,230 acres of pleasingly unmanicured trees and a vast spectrum of wildlife. It's well managed and easy to navigate for visitors; whether you're looking for a slow afternoon saunter or a more ambitious day-long ramble, this is a hassle-free place for jaded city-dwellers to get back to nature. A deserved pub lunch or drink in the nearby village of Hartwell is a lovely way to end the day out.

NATURE

Exactly what you'll see – or hear – depends on what part of the forest you decide to explore. A popular year-round attraction is the Elephant Pond. Local legend has it that this was a drinking hole for circus elephants used for timber logging in World War II. March is a great time to spot tadpoles and newts here – all three of Britain's native species can be seen, including the rare and BAP-protected great crested newt.

The other big draw at Salcey is the Tree Top Way. Nestled among the foliage just across from the pond, the entrance is so subtle it barely registers. Neatly co-existing with the natural habitat, this seven-foot-wide aerial flypath gently transcends the surrounding trees to reach a dramatic 66-foot peak, offering stunning views of Northamptonshire and neighbouring Buckinghamshire. In summer, the landscape is covered with oilseed rape and grazing meadows, making a clumsy jigsaw of neon yellows, shamrock greens and muted browns.

Salcey offers both an escape from the concrete sprawl and a refuge from what can at times be the most stressful feature of city living – people. To really lose the latter, though, you need to venture well away from the Tree Top Way, which is particularly crowded at weekends. Also busy are the two shorter trails, the Elephant and Church Path walks. These part-surfaced paths are popular with pram-pushing families, but do offer the chance to see the forest's fallen druids, or veteran oaks, said to be over 500 years old. For something a little closer to wilderness try the Woodpecker Trail, a near-deserted six-mile circuit of the forest that crosses various terrains (boots are a must in wetter seasons) and is by far the best route for seasonal wildlife spotting.

In winter, look out for small birds such as the coal tit, crossbill and the UK's smallest songbird, the orange and yellow-crowned goldcrest. All favour the stubborn survivalist conifers, a mix of Scots pine and Norway spruce, an expanse of which is an early feature on the trail. Wood pigeons feed on ivy berries at this time of year

while wandering white-speckled fallow deer and the smaller muntjac are a common sight at dusk. Salcey Lawn, a medieval wood pasture, is a great place to spot these as the trees clear and the view opens up. It feels like a natural place for a picnic (once popular with Henry VIII and Anne Boleyn), but, annoyingly, is privately owned.

Spring sees the forest blanketed with bluebells and the arrival of summer warblers including chiffchaffs and nightingales. Listen out for woodpeckers at this time of year too – three species live here, including the lesser-spotted woodpecker. Breathe in deeply in May when flowering ransoms give off a garlic-like scent.

Summer is the best time of year for spotting the rare butterflies that favour the forest's hides. Salcey boasts over half of all known species in the UK, including the white admiral, comma, Essex skipper and purple hairstreak. A recent survey by the Wildlife Trust showed that the super-rare black hairstreak can now only be found in belts of Northamptonshire, notably Salcey, where it feeds on the increasingly rare supply of blackthorn shrub. Dragonflies are very common in August, as are glow-worms, which freckle the thick foliage with a blue-green luminance after-dark.

The pick of the seasons, however, is autumn, when deciduous trees like oaks, beeches and field maples combust into a natural disco of yellow ochre, burnt umbers, deep russets, oranges and reds. October is the best time for fungi foraging; a wet summer will usually produce over 100 species here, including the edible jew's ear.

Sadly, there's no escape from the faint sound of the nearby M1, but a day out here still works as a gentle antidote for the toxic strains of city life. You'll wonder why you never thought to hop on the train here before.

Salcey Forest
Forest Road, Hartwell, Milton Keynes, Bedfordshire (01780 444920, www. forestry.gov.uk). Open 7am-dusk daily.

Exbury Gardens

You'd expect the Rothschilds to have a stately pile and grounds to house their potting sheds, and indeed they do; with more than 200 acres of riotous spring and autumn colour, Exbury Gardens should be high on every gardening fan's 'to-visit' list. Technicolour activity begins as early as March with daffodils, camellias, magnolias and primroses giving way to bluebells, rhododendrons and azaleas. Exbury isn't for those who think of garden visits as gentle strolls, though; more than

20 miles of paths mean an average visit time of over five hours in spring. Help is at hand, however, in the form of three steam locomotives (Mariloo, Rosemary and Naomi), which will take you on a one-and-a-quarter-mile tour in high season. Or, take a chauffeur-driven buggy tour, thereby saving energy to tackle the Exbury Maize Maze, open in July and August.
Summer Lane, Exbury, Southampton, Hampshire SO45 1AZ (02380 891203, www.exbury.co.uk).

Loseley Park. See p98.

NATURE

Painshill Park

Great Dixter

When the parents of Britain's most famous garden designer, Christopher Lloyd, moved to Great Dixter in 1910 there were no gardens to speak of. Which makes his achievements here seem all the more extraordinary, particularly when you see the imaginative plant combinations in his famous long border and the stunning hot summer colours of the subtropical plants that make up the exotic garden. The gardens surround the house, so a long circular walk through them gives you a terrific sense of the building and gardens working together, and also of the wide variety of interest. There are meadow flowers, dazzlingly colourful mixed borders, yew topiary, natural ponds, a formal pool and beautiful exotic plants, all complementing each other and working in perfect harmony.
Great Dixter, Northiam, nr Rye, East Sussex TN31 6PH (01797 252878, www.greatdixter.co.uk).

Loseley Park

Surrey's Loseley Park may be a minnow in the grand gardens stakes, but sometimes small and perfectly formed can be more enticing than huge and overwhelming. At less than three acres, the walled garden, based on a design by Gertrude Jekyll, is a little gem. Its series of 'rooms' (including a delightful rose garden planted with more than 1,000 bushes, many of them old-fashioned varieties; a colourful flower garden with a wealth of secure pathways; and a white garden with fountains and an organic vegetable garden) are perfect for to visit with kids who get easily bored and tired in toe. There's also an impressive vine walk, however, if you fancy something more energetic.
Nr Guildford, Surrey GU3 1HS (01483 304440, www.loseley-park.com).

Nymans Garden

Creativity runs through the veins of the three generations who cultivated the

romantic Nymans gardens in the Sussex Weald. The estate's last owner, the famous theatre set designer Oliver Messel, played a key role in shaping the lovingly tended and intimate garden, which is widely regarded to be one of the best gardens to visit in Britain. The plants are spectacular (and rare – the Messels sponsored great plant hunters to ensure as wide and interesting a variety of specimens as possible), and their setting is awe inspiring; there's even a wonderfully evocative ruin – the remains of a mock medieval manor house designed by the wonderfully named Sir Walter Tapper and Norman Evill.

Handcross, nr Haywards Heath, West Sussex RH17 6EB (01444 405250, www.national trust.org.uk/main/w-nymansgarden2).

Painshill Park
Gifted painter, plantsman and designer Charles Hamilton constructed this garden over a period of five years in the 18th century, with the aim of creating a garden that would be unique in Europe. And it's still pretty special. Filled with utterly fantastic follies, wandering around the 250-acre estate is huge fun. From the grotto to the abbey and the ampitheatre to the Gothic temple, everything here was designed to frame vistas or create interest on the skyline, all the while working in harmony with the planting and classical layouts of beds, borders and meadows. There's even an alpine valley and a vineyard. And given the presence of a temple of Bacchus, it might be worth sampling some of the estate-grown white, rosé and sparkling wine (on sale in the shop) on your way out.

Painshill Park, Portsmouth Road, Cobham, Surrey KT11 1JE (01932 868113, www.painshill.co.uk).

Rousham Manor
Pack a picnic if you're heading for this 18th-century masterpiece, for there are no tearooms or shops here, just glorious nature as man intended. One man in

particular made his mark here: renowned architect and designer William Kent, whose carefully constructed landscape remains much as he originally planned it. Through a series of focal points – such as ponds and cascades, and views framed through classical arches – and a landscape made more interesting by unusual additions, like a sham ruin known as the 'Eyecatcher', Rousham evokes a sense of space and tranquillity that's a joy to experience. And there are plants aplenty too; don't miss the walled garden with its herbaceous border. Note that under-15s aren't admitted.
Nr Steeple Aston, Bicester, Oxfordshire OX25 4QX (01869 347110, www.rousham.org).

Sheffield Park Garden

Many gardens are at their best in spring, but the confusingly named Sheffield Park Garden in East Sussex comes into its own in autumn, when four linked lakes offer dramatic reflections of the vivid autumn reds, golds and yellows created by the wealth of Japanese maples, nyssa, swamp cypresses, birches and tupelo trees. Designed by Capability Brown, the 18th-century landscaped garden is intriguing for its bold 20th-century planting by Arthur Soames – and for a rare cricket pitch, installed in the 1880s and site of the first England versus Australia international cricket match in 1884. Willow fans should take note: the historic cricket pitch has been restored for 2009, with matches planned thoughout the summer.
Sheffield Park, East Sussex TN22 3QX (01825 790231, www.nationaltrust. org.uk/main/w-sheffieldparkgarden).

Sir Harold Hillier Gardens

The name may not be as familiar to many as that of Christopher Lloyd, but to plant enthusiasts it's as important. Distinguished plantsman Sir Harold Hillier established these lovely gardens in 1953, and the 42,000 plants now growing here are a testament to his vision and creativity. The themed landscapes cover over 180 acres of beautiful rolling Hampshire countryside (between the villages of Ampfield and Braishfield, three miles north-east of Romsey, nine miles south-west of Winchester) and provide year-round interest, thanks to Hillier's focus on establishing hardy plants and shrubs from temperate regions of the world (particularly North America). Autumn is an especially

great time to visit, however, when the huge range of trees and massive shrubs put on a show that rivals New England for its spectrum of warm colours. A range of imaginative environmental games keeps younger visitors happy, while the restaurant and tearooms provide post-strolling sustenance.
Jermyns Lane, Ampfield, Romsey, Hampshire SO51 0QA (01794 369318, www.hillier gardens.org.uk).

Sissinghurst Castle Gardens

This most romantic of English country gardens is also England's most visited horticultural affair, and it's easy to see why. The intimate garden 'rooms' – a series of enclosed spaces created by writer Vita Sackville-West and her husband Sir Harold Nicolson (who designed the layout of the garden around the existing structures) in the 1920s – offers year-round interest and colour; yet the hordes come for the famous White Garden. It is indeed spectacular, but don't miss the other areas and walks – including the peaceful lakeside and woodland walk. And leave plenty of time to explore: afternoons are best once the crowds have thinned.
Beddington Road, Sissinghurst, nr Cranbrook, Kent TN17 2AB (01580 710700, www. nationaltrust.org.uk).

Stowe Landscape Gardens

Gardens don't come much bigger or much more classical than this. At 750 acres, and with 40 listed monuments and temples, you'll need a few hours to do it justice (the guided tours at 11am and noon on most days might help with orientation), but this 18th-century behemoth will repay your time in spades. With input from some of the biggest names in historical landscaping, among them Charles Bridgeman (who began work on the gardens in the 1710s), William Kent and James Gibbs, it's one of the most important gardens in Europe. And that's before you even factor in Lancelot 'Capability' Brown, who was head gardener here between 1741 and 1751. Highlights include the Temple of Concord and Victory (the largest and grandest of Stowe's temples), the Palladian Bridge and the wonderfully over-the-top Gothic Temple, designed by James Gibbs in 1741.
Buckingham, Buckinghamshire MK18 5DQ (01494 755568, www.nationaltrust.org.uk/ main/w-stowegardens).

RHS Wisley

Horticultural variety is the spice of garden life.

At some point between the arrival of guerrilla gardening and the discovery of fêtes, cakes and tea-dances by Shoreditch trendies, Londoners fell back in love with horticulture. And, for over a century, Wisley (reached by a 30-minute train ride from Waterloo to Woking, then a ten-minute taxi ride) has been a pioneer when it comes to the gardening arts. It was bought for the august Royal Horticultural Society from experimental gardener and RHS treasurer George Fergusson Wilson in 1902, and the 'Oakwood Experimental Garden' that Wilson set up to investigate how to make 'difficult plants grow successfully' today forms the basis of the deliciously shaggy Wild Garden. Serious development work is still being done here on new plant strains and composting and pleaching techniques.

All sounds a bit worthy? Relax. Past the car park and through frontage reminiscent of a suburban garden centre, Wisley is a thoroughly transporting place. Where Kew feels like a big park, Wisley is clearly a garden – or, rather, a series of different gardens spread out over 60 acres. It's the feeling of surprise as you peek from one garden into the next that makes a visit delightful; each section is different. Whichever season you choose, you'll be rewarded with sudden shifts of style and scale. Formal borders, wild undergrowth, neatly controlled rows of vegetables and a steamy jungle of outlandish orchids can all be found here, while venerable oaks and man-sized cacti contrast with bonsai trees and tiny, ground-level Alpine plants.

You enter the gardens between a sundial and the Laboratory, which looks like a dignified manor house – half-timbered, red-roofed and with classic tall chimneys and mullioned windows, despite having been built during World War I to house classrooms and lecture theatres. In front of it stretches the broad, lazy rectangle of the Canal, especially beautiful with water lilies in summer. The Walled Garden is discreetly charming with its hidden lovers' bench, trickling water features and a lovely little porthole cut through one of the hedges. It's clever too, with the westerly section using high walls to create a microclimate for tender, subtropical plants. Behind it you're suddenly in the Wild Garden, criss-crossed with paths twisting around a pond that settles surprisingly comfortably into this very English setting despite its Chinese-style mossy stone islands and bamboo grove.

The newest addition to the gardens is the Glasshouse, which opened in celebration of the RHS's bicentenary in summer 2007 at the cost of £7.7 million. It's a beautiful structure, 40 feet tall, with a rippling glass roof, crisp semicircular lake and coolly modern landscaping by renowned landscape architect Tom Stuart-Smith. Ignore the rather stagey fake rock outcrop and waterfall in the middle, and instead explore an interior that brims with exotic, colourful, sometimes disturbingly alien-looking plants. It's divided into four zones: the Dry Temperate Zone contains spiny and succulent desert plants of all shapes and sizes (including a giant Euphorbia ampliphylla); the Moist Temperate Zone is filled with the likes of charm and cascade chrysanthemums; the fiercely humid Tropical Zone has orchids, riotous houseplants and palm trees; and, in a cavern under the waterfall, the Root Zone elucidates undersoil happenings with child-friendly captions and speeded-up films.

At the extreme corners of the garden are the National Heather Collection, Jubilee Arboretum and the 16 acres and 670 apple cultivars of the Fruit Field. Along the southern side, meanwhile, a ridge of higher ground holds the Rose Borders (due to receive a thorough revamp and replanting through 2009 – they should be gorgeous in summer 2010), a lovely, shelved Rock Garden and an Alpine Display House full of sweetly modest rock plants. Hop like Peter Rabbit into Mr McGregor's garden to admire the cucumber frames of the Vegetable Garden, a dream allotment.

Throughout, the scientific basis of the gardens is clear. The Jubilee Arboretum is diligently laid out for easy comparison of the different types of trees, the excellent research library

NATURE

FIVE Things to see

The Glasshouse

A delight all year round, with towering cacti, a flower market's worth of blooms and strange exotics (orchids, red-hot cat's tails, phragmipedium). For fine views of the adjoining semicircular lake, climb the hill to the double spiral path of the Fruit Mount: you'll be sure you're about to collide with the people coming down, but it's an illusion – you're actually on separate paths.

Jubilee Arboretum

Carefully arranged to help you identify the different characteristics of the various families of tree, the arboretum is also a wonderfully tranquil area of woodland in which to wander and wonder. Come for sunshine through the new greenery in spring or for a thoroughly satisfactory crunch on fallen autumn leaves.

Late spring

Along the Canal Borders, the tulips are dazzling, while the rhododendrons and azaleas of Battleston Hill are a riot of colours. Watch out for irises below the Rock Garden, the Alpine Meadow's marigolds and buttercups, and fruit tree blossom in the Model Fruit Garden and Fruit Fields. Purple and white wisteria dominate the Loggia and oak trees in the Wild Garden.

High summer

The Mixed Border is stunning in July and August: bright red and purple cannas, dahlias and salvias, vivid blue delphiniums and agapanthus, yellow and cream hemoracallis and climbing clematis. In August, the Maize Maze is at its full height, hemmed in by nodding sunflowers.

Autumn

The flamingly bright, broad leaves of the 'Wisley Bonfire', Nyssa sylvatica, are visible for just a few, unpredictable October days (precisely when depends on the weather). For a mini-me that's more reliable, head to the Model Gardens to enjoy the leaf colours of the bonsai trees. Watch out in September for the asters and autumn-flowering crocus.

NATURE

The Glasshouse

(01483 212428) is open to all visitors to the gardens, while the Trial Gardens investigate new plants and growing conditions. But the horticultural knowledge of Wisley's experts is worn lightly; the information boards, for example, are sufficiently sparse to be ignored if you're only here for fun, but illuminating enough to provide dinner party factoids aplenty (did you know the banana is a perennial herb?) alongside plain-spoken growing tips.

Of course, what you can see changes through the year. Come for tulips and fruit blossom in spring, roses and lilies in summer, and don't neglect autumn and winter: January snowdrops, stunning autumn leaves, or apples in September.

And wherever there's such a wonderful array of plants, you'll also find wildlife. There are ducks and coots by the Butterfly Lovers' Pavilion, and finches, tits, nuthatches and jays among the strategically located bird feeders and nesting boxes. You might even glimpse a kestrel hovering over the grounds or a sparrowhawk in a tree, scrutinising the undergrowth for tasty morsels. In winter, there are fieldfares and redwings on flat ground, while summer offers dragonflies and damselflies over the Glasshouse lake.

If you want a bit more to do than just run through the leaves with the kids or stroll quietly among the trees, Wisley hosts numerous special events. We hope it will repeat its release of hundreds of butterflies in the Glasshouse in January and February this year, and be sure to put in your diary the Music Festival (three nights of outdoor concerts in June) and the Flower Show (normally) in September (and which attracted well over 20,000 visitors over the course of three days in 2008). You can also enjoy family activities in summer, Grow Your Own Weekend in early March or A Taste of Autumn in October. Then there are the likes of autumn Fungal Forays and regular morning bird walks, led by David Elliott and Frank Boxell (which will also handily get you into the garden before everyone else). For details of these and other events, check the website near the time of your visit.

For sustenance, it's easiest to join the family groups and elderly couples at one of several venues within the gardens. Nearest to the entrance, the Terrace Restaurant (01483 211773) serves two- and three-course lunches and afternoon tea. The adjacent Conservatory Café serves hot and cold snacks and own-made cakes, as does the brand-new self-service Glasshouse Café. In summer, the Orchard Café is an alfresco delight. There are also three picnic sites (one outside the gates). The shops (01483 211113) are another joy for keen gardeners: expert gardeners are on hand daily for advice in the Wisley Plant

NATURE

Centre, where there are over 10,000 types of plant to buy, and the gift shop has a wonderful book selection and a coffee shop right next door.

RHS Wisley
Wisley, Woking, Surrey GU23 6QB (0845 260 9000, www.rhs.org.uk). Open Mar-Oct 10am-6pm Mon-Fri; 9am-6pm Sat, Sun. Nov-Feb 10am-4.30pm Mon-Fri; 9am-4.30pm Sat, Sun. The Glasshouse closes at 3.45pm in winter. Admission £8.

Westonbirt Arboretum

Touch wood in Gloucestershire.

It's difficult to say when Westonbirt – which, along with Kent's Bedgebury Pinetum, has the official designation of 'National Arboretum' – is at its most glorious. There's certainly a strong case for autumn, when the arboretum's famed Japanese maple trees are aflame in every shade of crimson, pink and gold. The frozen stillness of winter is also magical; close to Christmas the Enchanted Wood opens after dark to visitors who follow a lit trail threading through majestic conifers and firs. Springtime bestows on Silk Wood a carpet of bluebells, primroses and wood anemones, while the Cherry Glade bursts forth with delicate blossom. By May Day, Westonbirt's renowned rhododendrons are in full,

gorgeous bloom, a mass of vivid pink and lilac marking the beginning of the arboretum's most colourful month. And then there's summer's long, lazy days, with walks through cool, sun-dappled glades and the annual Festival of the Tree, complete with wood carvers and tipis.

Whenever you visit Westonbirt, there is always something to wonder at. It's no surprise, then, that more than 350,000 people visit the arboretum each year. Westonbirt's 600 acres have the knack of never feeling too crowded or cramped, however, particularly in the older (free entry) part, where there's always a hidden copse or clearing fit for quiet contemplation.

Westonbirt's 16,000 trees are diverse not only in appearance but also in age: saplings have taken root alongside trees planted when the arboretum was first established (by Robert Stayner Holford in the mid 19th century). One of the oldest specimens is descended from an American tree, a native of Georgia discovered in 1765 beside a riverbank and named for Benjamin Franklin. Poignantly, it's now extinct in the wild.

When Robert Holford decided to create the arboretum, as well as rebuild the family pile (now a school) and add formal pleasure gardens, he was responding to a new craze for exotic flora. Botanists-turned-plant-hunters were bringing back from foreign lands weird and wonderful species never before seen on British soil, and one of the earliest additions to Westonbirt was a native of California. Those first Monterey pines still stand where Main and Circular Drives meet, though they are rather more statuesque these days.

In 1956, the Forestry Commission took charge of Westonbirt, not only making it safe for the public (it had become neglected by the end of World War II) but undertaking the daunting task of mapping and cataloguing every tree, and opening up new areas, such as Silk Wood. Though Westonbirt was originally conceived as homage to the Picturesque Movement, which favoured the aesthetic over the scientific, the contemporary arboretum is a harmonious blend of the two and is as pleasurable as it is educational (though some 10,000 schoolchildren descend annually).

Thanks to the Commission's meticulous care, there are now 110 'Champion Trees' here – that is, trees that are the largest of their kind growing in the UK. Visitors can often be spotted craning their necks to see the topmost blue-green fronds of one, an evergreen that, at a lanky 28 metres, still has some way to go to reach its maximum height of 70 metres. Another spectacle is the Bristol whitebeam on Broad Drive. Found only at the Avon Gorge, there are just 100 left there now.

Of course, some of Westonbirt's best-loved trees are not its biggest or rarest. Close to the Dewpond is a huge cedar of Lebanon, with its characteristic, schoolboy-tempting low-slung limbs. 'The Three Sisters', a group of redwoods planted two centuries ago by Holford's trio of daughters, are found at the head of Lime Avenue. Impressive as they are, in giant sequoia terms they are mere babies.

If you tire of the trees – and that's a big 'if' – there is a kaleidoscope of butterflies, moths and unusual birds such as the black cap and garden warbler to see. There are also 1,100 species of

fungi to count, rather than eat. If you do get peckish, the Maples restaurant serves up locally sourced food and boasts views over the Cotswolds. Alternatively, the Courtyard café is situated next to the Forest Shop, which sells handcrafted goods and local preserves and chutneys. The green-fingered or freshly inspired can buy good-quality shrubs, trees, seeds and gardening essentials in the Plant Centre.

It might only be a couple of hours down the M4 (parking is £5) but in a far-flung corner of Westonbirt you feel a long way from London. However, it was in the capital that the wealth used to create this unique environment was generated: the Holfords made their fortune in the 17th century by investing in the canal system that helped to clean up a polluted Thames. Perhaps it's rather fitting that some of that money has resulted in such a fine tribute to unspoilt nature.

Westonbirt National Arboretum

Nr Tetbury, Gloucestershire GL8 8QS (01666 880220, www.forestry.gov.uk). Open 9am-dusk Mon-Fri; 8am-dusk Sat, Sun. Admission Jan-Feb £5. Mar-Sept £7; Oct-Nov £8. Dec free.

NATURE

Conservation Volunteering

Muck in on a nature project.

Set up back in the 1950s as the Conservation Corps, the BTCV (British Trust for Conservation Volunteers) is now 'celebrating 50 years of mud, sweat and cheers', as its website boasts (www.btcv.org.uk). And celebrate it should; the organisation runs an admirably vast range of conservation activities for all ages, including thousands of placements for young people, conservation holidays and one-day volunteering projects where you can learn skills such as hedge-laying, making bird boxes, creating a wildlife garden or dry stonewalling. On top of these, there's an imaginative range of initiatives drawing in new volunteers through funky schemes like the Green Gym; more than 70 such classes were in operation throughout the UK in 2008. Events are free and the aim is to encourage local people to engage with, and thereby improve, their environment.

Projects cater for all ages, and adaptable leaders tailor activities according to who turns up on the day. Our day was predominantly family-based – which was fortunate, because as a primary-school teacher, artist and conservationist, Susan, our group leader and Wildlife Project Officer for Buckingham Community, was particularly well placed to put us through our paces in 'Wild Art'. Any initial shyness was dispelled as we stood in a circle, welly to welly, and got our instructions. Forewarned with visual aids as to what nettles and brambles look like and how to get out of them (the trick is to go backwards), we set off, clutching our clay balls and grabbing anything from the woodland to decorate. The lack of distractions like cafés to skulk off to was a real boon, and, inspired by some pictures of fabulous natural art by Andy Goldsworthy, we were soon all busily working away on our personal oeuvres without a care in the world. Apart from the cold winter weather, that is. Mercifully, there was a break for hot chocolate, provided by the magical Susan – who even stumped up soya milk and gluten-free biccies for those in need.

Children- and family-oriented events concentrate on developing observation skills through activities like bat- or badger-watching, learning about wildlife habitats, or gaining bushman skills through tree identification, fungi forays, hunting for wild food and uncovering what the hedgerow has to offer (rather than relying on supermarket snacks).

Adult events are geared more to construction and learning, offering volunteers the chance to pick up new skills and engage with nature in a positive way. Any number of walks and gentler tasks are available for less able volunteers too; simply choose your activity level and find something that suits it.

Signing up is easy; look at the interactive map on the BTCV's website, choose your area and find out which projects and task days are going on locally. In Kent, for example, recent projects included hedge-laying, creating a habitat to encourage reptiles, mammals and small invertebrates, and a woodland management event – surely a great opportunity to bring out your inner lumberjack. You decide which project is right for you, then make your own way there on the appointed day. A project leader is on site to organise and supervise, and more experienced volunteers are on hand to help out with advice and demos. There's little opportunity to get bored; there are always different tasks available, so if you hate what you're doing, you can have a go at something else. It's hard work, but exhilarating and hugely rewarding. Frequent breaks for tea and biscuits make it a sociable activity too, forcing you to engage with each other as well as the woodland. It costs nothing, and projects can play a really positive role in improving and conserving our local environment.

Many parents on the session we attended were regulars, and their kids clearly loved the freedom of it all. Just remember the wellies, and wrap up warm in the winter months; you won't necessarily move around as much as you do playing sport or walking. And don't forget your Monty Python *Lumberjack* song lyrics, to lead the group in a good old-fashioned singsong.

> ▶ Young people can get involved in conserving habitats for our feathered friends at the RSPB's Lodge; see p264.

The Stour Estuary

Birdwatching from a barge with the RSPB.

The RSPB (www.rspb.org.uk) claims more than a million members – a statistic that's even more impressive when you realise it means one in every 61 of us bird-crazy Brits has joined. One of the charity's most beguiling reserves is near Harwich, along the Stour Estuary. Here, the RSPB runs brilliant birdwatching boat trips on the *Victor*, a restored sailing barge that dates from 1895.

NATURE

At first sight, the estuary seems a bleak prospect – especially on a freezing January morning, when you know your £35 ticket has bought you four hours on the water. You board the *Victor* in an almost deserted marina and, to the untrained eye, the surrounding landscape seems utterly desolate, a monotonous streak of grey lacking any life at all, let alone birds. For our visit, the winter sky appears to have picked up on the bleakness of the estuary, its thick clouds letting through only a sliver of sunshine. It's almost unbearably cold too, but our well-wrapped companions and the RSPB guides all seem inexplicably jolly.

The fact is, there is a great deal of birdlife here – around 50 species have been spotted – you just need to acclimatise (or know what you're looking for). *Victor*'s engine is soon turned off and the vessel is carried quietly up one side of the estuary by the current, with the mainsail partly unfurled for a bit of extra push. Passing long stretches of mudflats on the right, two things happen as your eyes adjust. First, the apparently uninspiring landscape changes from an undistinguished slate into a surprisingly and delightfully vivid palette – still entirely grey, but in an unexpected range of shades and tones, shot with silver and white flecks and intonations.

As time passes, the sky and light change again, so that what seemed to be empty grey patches reveal many birds, disguised against unaccustomed eyes. The extremely well-informed site manager Rick Vonk, an inexhaustable source of information, has the keenest eyes of anyone – and he provides a thoroughly useful running commentary, skilfully pointing out birds of particular interest. The superstars of our trip are the great northern diver, the longtailed duck and the red-breasted merganser: these birds are rarely found in the south of

England, and only one or two live on the estuary, so our sighting is particularly special. Brent geese flap overhead, there are crowds of knots on the shoreline and the odd cormorant darts past, on the hunt for fish.

Suddenly, there is a commotion starboard: 'Did he say "teal" or "seal"?', asks my neighbour, an elderly lady whose zeal has remained markedly undamped by the cold. It's true: the head of a common seal is visible only 20 yards away from us. It is a wonderful sight and highlights an important aspect of the work here – although it is focused on the preservation of birds, the local RSPB centre spends a great deal of time protecting butterflies and dormice, for example, since the health of all species in a particular environment is interwoven. Your appreciation of the Stour's initially uninspiring mudflats increases dramatically as you begin to grasp the plethora of invisible shore species it harbours – many of them hungrily gobbled up by the smart black-and-white oystercatchers and avocets.

As we turn back, the wind really begins to bite. Many of our fellow birders now head below deck to warm up with tea and coffee, stamping their feet and happily sharing items of warm clothing with naïvely underdressed journalists. These cheerful folks are for the most part enthusiastic amateurs, easily distinguishing curlews, dunlins and redshanks. Many profess a lack of expertise, but all have brought their own binoculars – indeed, whether or not you own a pair (you are expected to bring your own, although this was not specified in advance) should give you a clue as to whether this trip is for you.

If you do decide to brave it, especially in winter, wear a hat (or two), gloves, two layers of trousers, two or three jumpers and a sensibly warm and waterproof coat. And bring binoculars: a good pair will hugely enhance the experience.

▶ The RSPB's Lodge runs introductory days for young twitchers; *see p264.*

Birds by Barge with the RSPB
01473 328006, stourestuary@rspb.org.uk, www.sbvictor.co.uk. Tickets £35.

If the concrete jungle is getting you down, go back to the land. The countryside around London is teeming with wild things: flora and fauna that don't flourish in the Big Smoke, or farmyard companions that haven't made it to the shelves of Sainsbury's. Here are ten tips on where to nurture your natural side.

Bluebells

If the snowdrop signifies the end of winter, the bluebell is synonymous with the arrival of spring. And, as with snowdrops, less is not more with bluebells: you need to see them en masse to experience the full blaze of glory. Coton Manor Gardens in Northamptonshire is a mecca for bluebell-watching. There, beneath a canopy of beech trees, a sea of bluebells shimmers in the dappled sunlight. And these are Class A bluebells – there are none of the so-called 'Spanish invaders', as the tabloids so sensitively christened them, despoiling the English purity.

For maximum colour, go the last week of April or the first week of May (contact the venue first as the bloom time varies depending on the severity of the winter). For an even more riotous display, go to Wakehurst Place Gardens in West Sussex and walk through the Himalayan Glade, which displays flowers that grow at 10,000 feet. Here, the soft shimmer of bluebells is backed by gaudy, early blooming rhododendrons.
Coton Manor Gardens, Coton, Northamptonshire NN6 8RQ (01604 740219, www.cotonmanor.co.uk); Royal Botanic Gardens, Wakehurst Place, Ardingly, nr Haywards Heath, West Sussex RH17 6TN (01444 894066, www.nationaltrust.org.uk, www.kew.org).

Butterflies

The fabled purple emperor is the holy grail of British butterflies, owing to its flamboyant colour and huge size. (With an 85mm wingspan, it's Britain's largest native species.) Despite its reputation for being elusive, 'His Majesty' can be found in abundance at Bentley Wood, a 2,000-acre butterfly conservation area between Winchester and Salisbury, during July. They are most active in the mornings on bright days. The car park is a good place to stake

them out; entice them with overripe fruit on the bonnet of your car, though some people use danish blue cheese or salty bacon. You can also spot them on damp patches on the ground of the car park, or nibbling on banana skins on top of the Bentley Wood sign, or just swirling among the oaks. But if you don't see purple, don't worry: there are more than 35 different species regularly seen here, with good populations of silver-washed fritillary, marsh fritillary, white admiral and duke of burgundy. The best months for viewing are between March and October, peaking in the warmer months – most butterflies start flying when the temperature reaches 17°C. Just wander the meadow and woodland and follow the flashes of colour.
Bentley Wood Car Park, West Dean Road, West Tytherley, Wiltshire SP5 (01929 400209, www.butterfly-conservation.org).

Deer

If you want to go deer stalking without getting blood on your hands, the creatures at Knole Park are easy prey. Situated outside a stately home in Sevenoaks, it's the only Tudor deer park remaining in Kent, and one of the few left in the country. With 800 fallow and Japanese sika deer roaming the grounds, it's Bambi a go-go at times. During the Middle Ages, they were introduced to keep the grass short. They still fulfil that function, even tending to the adjacent golf course; but they're also there to entertain the crowds. And they're remarkably tame, after years of being fed by visitors (this is strictly forbidden, but that's never stopped anybody).
Knole Park, Sevenoaks, Kent TN15 0RP (01732 450608, www.nationaltrust.org.uk).

Herons

For beginners, birdwatching can be a bore – especially if you don't like holding binoculars. But the grey heron is easy to spot, and these elegant creatures are easy on the eye too; with their long necks, slender beaks and bendy legs, they are grace epitomised. Now a new walking trail showcases the UK's largest colony of herons and egrets. Set amid the gentle marshland of the Hoo Peninsula in north Kent, the three-mile trail is the tranquil highlight of the RSPB's Northward Hill

NATURE

Nature Reserve. It's not all poetry in motion, though: be practical and bring a pair of boots, as some of the paths are muddy. And keep your eyes peeled for other breeds: woodpeckers and tits, nightingales, turtle doves and warblers are all resident. But the star of the show is the heron, all 200 pairs. They are visible for most of the year, but spring is prime time, when the young birds learn to fly.
RSPB Northward Hill, High Halstow, Kent ME3 8SF (01634 222480, www.rspb.org.uk).

Lambs

In the spring, the Seven Sisters Sheep Centre resembles a maternity ward, according to staffers. Lambing starts in March and goes on until May. So if you're feeling broody, you can bottlefeed a newborn, albeit a woolly one. There's never a shortage of mouths to feed: with 300 different ewes and over 40 varieties, the centre has one of the largest flocks in the world, including rare and traditional breeds that are no longer used in modern farming. From July to September, you can shear a sheep, milk one, weave some wool or make some cheese (the latter is agreeable for people who are lactose intolerant, apparently). And if you're tired of following the flock, take a tractor ride or feed the chicks, pigs, goats or rabbits.

Seven Sisters Sheep Centre, Gilberts Drive, East Dean, East Sussex BN20 0AA (01323 423302, www.sheepcentre.co.uk).

New Forest ponies

The wild ponies of the New Forest aren't, in fact, wild. They are privately owned by locals, but have roamed the common land for 1,000 years. Indeed, they have become an indelible part of the landscape, with 3,000 of them dotting the pastoral scene like objects in a painting. The phenomenon started back in 1016, when the rights of common pasture were granted to common people living in what was then a royal hunting ground. Back then, these were domesticated beasts of burden. Now they just roam freely, posing for pictures taken by passing motorists. And the breed has evolved too: over the centuries, several other breeds – Welsh, Arab and Hackney ponies – were introduced into the forest, and they have all intermingled with the originals. As a result, New Forest ponies really do have good breeding; they are renowned for their gentle nature and calm temperament. In the village of Burley, for example, they wander up and down the high street. So roll down your window and say hello.
New Forest, Hampshire (www.thenewforest.co.uk).

Otters and owls

The New Forest Otter, Owl & Wildlife Park was founded by the Heap family after a pair of Asian short-clawed otters set up camp in their garden. More than two decades on, the park now cares for Europe's largest groups of multi-specied otters and owls, as well as a whole menagerie of other indigenous wildlife. A day spent in the 25 acres of ancient woodland means time spent spotting polecats, minks, stoats, badgers, red foxes, wild boar and deer. Children in particular might enjoy learning about conservation and the work the park does with injured or orphaned otters. An animal house and night barn enable close encounters with otters, ferrets, harvest mice, snoring badgers and red foxes, but it's the great outdoors that's the most fun and natural way of seeing the animals in this lovely habitat. You can wander to your heart's content, or take a Wildlife Walkabout to the Owlery and see more otters, red deer, and Oden the lynx on his platform in the fir trees.
New Forest Otter, Owl & Wildlife Park, Deerleap Lane, Longdown, Marchwood, Southampton, Hampshire SO40 4UH (02380 292408, www.ottersandowls.co.uk).

Rhododendrons

If you want colour, the rhododendron is the showiest flower of spring. And for a truly flamboyant display, Leonardslee Gardens in Horsham is ablaze during the months of April and May, attracting visitors from around the world. No wonder it doubled as the Himalayas – where the rhododendron runs riot – in Powell and Pressburger's 1947 technicolor epic, *Black Narcissus*. And it doesn't stop with the rhodos. Camelias and magnolias brighten things up during April, and azaleas up the volume further in May, around the time the rhodos are peaking. Add in lush woodland, seven lakes, bonsai trees, and an Area of Outstanding Natural Beauty credential, and you've got Eden, Paradise and Shangri-La rolled into one. If you crave yet more colour, Sheffield Park Garden (*see p100*), also in Sussex, is another orgy of azaleas and rhodos. Bring your camera – and your shades.
Leonardslee, Lower Beeding, Horsham, West Sussex RH13 6PP (01403 891212, www.leonardslee.com); Sheffield Park Garden, nr Uckfield, East Sussex TN22 3QX (01825 790231, www.nationaltrust.org.uk).

Seal hunting

The sweet seals at the Hamford Water Nature Reserve in Walton-on-the-Naze may not be the most prolific breeders in the world, but the colony in these Essex backwaters has grown from five in 1986 to more than 70 now, meaning that sighting the little mammals bobbing in the Walton backwaters or basking on the mudbanks is fairly easy. Both common harbour and grey seals can be spotted by their dramatic russet colouring (they frolic on the backwaters' muddy banks, which are rich in iron oxide), making them even easier to spot in the water. Prebook a two-hour boat trip and you're likely to see lots of other wildlife too in this rich area of tidal creeks, mudflats, islands, salt marshes and marsh grasslands. The terrain is also great for plants, with rare coastal species like hog's fennel putting in an appearance along the banks and, in particular, on nearby Skippers Island, a 219-acre wildlife reserve accessible by prior booking with the Essex Wildlife Trust (01621 862960, www.essexwt.org.uk).
Hamford Water Nature Reserve, Walton-on-the-Naze, Essex (01255 677006, www.walton-on-the-naze.com). Boat trips May-Oct (07806 309460, www.nazeman.fsnet.co.uk).

Snowdrops

For such a small flower, snowdrops have a powerful effect on people. The *galanthus*, or milk flower, so captivated soldiers during the Crimean War that they brought them back to Britain in droves and planted them in their gardens, ensuring that this European species became a British icon. A number of country estates in the south-east have striking displays in February, but we have two favourites: Gatton Park in Surrey – once the estate of the Colman (as in the mustard) family – features a snowdrop scene in a Capability Brown-designed parkland; while Waterperry Gardens in Oxfordshire holds annual Snowdrop Weekends in February, when swathes of the little flowers shine out in the eight acres of historic ornamental gardens, and along the routes of the old orchard and riverside walks.
Gatton Park, Reigate, Surrey RH2 0TD (01737 649068, www.gattonpark.com); Waterperry Gardens, nr Wheatley, Oxfordshire OX33 1JZ (01844 339254, www.waterperrygardens.co.uk).

NATURE

Surrey Hills Llama Trek

Man's new best friend.

Surrey Hills Llamas, based just 40 miles from London and an easy ten-minute cab journey from Godalming station (a 50-minute trip from Waterloo), was started by Colin Stoneley and his partner Julie in 2003, after they experienced a llama trekking excursion while on holiday in Dorset. They were immediately taken by the woolly South American mammals, realising that they make incredibly endearing and strangely soothing trekking companions, and went about acquiring six llamas of their own; just six weeks after their initial experience with the animals, Surrey Hills Llamas was born. It's been based in its current location – the picturesque village of Hambledon – since 2008.

Exploring the beautiful undulating landscape and woodlands of the Surrey Hills – a designated Area of Outstanding Natural Beauty – is made all the more enjoyable with a llama in tow. And as your furry companion insists on stopping frequently to fill one of its three stomachs with the contents of a hedge, it's also a very relaxing experience, suitable for all levels of fitness.

NATURE

'We have all this amazing countryside to make the most of,' Colin says, arms outstretched towards the expanse of Surrey Hills surrounding the 16th-century Merry Harriers pub that he, Julie and the llamas call home. Since starting Surrey Hills Llamas, the couple's herd has grown to nine and they've gradually developed a number of trekking packages to suit all sorts of requirements. Feeling under stress? Opt for a gentle summer evening trek, a shortish walk that starts at 6pm, leading you through tranquil sun-dappled woodland right to the door of the Merry Harriers and a hearty main course from the Stoneley's delicious menu. In a romantic state of mind? Pop the question with an unashamedly nosey, furry-faced audience on a luxury champagne picnic trek for two. There's even an overnight camping trek for those looking for a more hardcore experience.

The festive Christmas Day trek is one of the longest running, and includes a sumptuous four-course dinner in the pub. But by far the most popular option is the English picnic trek – a day-long walk complete with slap-up picnic (handily transported by the llamas) that's perfect for birthday celebrations, get-togethers or just an unforgettable day in the countryside. Surrey Hills Llamas can cater for up to 20 people of all levels of fitness and ability on walks – just let them know any specific requirements beforehand and a walk can be tailored to your needs.

We opt for a bracing winter morning trek – just the ticket (even for the most adamantly non-outdoorsy of our group) for getting the blood flowing and for promoting lots of laughs. The promise of a hearty two-course pub lunch included in the price of the trek proved something of an incentive too.

We roll up to the Merry Harriers in heavy rain. 'We go whatever the weather,' Colin had warned us. 'So come prepared.' Prepared we are: our group is a festival of waterproofs, wellies, walking boots, umbrellas and hats. The llamas, however, appear less than bothered, greeting us with wet coats so speckled with field, hedge and tree detritus that grooming them – something all trekkers are encouraged to do to bond with their new-found friends – is rather like combing a rug that has been left out in the rain for a year. Our llama, Louis, isn't remotely fazed by his shabby appearance and stands calmly munching on a bit of tree while we work on his knots.

'The thing with llamas is that they're incredibly hardy,' notes Colin. 'We've only had the vet out twice.' He pats six-foot eight-inch Pandu, the tallest llama in the UK and leader of Surrey Hills Llamas' all-male herd. 'Basically, a llama is either alive, or it's dead,' he concludes. These llamas are very much alive. They're also very intelligent, curious and social creatures. Although famed for their habit of spitting, llamas rarely spit at humans, reserving this disciplining behaviour for members of their own species.

▶ More llama action close to London can be had at Ashdown Forest Llama Park; *see pp258-259.*

Louis, the youngest llama and – we are told – most mischievous of the herd, has to check out anything even vaguely edible that he encounters on the journey. He also sometimes just likes to run, while at other times he doesn't like to move at all. He definitely doesn't like puddles or umbrellas, and will in fact stop in his tracks and comfort eat should he be faced with either.

Even more comical is the fact that halfway up a very steep hill, in a silent wood deep with fallen leaves, the llamas stop, one by one, for a wee. This is their usual spot, apparently, and they like to take their time. Pandu holds the record with 25 minutes, but, thankfully, today they're all done after just ten and we carry on up to the highest point of the walk – Hydon's Ball (587 feet). From here you can see some 40 miles of rolling farmland stretching out towards Portsmouth. It is breathtaking and a

million miles away from grid-locked London. Louis seems to like it too, taking our moment of quiet contemplation as a prime hedge-nibbling opportunity.

An hour or so later, Louis and the other llamas are safely back in their paddock and we are warming our toes in front of the Merry Harrier's roaring fire. Our stomachs drum-tight with delicious comfort food and hands wrapped around pints of guest ale, we wonder if it's possible to transport a llama to a one-bed flat in south London. Amid the madness of city life, a day out with a six-foot furry friend is just what the soul requires.

Surrey Hills Llamas
Merry Harriers, Hambledon, Surrey GU8 4DR (01428 682883, www.surrey-hills-llamas.co.uk). Cost from £36; £18 concessions.

History

The Hell-Fire Caves 116
Hever Castle 117
Stonehenge & Avebury 120
Down House 121
FIVE Castles 122
LASSCO Three Pigeons 124
Battle 126
TEN Stately homes 129
Windsor Great Park 134

The Hell-Fire Caves

Ghost-hunting in the Chiltern Hills.

A unique site steeped in 18th-century political scandal and sexual intrigue, West Wycombe Caves (around two miles from High Wycombe in Buckinghamshire – a 40-minute train journey from Marylebone) is the perfect antidote to the traditional museum-based day-trip. An impressive Gothic church-like structure is the portal to a labyrinth of hand-carved tunnels that, among other things, harbour the enduring secrets of the notorious Hell-Fire Club – a mock 'gentleman's club' that, in its heyday, included some of the most high-profile politicians, artists and poets of the 1700s, and which met here twice a month for booze-fuelled 'immoral acts'.

The site was a chalk quarry until the 1750s, when, following a bout of poor harvests, local philanthropist and globetrotting playboy Sir Francis Dashwood decided to extend the tunnels in order to provide employment for impoverished local farmers. The chalk from the excavation was used to build a road from the village to High Wycombe. The caverns run for a quarter of a mile and at their deepest lie 328 feet (100 metres) beneath the ground's surface. It was here that Dashwood founded the Knights of St Francis of Wycombe club – posthumously baptised the Hell-Fire Club by outraged newspaper reporters of the time – which used the caves for alcohol-driven meetings supposedly involving pagan rituals and sexual debauchery.

The passageways of this former Iron Age mount are eerily dark and vary in height, while constant dripping sounds create a chilling atmosphere. Explorers are happily left to their own devices and there are no signs to direct your route – quite disconcerting at the first left-or-right option. But the first real conundrum comes in the form of Franklin's Cave, a kind of circular micro-maze named after a close friend of Dashwood's, Benjamin Franklin, the accomplished inventor and one of the founding fathers of America, who visited the caves in 1772.

The most impressive part of the caves is the Banqueting Hall, a circular room with a huge dome ceiling and an icy, demonic feel. Here it's said that club members (which included John Montagu, the fourth Earl of Sandwich) would practise mock religious ceremonies and pseudo-satanic rituals. Orgies with masked prostitutes (referred to as nuns) and wild, week-long parties were also rumoured to take place. Take time to read the placards attached to the wall: poems from the times give an excellent clue to the era's impish spirit, while the descriptions of the more risqué behaviour of club members have been reduced to amusing but short and polite anecdotes.

Not surprisingly, the caves are popular with ghost-hunters, and there are regular reported sightings of what they refer to as 'light orbs' or 'cosmic sneezes', as well as of the two resident ghosts. The most common sighting is of Sukie, a local bride-to-be who was apparently stoned to death by some local boys. Meetings, or rather 'investigations with high-tech ghost-detecting equipment', are regularly held here.

Of course, many of the stories surrounding the Hell-Fire Caves and the activities of the eponymous club are speculation. Paul Whitehead, the club's steward (and the other resident ghost here), is said to have burnt any records of the meetings, which ended in the 1760s, in the few days before he died. But half the fun is filling in the historical gaps with your own imagination.

The equally eccentric Dashwood Mausoleum, a few minutes' walk from the caves at the top of West Wycombe Hill, is also worth a visit. This bizarre hexagonal monument built in 1765 was inspired by Constantine's Arch in Rome and is a bold testament to Dashwood's love of neo-classical architecture. Its grandiose and slightly camp stature is upstaged only by the stunning views of the surrounding Chiltern Hills.

Also worth a look is West Wycombe itself, with its picturesque rows of 16th-century timber-framed cottages. Take a look at the Church Loft; it's the oldest building here and was once a pilgrim's rest house. Paul's Traditional Sweet Shop (36-37 High Street, 01494 529539) is a sugar-fest of over 400 kinds of retro confectionery, while the George & Dragon (High Street, 01494 464414) serves a decent range of ales and pub grub.

Hell-Fire Caves
Church Lane, West Wycombe, High Wycombe, Buckinghamshire HP14 3AH (01494 533739, www.hellfirecaves.co.uk). Open Apr-Oct 11am-5.30pm daily. Nov-Mar 11am-5pm Sat, Sun, bank & school holidays. Admission £5.

Hever Castle

A picture-perfect castle with a gruesome past.

Hever Castle has a fairy tale setting, but its pretty face belies a sordid history. If these walls could talk, what tawdry tales they'd tell: randy royals, extramarital affairs, incest, sibling rivalry, social climbing, gratuitous violence and restless ghosts, topped off with an appearance by an American millionaire and his celebrity guests. For such a tiny castle, then, Hever has plenty of talking points. And a huge legacy: indeed, it changed the course of English history. It's all down to one woman: Anne Boleyn. Hever Castle was her family home, and it has been trading on this connection ever since. With all the recent Tudor mania on screen – the juicy BBC mini-series *The Tudors* and the torrid film *The Other Boleyn Girl* – Hever Castle makes for a timely, and salacious, day out.

For such a classic castle, it's strange to think that Hever was just a plain old manor house when it was built in 1270. But its owner, Sir Stephen de Penchester, evidently needed to step up security: in 1272, Edward II granted him permission to convert it into a castle. He did a good job: it boasts crenellated towers, a moat, a drawbridge and a gatehouse complete with portcullis, plus winding stone staircases and secret rooms. And it would soon have royal credentials.

Anne Boleyn was born at Hever Castle in 1501. During her youth, Henry VIII would come to stay; Anne's father, Sir Thomas Boleyn, had married into royal circles, and was determined that his daughters would do the same. For a future queen, Anne sure had a tiny bedroom; the guest room for Henry VIII, by contrast, is the biggest in the house, complete with a whopping oak canopy bed. Anne was forced to share with her sister, Mary, whom she would later betray; if you believe the rumour-mongers, Anne stole Henry from under her sister's nose. Not content to be his bit on the side, she held out for marriage, setting in motion Henry VIII's divorce, the Reformation… and her own demise.

Hever Castle gives you all the gory details, including a rare portrait collection of all six of Henry VIII's unfortunate wives. All the juicy tidbits rescue Hever from stately-home stuffiness; Boleyn was described by a Venetian ambassador as 'not one of the handsomest women in the world…', her 1533 marriage to Henry VIII was apparently a shotgun affair, the crowds booed her at her coronation, and she was executed, with Henry citing an incestuous affair with her brother George (widely thought by historians to be untrue) as the reason. The potraits also highlight the plights of Anne of Cleves – whom Henry VIII married her on the basis of a beautiful miniature portrait only to discover she wasn't much of a looker in person – and Catherine Howard, the King's fifth wife; the former's marriage was annulled after six months but at least she kept her head, unlike the latter. The castle's desperate wives club is followed by a portrait of a more fortunate figure: Elizabeth I, Anne's daughter, resplendent in her trademark lacy collar and imperious stare.

If the history of the monarchy doesn't interest you, there are some cool visceral bits too. Behind a fake wall, there's a hidden chapel where Edward Waldegrave, a subsequent owner, used to worship in secret during the period when Catholicism was taboo in England; he also fashioned a clandestine priest's room. In the gatehouse there are murder holes (openings in the floor that allowed castle defenders to drop boiling water on to enemy attackers).

A garderobe, a medieval toilet, adds a touch of lewd entertainment. More alarming are the instruments of torture; here are hand choppers, thumb presses, leg manacles, flesh gougers, flails, scourges, neck traps, branding irons and beheading axes – at least Henry VIII brought in a French swordsman to give Anne a clean chop. Still, there have been frequent sightings of Anne's troubled ghost in the grounds of Hever, on the bridge over the River Eden, or under the great oak where Henry VIII courted her.

As for decor, Hever has all the requisite period trappings – majestic oak panelling, elaborate tapestries, stained-glass windows – but its glam 20th-century side holds the most appeal. William Waldorf Astor, the American tycoon, emigrated to England in 1890 – 'America was no longer a fit place for a gentleman to live' – and used his $100 million fortune to restore Hever Castle. The library is a real showpiece, with elegant antique lamps, leather-bound tomes and fantastical Grinling Gibbons-style wood carvings (the naked women are very Playboy mansion). The drawing room is another slice of 1920s chic, with a curvy satinwood commode that hides a record player, a secret panel that conceals a drinks cabinet and a rosewood baby grand piano, complemented by plush *Dynasty*-style furnishings. It was here that generations of Astors hosted the great and the good of British society; displays show correspondence with the likes of Queen Elizabeth II, Winston Churchill, Sir Arthur Conan Doyle and George Bernard Shaw.

Astor's greatest contribution to Hever Castle, however, was the lavish Italianate garden. Dotted with ornate fountains, columns, urns, statues and walkways, and overlooking a lake, it's like something out of *The Portrait of a Lady* – *la dolce vita* as imagined by an American millionaire. But a pair of mazes reminds you this is very much an English attraction; they will please the kids, as should the animal topiary hedges and the model dolls' houses in the gift shop. But adults should be wary of the water maze (*see p266*): it sprays you unexpectedly according to where you step. Getting wet during a cold English summer isn't fun; but try to keep things in perspective: think of what happened to poor Anne Boleyn.

Hever Castle

Hever, nr Edenbridge, Kent TN8 7NG (01732 865224, www.hevercastle.co.uk). Open Summer noon-6pm daily, last admission 5pm. Winter noon-5pm Thur-Sun, last admission 3pm. Garden open from 10.30am. Admission £12.

HISTORY

Stonehenge & Avebury

Prehistoric encounters without the crowds.

In high season, when the day-trippers descend in force, the roads leading to Stonehenge can be so hellish that it's tempting to turn around and head home. Yet there's no denying the wonder of the prehistoric site. Dodge the hordes by booking well in advance for a pre-opening or post-closing 'access' visit (01722 343834, www.english-heritage.org.uk). Only 26 people are admitted at a time, and you'll be able to go right inside the stone circle, bathed in morning or evening light. But if 26 people is 25 too many, you could instead explore Wiltshire's less visited prehistoric landscape, Avebury (on the A361/A4361, near Marlborough, 01672 539250, www.nationaltrust.org.uk), a quieter spot where wandering among the ancient stones can be a far more spiritual and peaceful experience. What's more, it's free (though there is a charge for the car park). Close by, you'll also find Silbury Hill and West Kennett Long Barrow, plus giant hill carvings of white horses at Manton and Cherhill.

Down House

See where Darwin got his inspiration.

Charles Darwin had noted down his preliminary thoughts about evolution a few years prior to moving from London to Kent in 1842. But it was the years of experimentation, correspondence and thinking at Down House, his Kent home for 40 years, that gave him enough evidence to contemplate publishing *On the Origin of Species by Means of Natural Selection*, the book that scandalised society and revolutionised biology. Despite the less-than-catchy title, the book was an instant and controversial bestseller when it was published in 1859. The house – extensively refurbished to celebrate 150 years since the book's appearance, and the simultaneous bicentennial of Darwin's birth – is a joy to visit, feeling like a peek inside the constantly enquiring mind of one of the world's greatest scientists.

In Darwin's day, Down House overflowed with playful children, piles of post and jars of exotic specimens. Even in the eerie stillness of the vacant rooms today, it's obvious Darwin was always at work: a jar of earthworms sits on his wife Emma's cherished rosewood piano; a skeleton lies on the billiard table; trailing plants and bees take over the greenhouses. It all combines to give a palpable sense of the environment as a lively, cherished place for research, experimentation and discovery. The restored rooms downstairs use as much original furniture as possible, including Darwin's study chair, the board he laid across his lap to handwrite *Origin*, the backgammon set used for twice-daily games with Emma, and the signed copy of *Das Kapital* on his bookcase. Sir David Attenborough describes Darwin's life and work in a hand-held multimedia tour.

Upstairs, displays explore Darwin's early years, his life-changing voyage on HMS *Beagle* (including a re-creation of his ship study), and the development of and controversy surrounding *Origin*. A handful of interactive exhibits illuminates the concepts of adaptation and evolutionary theory, and plenty of Darwin paraphernalia is on display. Look out for the panama hat that shaded Darwin's balding pate during his *Beagle* adventures, his compass and pistol, his beetle collections and a browsable digital version of his pocket notebooks. There's even a clinical diary of the debilitating illness that cursed his life at Down House, through the course of which Darwin noted daily changes in symptoms with characteristic fastidiousness.

The immaculately tended grounds served as Darwin's own personal outdoor laboratory. You can walk in his footsteps, following the 'thinking' sandwalk that he himself constructed and walked around three times a day like

clockwork, whatever the weather. With views across open countryside, it's hard to believe you're so close to London, but it's also easy to see how the routine cleared the scientist's head.

When Darwin died at Down House in 1882, aged 73, a little local funeral was planned. However, the science establishment had bigger ideas: the father of evolutionary theory was buried in Westminster Abbey, close to fellow science superstar Isaac Newton.

Down House
Luxted Road, Downe, Kent BR6 7JT (01689 859119, www.english-heritage.org.uk). Open Feb, Mar 11am-4pm Wed-Sun. Apr-June, Sept, Oct 11am-5pm Wed-Sun. July, Aug 11am-5pm daily. Admission £9 (incl multimedia tour).

FIVE Castles

Leeds Castle

Dover Castle

Perched solidly on the white cliffs of Dover, this castle has been guarding England since Roman times. It has a few claims to fame: its keep, or great tower, is the largest in England; it boasts a great Roman lighthouse; and its labyrinthine tunnels were used during World War II as an air-raid shelter, underground hospital and military command centre. The castle recaptures the excitement with tunnel tours, backed up by news clips, sound effects and interactive displays. Up above, meanwhile, you can see France from the highest tower.

Dover, Kent CT16 1HU (01304 211067, www.english-heritage.org.uk). Open Summer 10am-6pm daily. Winter 10am-4pm Mon, Thur-Sun. Admisson £10.

Kenilworth Castle

If Warwick (*see below*) is a theme-park castle par excellence, nearby Kenilworth is a wonderful romantic ruin. Though built in 1125, its heyday was the 1560s, when it served as a backdrop for the relationship between Robert Dudley, Earl of Leicester and Queen Elizabeth I (you can view a copy of the last letter he wrote to her in the gatehouse here). Most of the castle was demolished during the Civil War, but set amid rolling hills, the crumbling red sandstone remains are achingly pretty (Sir Walter Scott, one of the great romantics, was sufficiently moved to write a novel about it). *Kenilworth, Warwickshire CV8 1NE (01926 852078, www.english-heritage. org.uk). Open Summer 10am-5pm daily. Winter 10am-4pm daily. Admission £6.10.*

Leeds Castle
Surrounded by a mighty moat, Leeds boasts a magnificent medieval exterior (it was built around 1066), even if the interior – with antique furnishings from the 20th-century owner Lady Baillie – pales by comparison. The outdoor aviaryis remarkable, holding more than 100 exotic bird species, as is the duckery: black swans glide around the moat. The wildflower Wood Garden, the English Culpeper Garden and the Mediterranean Lady Baillie Garden are further natural assets. A dog collar museum adds a touch of quirk.
Maidstone, Kent ME17 1PL (01622 765400, www.leeds-castle.com). Open Summer 10am-5.30pm daily. Winter 10.30am-4pm daily. Admission £15.

Warwick Castle
Dubbed Britain's greatest medieval experience, Warwick Castle is pure theme park, but we like it that way. It does have real historical credentials, though; it was built in 917 and fortified by William the Conqueror during the late 11th century. But the Tussauds Group bought it in 1978, and ramped up the entertainment – the Royal Weekend Party is a waxwork scene featuring Edward VII and friends. There's also a torture chamber, a dungeon and a ghost show. Costumed medieval jousters and jesters dot the elaborate grounds, which include a peacock garden and an enchanting Victorian rose garden that is the stuff of Mills & Boon.
Warwick, Warwickshire CV34 4QU (0870 442 2000, www.warwick-castle.co.uk). Open Summer 10am-6pm daily. Winter 10am-5pm daily. Admission £15.

Windsor Castle
The Queen's weekend pad is actually bigger than Buckingham Palace (it's the world's biggest occupied castle). The State Apartments feature works by Rembrandt, Rubens, Gainsborough and Van Dyck; from October to March, you can also see the splendidly decorated Semi-State rooms. Inside St George's Chapel are the tombs of ten monarchs, including Henry VIII and Jane Seymour (and the Queen Mum). But the castle is perhaps most famous for Edward Lutyens's elaborate Queen Mary's Dolls' House, complete with flushing loos.
Windsor, Berkshire SL4 1NJ (01753 831118, www.royalcollection.org.uk). Open Summer 9.45am-5.15pm daily, last admission 4pm. Winter 9.45am-4.15pm daily, last admission 3pm. Admission £15.50.

HISTORY

Windsor Castle

LASSCO Three Pigeons

The salvage firm's Oxfordshire outpost offers more than architectural gewgaws.

If you're restoring or refitting a period home, you've probably heard of LASSCO – the London Architectural Salvage and Supply Company – already. Its London headquarters, Brunswick House in Vauxhall, is well known for its artfully chosen architectural antiques, large and small. So why drive out to this new Oxfordshire branch? Because you'll see a greater choice of pieces, of course, particularly for the garden, all displayed in the atmospheric setting of a converted Victorian pub. You'll also get to turn your shopping trip into a day out – there are plenty of enjoyable things to do in the surrounding area.

Most importantly, you get to eat the most atavistically good food in the adjoining Three Pigeons café, where cakes are baked, stews simmered and pie crusts crisped by Clare Assis, a former pastry chef at Le Manoir aux Quat'Saisons. In fact, having a house in need of restoration is not a prerequisite for a visit here. Lunch alone pretty much merits the trip, along with the chance to see some unique pieces of architectural art and pick up some decorative curios from a smattering of smaller objects.

HISTORY

LASSCO opened at Three Pigeons in May 2007. It's a former coaching inn located by the crossing of two major turnpikes (and now, handily, the M40), once the site of a gibbet (a gallows). Its salty past and beer-stained decor have yielded to a considerably classier country-cottage conversion. A stone eagle greets you in the porch, then architectural antiques and decorative objects jostle prettily for attention in a series of cosy room settings. Flocks of birdcages dangle from the ceiling, open fires crackle in unexpected nooks, museum display cases house drawers full of buttons for 25p each, a collection of ammonite fossils crawls from £5 tiddlers to £1,600 giants. It's all terribly charming.

On the architectural side, LASSCO offers pretty much everything except sanitaryware and radiators. It specialises in flooring – from a patch to a parquet – but can sort you out with anything from a log basket to an entire chimneypiece. It also has an entire outhouse filled with doors. Outside, an acre of garden displays a stoneyard's worth of cherubs and griffins, pergolas and domes, urns and amphorae, and ranks upon ranks of stone toadstools (from £400 to £600).

All the pieces are one-offs, of course, but some are more one-off than others, unique pieces of architectural and decorative art spanning several centuries. When we visited, one standout piece was a Victorian pulpit complete with stone staircase from a London church (for £18,000), a set of beautiful engraved windows by Helen Monro Turner from the 1960s, and a doorcase

from the Mappin & Webb headquarters at No.1 Poultry (demolished in 1994 and replaced with a James Stirling building voted by *Time Out* readers the fifth worst building in London).

The café is at the back, a cosy place of low light and homely rustic furniture infused with the cheerful personality of chef Clare Assis, who cooks often singlehandedly in the open kitchen and still finds time to natter with regulars or pass on the ingredients of her biscuits. (Her deep, dark brownies are revered by the locals.) The food, as she says, is 'simple, seasonal and nice', but don't let her WI down-to-earthness fool you; this is cooking of the highest order. The simple things are the hardest to get right, and our 'simple' steak and kidney pie with its hand-made water crust was the stuff of pie-obsessives' dreams. The other dishes we tried – beetroot salad, onion soup and sausage and mash – were almost as good. The ingredients are free-range and organic, and sourced as locally as possible, which means very locally indeed; Clare picks up the veg from a farm on the next lane along from the café, and the pork is from gastro hotspot Britwell Salome ten miles away.

Lunch and a browse here only take a morning, but if you want to extend your visit there's plenty to do within easy reach. Oxford, of course, or a walk in the Chilterns, which you pass en route. Or, if you want to extend the history theme, cross the M40 to investigate the Swan at Tetsworth (High Street, 01844 281777, www.theswan.co.uk), another converted coaching inn that sells antiques, this time of the

fine variety, plus some interesting vintage clothing. Or, drive a dozen or so miles into Hertfordshire to visit Waddesdon Manor (Waddesdon, near Aylesbury, 01296 653226, www.waddesdon.org.uk), the very stately home of the Rothschilds' amazing decorative arts collection. Alternatively, if you came to LASSCO looking for garden furniture, you could do

further horticultural research – or even a class – at Waterperry Gardens (near Wheatley, 01844 339254, www.waterperrygardens.co.uk).

LASSCO Three Pigeons
London Road, Milton Common, Oxfordshire OX9 2JN (01844 277188, www.lassco.co.uk). Open 10am-5pm Mon-Sat.

Battle

Go Norman in East Sussex.

Squint hard, and you can almost imagine yourself back in 1066 – despite a few modern anachronisms. The clanking English army are defending the side of Senlac Hill (giving spectators a good view from the top), while King Harold is getting an eyeful of arrow, right by the plaque that marks the historic spot. Once the battle has been fought, the Conqueror's hordes go on to pillage the craft tents and merrye refreshment stalls. This Battle of Hastings may be a remake – shown in the auditorium at the new visitor experience in the small town of Battle (about an hour and 20 minutes from Cannon Street or Charing Cross) – but the sight of 1,500 colourful archers, cavalry and footsoldiers, plus a whole ramshackle village of 'living history' extras, leaves an indelible impression. Whether you come to participate or to spectate, escapism doesn't get much better than this.

But come here on a normal weekend and you can still immerse yourself in history with the 1066 Battle of Hastings, Abbey & Battlefield experience, organised by English Heritage. It includes an exhibition and a monastic life tour, but by far the best part is the ability to spend a couple of hours wandering around the battlefield and abbey ruins. Roaming over a former battleground is intensely evocative, and, treading the soils of one of the most pivotal moments in English history, you feel privileged, proud and undeniably part of the action.

The audio tour is packed with fascinating details and anecdotes that paint a vivid picture of the battle that changed the course of English history. Over 14,000 troops were involved in the brutal conflict between Saxon King Harold and William of Normandy on 14 October 1066 – a battle for the English throne. You'll learn about the tactics used by each side, the advantages and disadvantages of their positions and, ultimately, the reasons for Harold's defeat.

Standing on the spot where Harold was slain, and gazing up the hill at the abbey you'll find yourself drifting into another world – complete with spears, shields, clubs and armour. Before you know it, you'll have gone back almost 1,000 years, when English history changed forever.

1066 Battle of Hastings, Abbey & Battlefield

Battle, East Sussex TN33 0AD (01424 775705, www.english-heritage.org.uk/1066). Open April-Sept 10am-6pm daily. Oct-Mar 10am-4pm daily. Admission £6.40.

HISTORY

award-winning sculpture set in stunning woodlands

bring this advert for two-for-one admission to the sculpture estate

cass sculpture
foundation
at goodwood

registered charity number 1015088

open april – october every year
10:30 to 5pm, last entry 4:30pm
directions at **www.sculpture.org.uk**

i'm alive by tony cragg, photography simon norfolk

Cliveden

Audley End House

The first Earl of Suffolk and Lord Treasurer Thomas Howard built this Essex mansion on the scale of a great royal palace, so it's no surprise that Charles II snapped it up in 1668 as a stopover for the Newmarket races. Shortly after, much of it was demolished but what's left, less than a third of the original, is still one of the best examples of Jacobean neo-classical architecture in Britain. The chief fun here is trying to work out what's happened in the ensuing 300 years, as successive owners have imposed their own individual styles and tastes on the 30 rooms open for exploration – look out in particular for the architectural foibles of Robert Adam in the ground-floor reception rooms. *Audley End House, Saffron Walden, Essex CB11 4JF (01799 522399, www.english-heritage.org.uk). Open House Mar-Sept 11am-5pm Wed-Fri, Sun; 11am-3.30pm Sun. Oct 11am-4pm Wed-Sun. Gardens Mar-Dec 10am-dusk Wed-Sun. Admission £7.30. Gardens only £5.40.*

Charleston

The Bloomsbury Set go mad in the country: in 1916 the artists Vanessa Bell and Duncan Grant moved to Sussex where, inspired by Italian fresco painting and the Post-Impressionists, they painted the walls, doors, furniture and ceramics, to create what's now regarded as a fascinating example of belle époque decorative arts. Outside, they redesigned a walled garden in a style reminiscent of southern Europe, with mosaics, box hedges, gravel pathways and ponds. Inside, they covered their decorated surfaces with art by greats like Renoir, Picasso, Walter Sickert and Delacroix, as well as the Bloomsbury contemporaries who were regular guests. *Charleston, Lewes, East Sussex BN8 6LL (01323 811265, www.charleston.org.uk). Open Mar-June, Sept, Oct 11.30am-6pm Wed, Sat; 2-6pm Thur, Fri, Sun, bank hols. July, Aug 11.30am-6pm Wed-Sat; 2-6pm Sun, bank hols. (Guided tour only Wed-Sat.) Admission £7.50. Grounds only £3.*

Cliveden

If you like your stately homes close to your own home, Cliveden, just 45 minutes away from London, will definitely hit the spot. Most of the Italianate house, built in 1851 and once the home of American socialite Nancy Astor, is now a hotel and generally off-limits (though a part of it is open for a few hours every week), but the reason to come to Cliveden is to leisurely explore one of southern England's most amazing estates. Overlooking a beautiful stretch of the Thames is a series of formal gardens, each with its own character, featuring topiary, statues, water gardens, a parterre and woodland and riverside walks with stunning views.

Petworth. See p131.

Charleston . See p129.

Cliveden House, Taplow, Maidenhead, Berkshire SL6 0JA (01494 755562, www. nationaltrust.org.uk). Open Grounds Mar-Oct 11am-6pm daily. Nov, Dec 11am-4pm daily. House Apr-Oct 3-5.30pm Thur, Sun. Admission Grounds £8. Grounds & House £9.

Elton Hall
A little off the stately home beaten track, and often overlooked because of it, Elton Hall is nevertheless one of the most unusual stately homes in the area, and its peculiar mix of styles makes for great exploration. Its earliest parts – a front hall tower and chapel – date back to the 15th century, and later wings and additions cover another 300 years of architectural styles (including an 1860 dining room designed by Henry Ashton and a library situated in a medieval tower), creating a whole that's decidedly romantic, with extensive parkland and lovely gardens. Elton Hall, Elton, Cambridgeshire PE8 6SH (01832 280468, www.eltonhall.com). Open June 2-5pm Wed. July, Aug 2-5pm Wed, Thur, Sun. (May & Aug bank hols 2-5pm.) Admission £7.50. Gardens only £5.

Knole
With its seven courtyards, 52 staircases and 365 rooms, the seriously grand Knole house really does warrant the tag 'stately'.

Granted to Thomas Sackville by Elizabeth I in 1566, every aspect of Knole is superb, from the craftsmanship evident in its furniture, textiles, tapestries and carved woodwork to the superior masonry of the ornate plaster ceilings and magnificent carved marble chimneypieces. The literary

Polesden Lacey. See p132.

Snowshill Manor. See p133.

Sissinghurt Castle. See p132.

connections are interesting too (it's fun to think of Vita Sackville-West growing up here, and Virginia Woolf's *Orlando* is largely based on the history of the house and family) and you can ponder them as you explore the extensive gardens and the lovely 1,000-acre parkland, keeping an eagle eye out for the large herds of Japanese deer.

Knole, Sevenoaks, Kent TN15 0RP (01732 450608, www.nationaltrust.co.uk). Open House Mar noon-4pm Sat, Sun. Apr-July, Sept, Oct noon-4pm Wed-Sun. Aug 11am-4.30pm Tue-Sun. Gardens Apr-Sept 11am-4pm Wed. (Park open daily.) Admission £9. Gardens only £2.

Petworth

Art lovers will find a veritable cornucopia of wonder at this impressive late 17th-century mansion set in a 700-acre Capability Brown-landscaped park. Turner made Petworth famous and many of his works are on show here, as well as exemplary pieces by Van Dyck, Titian, Gainsborough, William Blake, Bosch and Reynolds, all amassed by one family over 350 years. Look for carvings by Grinling Gibbons throughout the house, as well as exquisite sculpture, furniture and porcelain. It's worth coming on a weekday, when owners Lord and Lady Egremont allow extra family rooms to be opened.

Petworth House & Park, Petworth, West Sussex GU28 0AE (01798 343929, www.nationaltrust.org.uk). Open House Mar-Oct 11am-5pm Mon-Wed, Sat, Sun. Grounds Mar-Oct 11am-5pm Mon-Wed, Sat, Sun. Nov, Dec 10am-3.30pm Wed-Sun. Admission £9.40. Grounds only £4.

Knole

Polesden Lacey

From its lofty perch on the North Downs, Thomas Cubbit's Regency country house – set in a 1,400-acre estate – lords it over the surrounding terrain, just as it did when it was home to poet Richard Brinsley Sheridan. It's a lovely place to explore, particularly in the summer, when outdoor Shakespeare performances are held in the grounds. But it's the interiors that really shine, in a decidedly over the top French rococo style that you're unlikely to see in many other stately homes. *Polesden Lacey, Great Bookham, nr Dorking, Surrey RH5 6BD (01372 458203, www.nationaltrust.co.uk). Open House Mar-Oct 11am-5pm Wed-Sun. Gardens Feb-Oct 10am-5pm daily. Nov, Dec 10am-4pm daily. Admission £9.95. Gardens only £6.35.*

Sissinghurst Castle

Everyone knows Vita Sackville-West's home for its outstanding gardens, but the home she shared with husband Harold Nicolson is just as enchanting, including an oast house, a priest's house and a pink-brick Elizabethan prospect tower. The study and library are the only parts of the house open to visitors, but it's included in our favourite stately homes because the gardens alone are some of the loveliest in England. Designed by Sackville-West and Nicolson, the series of warm intimate spaces are themed by season (making them worth visiting at almost any time of the year) and supplemented by such sweet architectural features as the medieval moat (which houses an orchard) and gorgeous woodland walks. *Sissinghurst Castle Garden, Sissinghurst, nr Cranbrook, Kent TN17 2AB (01580 710701, www.nationaltrust.org.uk). Open House Mar-Oct 11am-5pm Mon, Tue, Fri-Sun. Nov 11am-4pm Mon, Tue, Fri-Sun. Garden Mar-Oct 11am-6.30pm Mon, Tue, Fri; 10am-6.30pm Sat, Sun. Nov 11am-4pm Mon, Tue, Fri; 10am-4pm Sat, Sun. Admission £8.80.*

Audley End House. See p129.

Snowshill Manor

This wonderfully idiosyncratic Cotswold manor house dates back to 1539, but it's the owner who arrived in 1919 that makes it one of our favourite historical homes. The cottagey architecture is the perfect home for the collections of Charles Paget Wade; the architect, artist-craftsman, collector and poet spent his family fortune on his mania for collecting examples of craftsmanship from around the world. The 21 rooms of the house are consequently filled with more than 22,000 objects, including one room full of clocks, one full of life-size Samurai warriors, another packed with dolls' houses, and a 2,000-piece costume collection. The garden is also charming, with terraces, ponds and great views over the Vale of Evesham.
Snowshill Manor, nr Broadway, Gloucestershire WR12 7JU (01386 852410, www.nationaltrust.org.uk). Open Manor Mar-Oct noon-5pm Wed-Sun. Garden Mar-Oct 11am-5.30pm Wed-Sun. Admission £7.70. Garden only £4.10.

Wilton House

If you like your stately homes to look just as they do in costume dramas, the 450-year-old Wilton House won't disappoint; in fact, as you approach what's regarded as one of Britain's finest Palladian-style houses through the 21 acres of parkland and gardens, it might feel distinctly familiar from films like *Pride and Prejudice*, *Sense and Sensibility*, *The Madness of King George* and *Mrs Brown*, all filmed here. The grandeur carries on inside, where rooms like the Gothic Revival upper cloisters are breathtaking, but we love wandering around the grounds of this truly stately pile, admiring the elegant Palladian bridge over the River Naddar and, of course, pretending the whole thing's ours.
Wilton House, Wilton, Wiltshire SP2 0BJ (01722 746714, www.wiltonhouse.co.uk). Open House Easter weekend, May-Aug noon-5pm Mon-Thur, Sun. Grounds Apr-Aug 11am-5.30pm daily. Admission £12. Grounds only £5.

Windsor Great Park

A long walk through history.

Leave the changing guards, castle tours and shops full of tat to the tourists and make the most of Windsor local-style, with a stomp through the Great Park to soak up some history, and a hearty pub lunch to soak up an accompanying pint.

The most relaxing way to arrive is by train, and the direct line from Waterloo to Windsor & Eton Riverside (taking just under an hour) offers pleasing views of Windsor Castle as you roll into town. Step on to the platform and a short stroll past the castle (Her Majesty is in residence if the royal standard is flying) takes you to the start of the 4,800-acre Great Park's Long Walk – a three-mile stretch of surfaced path that leads from the castle to the Copper Horse statue atop Snow Hill depicting George III.

HISTORY

You won't have it to yourself, however. This is prime strolling, jogging, dog-walking and pram-pushing territory – and for good reason. There are few things that better encapsulate the sedate grandeur of this well-to-do tourist town than the expanse of green and castle views here. Depending on the timing of your walk, you might want to stop by the lovely Two Brewers (34 Park Street, SL4 1LB, 01753 855426) for a fortifying pre-stroll beverage or two. Despite its location, seconds from the park gates, this homely pub (all low ceilings and wonky floors) somehow manages to defy the tourist masses, serving gigantic Sunday roasts, an evening tapas menu and a solid pint of London Pride or Spitfire to a loyal local crowd.

Get back on track and the greatest joy of the Long Walk promenade soon becomes clear. You don't need a map. You don't need instructions. You don't even need to concentrate. Simply relax and let your mind wander as you march ahead admiring gnarly old oak trees and – a little further along – the resident red deer.

Should you fancy straying from the path there are ample, well-signposted diversions. One of the most fascinating is Frogmore House and the Royal Mausoleum (final resting place of Prince Albert and Queen Victoria), set in the private Home Park. You'll have to plan ahead to visit it as the former royal residence is only open to the public for two weekends a year – typically August bank holiday weekend and another in either May or June (www.royalcollection.org.uk) – but the house and its art collections, featuring works by several generations of royals (including George III's consort Queen Charlotte, Queen Victoria and her daughters Princesses Victoria and Louise), are well worth a look.

The landscaped gardens are vast and impressive, with tulip trees and giant redwoods among the many historic plantings. Queen Charlotte was a keen botanist and takes cred it for many of the rare and unusual plants that can be admired here.

Frogmore House was adored by Queen Victoria, and the tranquil setting of the Tea House installed in the grounds during her reign offers some insight into what might have inspired her to write the words 'all is peace and quiet and you only hear the hum of the bees, the singing of the birds', in reference to the residence.

Stay away from such detours and your walking efforts will be rewarded as you ascend Snow Hill for stunning views of the castle and beyond (the arch of Wembley Stadium can be seen on a clear day). From here you could opt to walk another couple of miles to Savill Garden (Wick Lane, 01784 435544, www.theroyal landscape.co.uk), a woodland and ornamental garden complete with 35 acres of trees, ponds, lawns, meadows and flowerbeds. The award-winning Savill building is home to a decent restaurant with a large terrace.

For lunch with the locals, however, you'll need to take a left as you face the Copper Horse and walk towards Bishops Gate and the cosy Fox & Hounds (*see p188*). Settle in for the afternoon (you can always call a taxi back to the station later) or simply relax and refuel before embarking on the walk back to the town centre.

▶ For further walks, *see p112* Surrey Hills Llama Trek; *p243* Beachy Head Walk; *p244* Five Interesting walks; *p95* Salcey Forest; and *p46* Grantchester. For more castles, *see p122* Five Castles and *p116* Hever Castle.

If you've time to spare before you head back to the capital, Windsor town centre offers high-class shopping (Jo Malone, Ghost, Whistles) at a pace that makes you wonder why anyone would ever set foot on Oxford Street – check out Windsor Royal Shopping (www.windsor royalshopping.co.uk). And if you can't bear to leave without snapping a few sights, there's always the Guildhall (completed in 1689) with its famed Wren pillars. Look closely and you'll see they stop short of the floor they're meant to support – it is believed that a nervous council insisted they were necessary to ensure the chamber above didn't collapse and Sir Christopher Wren only semi-obliged to prove a point. Eton College (www.etoncollege.com) and the River Thames also offer pleasant diversions.

Eating & Drinking

Fox & Hounds

Bishops Gate, Englefield Green, Surrey TW20 0XU (01784 433098, www.thefoxandhounds restaurant.co.uk). Open 11am-3pm, 5.30-11pm Mon-Thur; 11am-11pm Fri, Sat; noon-7pm Sun.

Warming in winter and spot on for summer alfresco drinking (there's a garden out front and a lovely enclosed terrace at the rear), this atmospheric pub is a popular local choice. Booking is advisable for weekend lunches where the organised are rewarded with well-executed classics such as braised pork belly, ribeye steak and traditional fish and chips. A fine place to lose an afternoon.

Culture

Cambridge 138
FIVE Galleries 143
Constable Country 144
TEN Architectural marvels 146
FIVE Festivals 148
Garsington Opera 150
FIVE Works of art 151
Cheltenham Literature Festival 154
Snape Maltings & Aldeburgh 156
FIVE Sculpture parks 160

Cambridge

Oxford may have dreaming spires, but for culture, head to Cambridge.

Turn your back on the Gothic outline of King's College to head down narrow St Edward's Passage and you immediately know what a day out in Cambridge is all about: two theatres, a tiny café and a dreamy old bookshop are all within a few steps. That's just the start – there really is something of cultural interest on nearly every corner of this city.

Best of all, it's wonderfully compact. You won't even need a bus ticket, if you don't mind the ten-minute walk to the centre from the train station. In fact, if you want to feel like a local straight away, hire a bicycle (www.citycyclehire.com). Whether you cycle or walk, however, you should find this an ideal destination for a stress-free day out. Inside the Fitzbillies bakery (2 Trumpington Street, 01223 352500, www.fitzbillies.co.uk), source of estimable chelsea buns, staff even refuse to serve you if you're talking on your mobile.

Halfway between the station and the delightful colleges that cluster around the city centre is the superb Fitzwilliam Museum (*see p140*), its palatial façade stretching along Trumpington Street. Further west across the River Cam looms the monolithic brick tower of the University Library (West Road, 01223 333000, www.lib.cam.ac.uk). Recognisably by Giles Gilbert Scott, the architect responsible for the power station that became Tate Modern, you can see some of the stacks of books from outside. The library is one of the few in the country entitled to a free copy of any book published in Britain or Ireland and the collection already holds some seven million volumes; non-cardholders can see a small, changing exhibition inside. Just up the road, the music faculty's West Road Concert Hall (11 West Road, 01223 335184, www.westroad.org) and its three resident ensembles host lively lunchtime concerts, a Cambridge habit that is very handy for day-trippers – check the posters that hang outside most churches and colleges for options as you wander about. To get back to the centre of town, take the footbridge leading to the back of King's College for your snapshot view: the river, the lawn, the 'chapel' that's as big as many cathedrals… you'll recognise them from a million postcards, but your heart will leap to see them for real.

A cultural buzz permeates the whole city. Art galleries mix with small shops, delis and cafés in the centre, but don't be afraid to venture a little further out; watch members of the local collective Cambridge Artworks at work in their studios (5 Greens Road, 01223 309393,

www.cambridgeartworks.com), or seek out the student shows at the airy Ruskin Gallery (East Road, 01245 493131, www.anglia.ac.uk).

But in Cambridge the best places are often not the most obvious – after all, it's a city known for thinking, not shouting. So it is with the Shop on Jesus Lane (18 Jesus Lane, www.theshopjesus lane.co.uk), a bright, white gallery on an unassuming stretch of road that attracts some of the city's most exciting exhibitions, and the magnificent Kettle's Yard (*see p141*), surely the most beguiling museum in Cambridge. Likewise, ordinary neighbourhood boozers turn into the finest stages for live music (witness 'The Back Room' of the Man on the Moon, 2 Norfolk Street, 01223 474144, www.myspace.com/ manonthemoonuk) and what looks like an undergraduate office is, in fact, the excellent, 264-seat Mumford Theatre (Anglia Ruskin University, East Road, 0845 196 2320, http://web.anglia.ac.uk/mumfordtheatre/).

Whatever else you do, don't rush. There's more to do here than is possible in a day, so don't try and cram too much in: a visit to Cambridge is just as much about lingering in Auntie's Tea Shop (1 St Mary's Passage, 01223 315641, www.auntiesteashop.co.uk) or Agora at the Copper Kettle (4 King's Parade, 01223 308448, www.agoraatthecopperkettle.co.uk). With its big windows facing King's College, it's perfect for lazily sipping a cappuccino, while some poor soul next to you is correcting coursework. Hungry? St Andrew's Street and Regent's Street are lined with restaurants, but again curiosity is rewarded: our favourites are on the top floor of the Arts Theatre (Arts

Restaurant, *see p141*) and tucked away in a basement (Rainbow Café, *see p141*).

If you're happy with a later return home, you could attend the famous evensong services at King's College Chapel (01223 331100, www.kings.cam.ac.uk, 5.30pm Tue-Sat during term), when the enchanting voices of the college choir echo through the candlelit nave. If that's not your style, try an intimate acoustic gig at the Portland Arms (129 Chesterton Road, 01223 357268, www.theportland.co.uk), or chunkier names from rock, pop and even opera over at the Corn Exchange (Wheeler Street, 01223 357851, www.cornex.co.uk). The Junction (*see p140*), meanwhile, nonchalantly mixes hard rock, comedy, electro nights and experimental theatre into a typically satisfying cultural stew.

If one cultural activity stands out here, it's drama. The options range from high-profile productions at the Arts (6 St Edward's Passage, 01223 503333, www.cambridgeartstheatre.com)

all the way to daring student shows (Corpus Playroom, www.srcf.ucam.org/fps). The city's oldest university stage, the ADC Theatre (*see p140*), neatly combines both tendencies – and it's fun to mingle with future Oscar-winners in the busy ADC bar after a show. If you're after something more traditional by way of drinking, Cambridge has plenty of creaky old hostelries: the Eagle on Bene't Street (8 Bene't Street, CB2 3QN, 01223 505020) and the Pickerel Inn (*see p141*) are two of the best. Surely it's only in Cambridge that you find yourself drinking beside a bunch of literature students in avid debate over the erotic in Whitman, only for a total stranger (a professor, it turns out) to join in with equal fervour.

Finally, what better way to reflect on your day of culture then a quiet punt along the River Cam. Punts can be hired from Scudamores (01223 359 750, www.scudamores.co.uk, £16 per hour) at any of its three central Cambridge stations .

CULTURE

Diary Dates

Wordfest
www.cambridgewordfest.co.uk.
A biannual festival that celebrates all things wordy in spring and autumn each year. Heavyweight guest speakers have included Kate Adie, Ali Smith, Tony Benn and Jonathan Coe.

Super8 Film Festival
www.cambridge-super8.org.
Under constant threat of extinction from digital camcorders, Super8 remains a brilliantly expressive film format, instantly evocative of home movies. Nostalgists and experimentalists alike are drawn to this annual festival held in April/May.

Strawberry Fair
www.strawberry-fair.org.uk.
A fair and carnival parade held in June, organised and run by volunteers. It that's particularly popular with East Anglia's teenagers who flock in from miles around. There are four music stages, great food and even a mini-film festival.

Summer in the City
www.cambridge-summer.co.uk.
A catch-all programme that includes the 800-year-old June fair on Midsummer Common, Big Weekend's three-day music and dance extravaganza on Parker's Piece in July, and the comedy and children's events of Jesus Green Live each August.

Cambridge Folk Festival
www.cambridgefolkfestival.co.uk.
Still going strong after more than 40 years, this is a genuinely eclectic and always impressive international music festival. Judy Collins, Allen Toussaint, Tunng and, er, the Levellers have found themselves on the same bill in previous years. Late July, early August.

Cambridge Music Festival
www.cammusic.co.uk.
The best of classical music and jazz in a triennial festival that features local as well as international artists. November.

Eating & Drinking

Arts Restaurant
6 St Edward's Passage, CB2 3PJ (01223 367333, www.cambridgeartstheatre.com).
Open 5-10.30pm Mon; noon-10.30pm Tue-Sat.
Housed on the fourth floor of the Cambridge Arts Theatre, the Arts Restaurant serves contemporary European fare – the likes of pan-fried duck breast, salmon steaks or an extravagant vegetable moussaka – in a light, modern interior. Come for lunch (when the menu's slightly slimmer) or check out the full pre-show menu – whether you have tickets for the theatre downstairs or not.

Pickerel Inn
30 Magdalene Street, CB3 0AF (01223 355068). Open noon-midnight daily.
This atmospheric old pub serves a great selection of real ales – and rarely gets as crowded as places closer to the centre. Grab a window seat to watch people stroll in and out of the pretty River Court of Magdalene (pronounced 'Maudlin') College, or take your pint to the dimly lit, cosy backroom. There's mulled wine and a fire in winter and a small courtyard in summer.

Rainbow Café
9A King's Parade, CB2 1SJ (01223 321551, www.rainbowcafe.co.uk). Open 10am-9.30pm daily.
This sweet little vegetarian eaterie, tucked away in a basement off King's Parade (it's the white door), delights diehard vegans as much as meat-eaters. Everything is locally sourced and freshly prepared. The menu might feature spinach lasagne, a crunchy Latvian potato bake or Caribbean-style pumpkin curry.

Shopping & Attractions

ADC Theatre
Park Street, CB5 8AS (01223 359547, www.adctheatre.com). Open (box office) 12.30-7pm Tue, Fri; 3-7pm Wed, Thur, Sat.
Britain's oldest student theatre, the Amateur Dramatic Club was founded in 1855 and its playhouse has finally emerged from several years of step-by-step refurbishment. It hosts West End transfers, high-quality student performances – from the ADC itself (alumni include Sir Ian McKellen and Emma Thompson) and Footlights (most of the comedy establishment) – and seasons such as the annual WordFest. The Lateshows are

one-hour, unreserved performances of comedy, drama or music, taking place at 11pm most nights.

Fitzwilliam Museum
Trumpington Street, CB2 1RB (01223 332900, www.fitzmuseum.cam.ac.uk). Open 10am-5pm Tue-Sat; noon-5pm Sun. Admission free.
This under-visited museum has brought together a superb collection of paintings, sculpture and antiques behind a broad neo-classical façade. Upstairs, the various pieces – some of them dating back to the 14th century – blend beautifully with the imposing museum interiors, especially the furniture exhibits. Artistic highlights include masterpieces by Titian, Modigliani and Picasso, while the downstairs is full of relics from Egypt, Greece and Rome, as well as fine literary and musical manuscripts. There's also a great programme of lunchtime talks, drop-in events and concerts.

The Junction
Clifton Way, CB1 7GX (01223 511511, www.junction.co.uk). Open (box office) noon-6pm Mon-Sat.
The Junction opened in 1990 as a standing-only auditorium. This 1,050-capacity main hall continues to host club nights, where you can see the likes of Andy C and Sinden minus the crazy crowds that they pull in bigger towns. There are also a decent selection of bands – from established student-pleasers like the Only Ones and Robyn Hitchcock, plus some up-and-comers – but in 2005 it was joined by two subsidiary spaces. J2 stages drama, comedy and dance in an adaptable theatre that accommodates 220 seated or 300 standing, while the J3 studio space also hosts enterprising performing arts workshops on its sprung floor. Three bars and a café complete the picture.

Kettle's Yard
Castle Street, CB3 0AQ (01223 748100, www.kettlesyard.co.uk). Open (House) Summer 1.30-4.30pm Tue-Sun & bank holiday Mon. Winter 2-4pm Tue-Sun & bank holiday Mon. (Gallery & bookshop) 11.30am-5pm Tue-Sun & bank holiday Mon. Closed Good Friday.
When former Tate curator Jim Ede lived here, he held an 'open house' each afternoon so visitors could enjoy his collection of early 20th-century artists – Miró, Brancusi, Hepworth and Moore among them. Ring the doorbell and you can do the same. A bookshop and gallery for temporary exhibitions occupy a separate building; both close while new exhibitions are set up.

Kettle's Yard

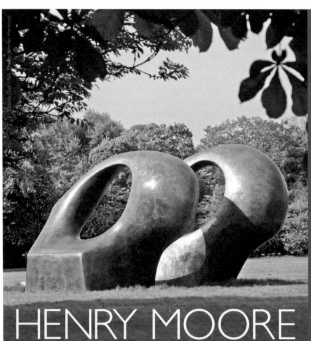

FIVE Galleries

Beecroft Art Gallery, Westcliff-on-Sea

From the outside, this unprepossessing townhouse looks less than promising. Inside, though, is a collection of more than 2,000 pieces, taking in portraits by Constable and Rossetti, a Jacob Epstein bronze and a landscape by Edward Lear, as well as an impressive array of 17th-century Dutch works. Local views figure prominently in the Thorpe Smith Collection, a surprisingly varied collection of local landscapes dating back to 1803.
Station Road, Westcliff-on-Sea, Essex SS0 7RA (01702 347418, www.beecroft-art-gallery.co.uk). Open 10am-1pm, 2-5pm Tue-Sat. Admission free.

Fry Art Gallery, Saffron Walden

If the Towner (*see below*) could be said to be the home of Eric Ravilious, the Fry is that of Ravilious's good friend Edward Bawden, who is represented here by almost 600 works of art. All of the work displayed here is by artists who were part of a creative community that flourished in and around the nearby village of Great Bardfield before and after World War II. It's a terrific collection, stuffed with prints, paintings, , illustrations, wallpapers and decorative designs that offer a glimpse into the lives of working artists we might not be entirely familiar with. The name of Chilean artist Olga Lehmann may not ring a bell, for example, but her paintings were seen by millions as the art hanging on the walls of the Colbys in *Dallas*, and her private portrait commissions included Dirk Bogarde, Errol Flynn and Marlene Dietrich.
Castle Street, Saffron Walden, Essex CB10 1BD (01799 513779, www.fryartgallery.org). Open Apr-Oct 2-5pm Tue, Fri, Sun; 11am-5pm Sat. Admission free.

Russell-Cotes Art Gallery & Museum, Bournemouth

The Russell-Cotes is housed in one of Bournemouth's few remaining Victorian villas – an eccentric-looking turret-topped affair, filled to the rafters with treasures. A rare survivor as the residence of a Victorian private collector, planned and perpetuated as a permanent art museum, it's as utterly absorbing as its exterior would suggest, and packed with thousands of curios, artefacts and artworks from around the globe – including more than 1,000 oil paintings and an awful lot of female nudes. It's perched on the clifftops, and the café and gardens have great views.
Russell-Cotes Road, East Cliff, Bournemouth, Dorset BH1 3AA (01202 451858, http:// russell-cotes.bournemouth.gov.uk). Open 10am-5pm Tue-Sun. Admission free.

Stanley Spencer Gallery, Cookham

Sir Stanley Spencer lived in Cookham for much of his life, and made it the subject of many of his paintings and drawings, some 100 of which are gathered here. While the big guns – the likes of *The Resurrection, Cookham* and *Shipbuilding on the Clyde* – are housed in galleries such as the Tate and Imperial War Museum, there's a very impressive collection of work on display. It's also a rare delight to be able to explore the relationship between an artist and his surroundings. The gallery's website details an hour-long ramble you can take around the village that passes many of the subjects and locations of Spencer's paintings.
High Street, Cookham, Berkshire SL6 9SJ (01628 471885, www.stanleyspencer.org.uk). Open Apr-Oct 10.30am-5.30pm daily. Nov-Mar 11am-4.30pm Thur-Sun. Admission £3.

Towner Gallery, Eastbourne

The town's new £8.5m Rick Mather-designed, purpose-built gallery becomes home to more than 4,000 works of art in 2009, with pieces by the likes of Vanessa Bell, Tacita Dean, Olafur Eliasson, Anya Gallaccio, Picasso, Wolfgang Tillmans and Eric Ravilious. Ravilious is the name anyone who's ever heard of the Towner associates it with, and with good reason; having studied and taught at Eastbourne School of Art, the artist's work is a key element of the collection, and includes everything from woodcuts to the posters he designed for London Transport and the ceramics he created for Wedgwood.
Devonshire Park, College Road, Eastbourne, East Sussex N21 4JJ (01323 434660, www.townereastbourne.org.uk). Open 10am-6pm Tue, Wed, Fri-Sun; 10am-8pm Thur. Admission free.

CULTURE

Constable Country

Put yourself in the picture, at Suffolk's Dedham Vale.

The work of Britain's most famous romantic landscape painter has been distorted by thousands of chocolate box imitations but, two centuries on, John Constable's depictions of Dedham Vale and the countryside around the Suffolk–Essex borders still remain true to his belief that 'I should paint my own places best'.

It's possible to trace Constable's life and times – maybe trying to put yourself in exactly the spot from which he painted one of his masterpieces – in a day spent in the triangle formed by the pretty village of East Bergholt, the ravishing small town of Dedham and the intriguing adjacent settlements of Manningtree and Mistley (to where there are direct trains from Liverpool Street station, taking just over an hour).

Constable was born in 1776 in East Bergholt on the Stour estuary, the son of a wealthy corn merchant who owned Flatford Mill. Golding Constable managed his business interests from the mill, so it's easy to appreciate why the budding young artist, in search, as he put it, of 'the sound of water escaping from mill dams et cetera, willows, old rotten planks, slimy posts, and brickwork', was inspired by the stream in front of the building. He was to place it at the heart of many of his greatest works. You can stand at the exact spot where masterpieces such as the *Haywain*, the *Mill Stream* and *Flatford Mill from the Lock* were conceived; the landscape is remarkably unchanged.

Flatford Mill itself, along with Valley Farm and Willy Lott's Cottage that also feature in many of Constable's works, are leased to the Field Studies Council, which runs arts and environmental courses for all age groups (0845 330 7368, www.field-studies-council.org). There's no public access to the mill, but the 16th-century Bridge Cottage (01206 298260, www.nationaltrust.org.uk) houses an exhibition about the artist, plus a riverside tearoom.

Back in East Bergholt, St Mary's Church reveals a history of religious insurrection. Several Protestant inhabitants were martyred during the 16th-century reign of Catholic Queen Mary, their fate recorded by John Foxe in his famous *Foxe's Book of Martyrs*. The church has a fine set of bells – in an extraordinary location. Work on building a bell tower started in 1525, but Cardinal Wolsey's fall from grace five years later brought construction to a halt. In 1531, a temporary wooden bellcage was erected in the churchyard, and it's still there. Nearby is Old Hall (www.oldhall.org.uk), occupied by some 60 people living communally and cultivating 70 acres of land organically. The community holds occasional open days and festivals.

Constable went to school in what is now the Old Grammar School in Dedham, walking along the river from East Bergholt each day. The wool and cloth trades made Dedham rich, and the opulent church of St Mary the Virgin bears testament to this elevated status. It was the last of the region's magnificent late-medieval 'wool churches' to be completed, where, as Nikolaus Pevsner put it, 'nothing hurts the eye'. Its pleasing spire features in many of Constable's best-known compositions.

There's further evidence of Dedham's prosperity in the grand houses along the High Street, notably the Grade I–listed Sherman's Hall. The frontages are Georgian but the structures behind are in most cases far older, a striking example of the newly wealthy wanting to disguise their village's more humble fabric.

From the late 19th century, Constable's reputation attracted other artists to the area. Chief among these was Sir Alfred Munnings, who lived at Castle House in Dedham from 1919 until his death in 1959. Munnings was one of Britain's greatest equestrian artists and an arch-opponent of modernism; he once famously declared: 'What are pictures for? To fill a man's soul with admiration and sheer joy, not to bewilder and daze him.' However, the collection of his paintings and sculptures beautifully displayed at the house, now home to to the Sir Alfred Munnings Art Museum (01206 322127, www.siralfredmunnings.co.uk), makes an excellent case for Munnings as an artist with an interesting and broad palette, rather than a mere painter of horses.

Still, he was no fan of the East Anglian School of Painting & Drawing, set up in an old house in the village by Cedric Morris and Arthur Lett-Haines in 1937. Idiosyncratic, radical and calling itself 'an oasis of decency for artists outside the system', Lucian Freud was among the first intake of students. However, the building burned down in 1939 – much to the delight of traditionalist Munnings.

More contemporary work can be found at Dedham Art & Craft Centre on the High Street (01206 322666, www.dedhamartandcraftcentre. co.uk), which houses a pleasant vegetarian tearoom. Another decent High Street lunch spot is the comfy Essex Rose Tea House (01206 323101, www.trooms.com), where you can sample the superior Tiptree conserves manufactured by Wilkin & Sons 20 miles back down the A12. The jam factory, museum and visitor centre in Tiptree itself (01621 814524, www.tiptree.com) is an unusual alternative stop-off on the way back to London – and a rare chance to indulge in a superior jam sandwich.

Meanwhile, the Sun Inn (01206 323351, www.thesuninndedham.com), also on the High Street, is a former coaching inn serving a classy modern British menu with a Mediterranean twist, amid beams, flagstones, panelling and big fireplaces. In the pub's Archway Annex, Victoria's Plums sells locally grown fruit and veg and some organic produce.

Constable's father owned a small ship, the *Telegraph*, which he moored at Mistley and used to transport corn to London. The village acquired its Georgian character from local bigwig Richard Rigby, Secretary of Ireland and Paymaster of the Forces, who in the 1760s had lavish plans to turn Mistley into a port and spa.

He engaged Robert Adam as architect, but his grandiose plans never came to fruition as the money ran out when Rigby was found to have abused his position as Paymaster. All that remains are Mistley Towers, two imposing but rather wan structures that formed part of Adam's unconventional remodelling of the parish church. You can have a peek inside by collecting the key from Mistley Quay Workshops (01206 393884).

Manningtree, by contrast, was already a thriving port by Tudor times. Like Dedham, the cloth trade brought prosperity, and there are good examples of weavers' cottages, built by craftsmen fleeing the Netherlands, in Brook Street and South Street.

The White Hart (01206 392768, www.white hartmanningtree.co.uk) is Manningtree's oldest inn, and notorious as the venue of the trials and interrogations of self-appointed 'Witch Finder General' Matthew Hopkins, during the 1640s. Nineteen women were put to death on the village green and four more died in prison. The Manningtree Local History Museum (01206 395548) features both the area's glories and ghoulishness.

How best to complete your exploration of 'Constable Country'? Back in the capital, head for Tate Britain and view many of those familiar landscape paintings with an entirely fresh eye; for the *Haywain* itself, head instead for the National Gallery.

TEN Architectural marvels

American Air Museum

Norman Foster's sleek 1997 glass structure stands as a memorial to the 30,000 American airmen who lost their lives flying from UK bases during World War II. A huge and impressive collection of American war planes is suspended from the arched glass roof.
Imperial War Museum Duxford, Cambridgeshire CB22 4QR (01223 835000, www.iwm.org.uk). Open end Mar-Oct 10am-6pm daily. Nov-early Mar 10am-4pm daily. (Last admission 1hr before close.) Admission £16.

Art Deco in Frinton-on-Sea

Tucked away in seaside suburbia are some of England's best art deco buildings, unsung and often unnoticed. Essex estuary town Frinton-on-Sea is awash with terrific examples, thanks largely to architect Oliver Hill, who conceived the 200-acre Frinton Park Estate: 1,100 houses grouped together in different styles by leading invited architects of the day, among them Erich Mendelsohn & Serge Chermayeff, Tecton, and Wells Coates. That Hill's vision was only partially realised isn't necessarily a bad thing; most of the remaining 30 houses haven't worn that well, but the likes of the Round House (7 Cliff Way), Dawn (55 Quendon Way), Willingale (16 Warley Way) and Thalia (11 Graces Walk) still call to mind a bygone era of elegance.
Frinton Park Estate, off Walton Road, Frinton-on-Sea, Essex CO13.

Arts and Crafts around the Downs

A triumphant triumvirate of Arts and Crafts splendour lies within easy distance of London, making a memorable day out for anyone into the architecture of the early 20th century. The Watts Gallery in Surrey is closed for extensive refurbishment until 2010, but you can still take a fascinating one-hour guided tour of the Watts Cemetery Chapel (Down Lane, Compton, 01483 810235, www.wattsgallery.org.uk), a Celtic and art nouveau masterpiece created by Mary Seton Watts. From there it's a short drive to Standen (West Hoathly Road, East Grinstead, 01342 323029, www.nationaltrust.org.uk), a showpiece

De La Warr Pavilion

Arts and Crafts home designed by Philip Webb, with William Morris furnishings, textiles and wallcoverings at every turn. Then it's off to Charleston to explore the walled garden designed by Roger Fry, before joining a guided tour to admire the interiors created by Vanessa Bell, Duncan Grant and other Bloomsbury Set pals (Charleston Firle, Lewes, 01323 811265, www.charleston.org.uk).

De La Warr Pavilion

Reopened in 2005 following an £8 million restoration project, Erich Mendelsohn and Serge Chermayeff's 1935 modernist masterpiece looks better than ever. Admire the clean lines, take in the sea views and make the most of this thriving arts centre's vibrant programme of exhibitions, music and comedy.
Marina, Bexhill-on-Sea, East Sussex TN40 1DP (01424 229111, www.dlwp.com). Open 10am-5pm Mon-Fri; 10am-6pm Sat, Sun. Admission free.

Georgian Bath

Bath's elegant Circus and Royal Crescent are glorious examples of 18th-century Georgian architecture. At the former, look out for architect John Wood's frieze of 528 carvings taken from a 17th-century fortune- telling book, then walk down Brock Street to the magnificent Royal Crescent, designed by Wood junior and completed in 1767. From here, the views of the surrounding countryside are stunning, but nothing beats the view of the Crescent itself. Look out too for the Ha-ha, a sunken fence that kept the sheep, cows and peasants from the front lawns of the gentry inside, but didn't interrupt their expansive vistas. If you've time, picnic in the nearby Royal Victoria Park and take in the lovely townhouses at Lansdown Crescent, all built in the same Bath stone that gives the city its rare architectural unity. (*See also p188* Bath Thermae Spa and *p41* Five Shopping extravaganzas.) *www.visitbath.co.uk.*

Medieval marvels in Lavenham, Suffolk
With more than 300 listed buildings, deciding to paint your front door must be a real pain if you live in Lavenham. But for non-resident architecture fans, this quaint Suffolk town is a must. It's often cited as England's finest example of a medieval town, and with good reason. Wandering around enjoying the buildings and streets – with breaks for a fantastic lunch in the multi-award-winning Great House Restaurant & Hotel (Market Place, 01787 247431, www.greathouse.co.uk) or tea at the Tickled Pink Tea Rooms (17 High Street, 01787 249517) – is rewarding, but you'll get additional historical and cultural insights if you invest in the 90-minute audio tour (£3 from Lavenham Pharmacy & Perfumery, 3 High Street, 01787 247284) or one of the summer walking tours that start at the Tourist Information Centre (Lady Street, 01787 248207, www.discoverlavenham.co.uk).

Radcliffe Camera
With its smooth curves and domed roof, James Gibbs's 1749 library is one of Oxford's most imposing and inspiring buildings. There's no public access to the reading rooms it now contains so unless you did very well in your A Levels, you'll have to make do with gazing at the exterior. *See also p20.*
Radcliffe Square, Oxford, Oxfordshire OX1 4AJ (01865 277000).

Regency Brighton
Come and do the Princess Di moonface pose in front of Brighton's Royal Pavilion and, with some judicious cropping, pretend you went to the Taj Mahal. The Prince Regent's ornate, outlandish country farmhouse-turned-mock-Mughal palace never ceases to amuse and amaze, not least for architect John Nash's happy pilfering of not just Indian but also Chinese and Gothic notes in this splendid example of joyful excess. The interiors are well worth a tour too; if anything their lavishness even exceeds the minarets, towers and materials of the exterior. Here are Chinese-style decorations with magnificent furniture and furnishings, columns topped with palm fronds, gilded dragons, imitation bamboo staircases and vibrant colours everywhere. *See also p13.*
Royal Pavilion, Brighton, East Sussex BN1 1EE (0300 029 0900, www.royalpavilion. org.uk). Open Apr-Sept 9.30am-5.45pm daily. Oct-Mar 10am-5.15pm daily. Admission £8.30.

Rushton Triangular Lodge
A little bit weird but definitely wonderful, Thomas Tresham's 1597 folly pays homage to the number three, symbolising the Holy Trinity. Three floors, three walls, triple gables – give yourself a few minutes to take it all in and you can stop counting.
Rushton, Northamptonshire NN14 1RP (01536 710761, www.english-heritage. org.uk). Open Mar-Oct 11am-4pm Mon, Thur-Sun. Admission £2.60.

Saltdean Lido
There's only one way to truly appreciate Richard Jones's curvaceously glam 1938 lido and that's to dive in. A refreshing throwback to the lido's Golden Age. Fans of this style might want to combine a visit with a trip to De La Warr; *see left.*
Saltdean Park Road, Saltdean, Brighton, East Sussex BN2 8SP (01273 888308, www. saltdean.info). Open May-Sept 7am-9pm Mon-Fri; 10am-6pm Sat, Sun. Admission £4.

CULTURE

Latitude

Cambridge Folk Festival

An ongoing folk renaissance is bringing even bigger audiences to this long-running festival that attracts veterans of the scene such as Altan, as well as hip young things like Laura Marling. The Radio 2-sponsored event may not be strictly folk – last year's line-up included Texan Latin band Grupo Fantasma, Mali's Bassekou Kouyate and Ngoni Ba, and New Orleans legend Allen Toussaint – but all performers are accomplished and quality musicians and singers. *Cherry Hinton Hall, Cambridge, Cambridgeshire CB1 8BW (01223 357851, www.cambridgefolk festival.co.uk). £45 day ticket. Late July/early Aug.*

Dot to Dot Festival

Venue-hop around intimate Bristol hangouts to take in both the laid-back city and up-and-coming indie-dance acts.

Previous acts over the last four festivals have included Alphabeat, Glasvegas, Gallows, British Sea Power, Foals, Santogold, Long Blondes, Erol Alkan and Kissy Sellout in eclectic bills that eschew the stadium acts in favour of intimate performances. It's over two days (the last bank holiday weekend in May) and twinned with Nottingham, so zoom across the country if you want to see an equally original line-up there. *Venues across Bristol and Nottingham (www.dottodotfestival.co.uk). Late May.*

The Great Escape

If you can't get to Texas for South by Southwest, take the London to Brighton train to catch the next big indie thing. In between the mayhem, wander the Lanes or lie on the beach as you pick who to enjoy from 300 bands that in the past have included Crystal Castles and the

Subways. 2008 saw more than 300 new local and international artists perform in 34 venues over the three-day event, plus a whole host of outdoor gigs, afternoon shows, club nights, after-parties and fringe events around the city, many of them free.
Venues across Brighton (020 7688 9000, www.escapegreat.com). £22.50 day ticket. May.

Latitude
The ultimate extra-curricular festival offers more music, theatre, poetry, literature, comedy and film than you'll probably see in a year. Big names like Franz Ferdinand, Elbow, Bill Bailey and the Royal Court share the bill with hundreds of smaller acts at this lovely, friendly culture fest. There's as much loving attention paid to the literature, comedy and cabaret line-ups as the

music ones, making the whole thing a lot more entertaining – and the crowds a lot more varied – than your usual spotty-herberts-drinking-beer music fest.
Henham Park, Suffolk NR34 8AN (0871 231 0821, www.latitudefestival.co.uk). £55 day ticket. July.

Lounge on the Farm
If avoiding crowds is your priority, this 5,000-capacity, locally focused affair is just the ticket. But boutique doesn't equal lame line-up: past headliners have included Super Furry Animals, the Bees, New York Dolls and Black Kids. Food is locally sourced, the booze (cider) comes from just down the road, and there's even a Battle of the Bands for kids.
Merton Farm, Canterbury, Kent CT4 7BA (www.loungeonthefarm.co.uk). £35 day ticket. July.

Garsington Opera

Open-air arias in intimate surroundings.

CULTURE

When Leonard and Rosalind Ingrams moved into their new pad in rural Oxfordshire in 1989, they made a happy discovery: the terrace of Garsington Manor lent itself surprisingly well to opera performances. Twenty years on, Garsington hosts a summer season of intimate opera in its fabulously quaint gardens, to rival anything you'll hear in the UK's best opera houses. Its productions have been well received not only at home but also on tour in some of the world's top venues, including the Met in New York. The performances have a deliberately long interval, during which it is customary to go for a walk around the gardens (à la Glyndebourne), open a bottle of something fizzy and consume one's picnic (in evening dress) on one's picnic rug. Lovely.

Garsington Opera
Garsington Manor, Garsington, Oxford, Oxfordshire OX44 9DJ (01865 361636, www.garsingtonopera.org).

FIVE Works of art

Marc Chagall's stained-glass windows

In a battle of artistic merit between Chichester Cathedral and the 12th-century All Saints Church in Tudeley, you might expect the former to win hands down. But while the cathedral does boast one window by Russian émigré artist Marc Chagall, Tudeley has 12 of them, all commissioned as a memorial tribute to local resident Sarah d'Avigdor-Goldsmid. The first, in the east window, was installed in 1967; the subsequent 11 windows were made and installed over the next 18 years, until Chagall's death in 1985. Come during one of the dozen or so chamber concerts that make up the annual Tudeley Festival (www.tudeleyfestival.org.uk) to enjoy this beautiful, magical art with soothing background music.
All Saints Church, Tudeley, nr Tonbridge, Kent TN11 0NZ (01732 357648, www.tudeley.org). Open Summer 9am-6pm Mon-Sat; noon-6pm Sun. Winter 9am-dusk Mon-Sat; noon-dusk Sun. Admission (voluntary) £2.

Prospect Cottage Garden

The garden that filmmaker and artist Derek Jarman designed and created in the eight years he lived at Dungeness should be obligatory viewing for anyone interested in the history or practice of art. Dungeness itself makes for a highly original day trip (*see p73*), but it's the little black and yellow cottage that was a haven for Jarman until his death in 1994 that's the lure for art-lovers. Nowadays, it doesn't look that different to many of the other gardens around it, but that's because Jarman pioneered a trend, with a design that looks effortless. Shells, bits of broken tools, fishing kit and unrecognisable shards of corroded metal decorate sticks of driftwood and standing stones sit alongside plants chosen for their ability to withstand the raging winds, salty spray and inhospitable terrain – like bonsai aloes, lavenders, santolinas, poppies and crambes. The designs sometimes echo garden cottages and sometimes look like higgledy-piggledy randomness, but, seen as a whole, it's a piece of conceptual art that's absolutely in tune with its surroundings. The garden featured in many of Jarman's later films, including *War Requiem* and *The Garden*, where it was both the Garden of Eden and the garden at Gethsemane.
Prospect Cottage, Dungeness Road, Dungeness, Romney Marsh, Kent TN29 9NB.

Sir Stanley Spencer's war murals

The highly decorated Sandham Memorial Chapel, designed by Lionel Pearson in 1920 specifically to house the war paintings of Sir Stanley Spencer, is well worth a visit even if you're not here for the art; the idyllic grounds are also incredibly soothing. But to miss the extraordinary set of murals inside would be a huge shame. Inspired by Spencer's experience as both a medic and front line soldier during World War I – and influenced by Giotto's Arena Chapel murals in Padua – these wonderful examples of the artist's trademark naïve style took six years to complete and are considered to be among his finest work. And in their depiction of the humanity of war as opposed to its horror, they're a world away from what you'd expect of war art. If they inspire you to see more, head for the Berkshire village of Cookham, the birthplace of Spencer and home to a lovely gallery dedicated to his work (*see p143*).
Sandham Memorial Chapel, Harts Lane, Burghclere, nr Newbury, Hampshire RG20 9JT (01635 278394, www.nationaltrust.org.uk). Open Mar, Nov, Dec 11am-3pm Sat, Sun. Apr-Sept 11am-5pm Wed-Sun. Oct 11am-3pm Wed-Sun. Admission £4.

Sitooterie

Architect, designer and artist Thomas Heatherwick has done much to enliven the natural environment of south-east England, notably via his lovely East Beach Café (*see p79*) in Littlehampton, which exhibits his trademark organic shapes and sculptural ribbons in unusual materials. But there's another Heatherwick piece that's a very different kettle of fish; the *Sitooterie II*. This inventive reinvention of a traditional Scottish summer house (or 'sitooterie', in which to literally 'sit oot'), commissioned by the directors of the National Malus (crab-apple) Collection, takes the form of a fantastic, futuristic metal and glass cube punctured by more than 5,000 long thin windows that project from all its surfaces and lift it off the ground. A single central light source sends light through every tube,

CULTURE

Sitooterie. See p151.

causing all the windows to glow a shimmering orange. Best of all, a small number of them project into the cube to form seating. The whole looks like some alien spaceship that's incongruously found itself plonked in an Essex field, providing surely one of the most original places to sit... anywhere. And once you've had enough of sitting and thinking, there's plenty of other art to enjoy around the 42 acres, including works by Elizabeth Frink, Antony Gormley, Nicolas Lavarenne, and Monica Young.
Barnards Farm, Brentwood Road, West Horndon, Essex CM13 3LX (01277 811262, www.barnardsfarm.eu). Open Apr-Aug 11am-4pm Thur. Admission £5.

William Lyngewode's medieval carvings

While there's no single outstanding piece of art in Winchester Cathedral, the 11th-century building does boast some of the finest medieval wood carvings in Britain, if not Europe. You're immediately drawn to

the intricacy of the fine-grained limestone 15th-century Great Screen (the statues are Victorian replicas of the originals, destroyed in the 16th century), but the real draw here lies in the cathedral's stalls, where, in the 13th century, Norfolk-born carpenter William Lyngewode spent four years meticulously decorating the choir-stalls with witty scenes from secular life and with characters from an enchanted woodland scene (a knight with his sword at the ready here, a falconer with his bird of prey there).

Other artworks here include a lyrical modern *Pietá* by Eugene Ball, a spectacular example of early mosaic glasswork in the huge west window (made up of randomly patterned fragments from original panes destroyed by Cromwell's troops), the 12th-century stone font carved from a single block of black marble and Britain's largest area of medieval tiling.
1 The Close, Winchester, Hampshire SO23 9LS (01962 857200, www.winchester-cathedral.org.uk). Open 8.30am-6pm Mon-Sat; 8.30am-5.30pm Sun. Admission £5.

Prospect Cottage Garden. See p151.

Cheltenham Literature Festival

Wise words, in England's most complete Regency town.

Cheltenham is no stranger to festivals: it holds more than five annually, all of them well regarded and all of them different. The Literature Festival, held in October, is the last in the calendar, following jazz and folk in spring, science in early summer and the Cheltenham Music Festival (whose first melodic strains were heard two weeks after the end of World War II) in July.

Say the word 'Cheltenham' to a Londoner and the same shorthand images normally emerge; that heady combination of the famous Ladies' College, the 'Spa' suffix, the abundance of Regency terraces and its proximity to the Cotswolds all contribute to making the place sound unequivocally posh. And you know what? That's exactly what it can be like during the Lit Fest, when you queue up for author events behind ladies in pearls and fine coats, lunch at Raymond Blanc's brasserie (Promenade, 01242 266800, www.brasserieblanc.com) in the imposing Queen's Hotel, or stumble across Ann Widdecombe being interviewed by Radio 4 on a manicured lawn.

Hay-on-Wye may receive more hype (you can hardly move for 'those-in-the-know' mentions of 'Hay' in a certain broadsheet each spring), but the UK's oldest literature festival presents a hugely diverse range of authors and personalities and is extremely well planned, run and sponsored.

In 2008 alone the Cheltenham Literature Festival boasted a roster of well-known names such as Richard Attenborough, Toni Morrison, David Starkey and Gordon Brown, which goes some way to explaining how ticket sales reached 100,000 over 350 events. The list of past speakers includes the likes of Andrew Motion, Alice Walker, John Betjeman and VS Naipaul – and the list goes on.

Cheltenham's best-loved festival sprang into life on 3 October, 1949. Back then it advertised just nine events compared to today's three-figure myriad, which includes fringe events, children's activities, writers' workshops and live poetry battles. According to Nicola Bennett's 1999 book *Speaking Volumes*, celebrating 50 years of the festival, Elizabeth Jane Howard met her future husband Kingsley Amis there in 1962, the year she was appointed festival director. Further back in 1954, CP Snow 'rejected out of hand' a strange tale by a William Golding called *Lord of the Flies*, after Golding entered it for the festival's First Novel Competition. That same year, the runner-up was Iris Murdoch for *Under the Net*.

Now, just as then, the festival's hub is the town hall, a honey-coloured Edwardian building sandwiched between the well-heeled neighbourhood of Montpellier and the town's main (and copious) shopping area. Such is the overspill these days that enormous white marquees are also erected on the adjoining Imperial Gardens. Thanks to these, you can't miss the most visible sponsors and collaborators – chiefly *The Times* (whose newspapers are distributed gratis throughout the festival) and Waterstone's, whose temporary bookshop in one of the largest tents sells in the region of 25,000 books during the ten-day event. Other satellite venues are also used – most notably the Centaur at Cheltenham Racecourse, which holds 2,000 people, making it the largest venue for purely literary events in the UK.

The main, crowd-drawing speakers are, conveniently, scheduled over the two weekends, with the second weekend normally hosting the cream of the literary heavyweights. This is also when some of the most light-hearted events take place. In 2008, Radio 4 broadcast live shows such as the *News Quiz* and *Poetry Please*, while Sue Perkins and Giles Coren discussed their next *Supersizers* TV series.

If you can visit midweek, however, you'll find the festival at its most intimate and charming, with the vibe of a private gathering. Unsurprisingly, the audience sizes are less

▶ The Roald Dahl Museum (*see p260*) provides a literature-related day out for children.

daunting at 10am on a Tuesday morning, and even the shyest fans are emboldened to ask a question of their favourite writer.

Cheltenham has enough scenery, shopping and stylish dining to keep even the most hard-to-please day-tripper satisfied (during festival season or otherwise). Everyone living within a 30-mile radius heads here for a shopping session when they want to buy something special. High-class chains are found on the Promenade, but for pricey but tempting independents, head up the hill to Montpellier's Rotunda Terrace, where lifestyle shops such as Skandic Hus (no.4, 01242 233391, www.skandic-hus.co.uk) and Pod (no.7, 01242 541300, www.thepodcompany.co.uk) sell their chic and understated wares. The nearby 'Suffolks', an enclave of elegant houses and smart antique shops that could be mistaken for Chelsea, is where you'll find two good eateries. One, Le Champignon Sauvage (24-26 Suffolk Road, 01242 573449, www.lechampignonsauvage. co.uk), is Michelin-starred, while the other, the rather decadent Daffodil (18-20 Suffolk Parade, 01242 700055, www.thedaffodil.com), is a converted art deco cinema that looks like an ocean liner's dining room inside. An after-dinner stroll to the station down Cheltenham's gracious avenues will round off the day nicely, and then it's only a couple of hours back to Paddington on the train – plenty of time to scribble down that idea for a novel.

Cheltenham Literature Festival
(0844 576 8970, www.cheltenhamfestivals.com). Annually in October.

Snape Maltings & Aldeburgh

Benjamin Britten's home county is a fitting setting for this world-class concert hall.

Snape Maltings is an unusual sort of place – an odd, often rather forbidding, set of buildings situated on a hushed, peaceful, marshy expanse of the River Alde. It's beautiful; a reedy, wet, windy, salty and enchanting nook of England. The Victorian complex, proximate to – and dwarfing – the tiny village of Snape, was originally a factory and series of transport links for one of Europe's busiest malting operations (the process where barley is turned into malt). Today, the privately owned, Grade-II listed Maltings is home to a world-renowned concert hall and a selection of cafés and artisan craft shops ideal for a day's casual browsing.

Snape's most famous feature, its 832-seat concert hall, is the home of June's annual Aldeburgh Festival (box office 01728 687110, www.aldeburgh.co.uk), the brainchild of one of England's pre-eminent modern composers, Benjamin Britten; his life companion, tenor Peter Pears; and long-time collaborator, the director and librettist Eric Crozier. It's also the headquarters of Aldeburgh Music, which, in addition to producing the festival, organises a year-round series of concerts and runs the Britten Pears Young Artists Programme, one of the world's best professional music development schemes. Aldeburgh Music is nearing the end of a major redevelopment with new facilities, including small studios and concert spaces, being unveiled at Easter 2009.

Britten's home county, particularly its coast, served as a major muse throughout his career. He composed in most genres – chamber, symphonic, solo instrumental, song and, notably, opera: he is perhaps best known for his three 'English' operas, *Peter Grimes* (after the writings of Aldeburgh poet George Crabbe), *Billy Budd* (Herman Melville) and *The Turn of the Screw* (Henry James), and his mighty, still frequently performed *War Requiem* (Wilfred Owen, among others).

> ▶ Nearby Woodbridge (*see p31*) provides market town pottering-about pleasures en route.

In 1947, Britten, Pears, Imogen Holst (daughter of Gustav, who composed *The Planets*) and others formed the English Opera Group and, a year later, the Aldeburgh Festival, frustrated at how few opportunities there were for Britten's music to be performed in London. The first performances – which also took in gallery shows, literature and poetry readings, plays and lectures – took place in Aldeburgh's Jubilee Hall, before spilling out into nearby halls and churches and, eventually, the surrounding villages. Instantly popular with locals and visitors, it quickly became a permanent fixture on the European summer music calendar, and had thoroughly burst its banks by the mid 1960s.

By 1965, Snape Maltings' then owner George Gooderham was looking to repurpose its buildings and gave a 999-year lease to Aldeburgh Music to convert the biggest building and surrounds into a world-class concert hall and theatre. The Queen opened the 20th Aldeburgh Festival on 2 June 1967. On the first night of the 1969 festival, the concert hall was largely destroyed by fire. Within a year it had been rebuilt, and has hosted the festival every June since – though even now you can see scorch marks on the walls.

The festival runs for two weeks every June, with the programme announced in early February. Prompt booking and advance planning is required. Aldeburgh is not only popular but also very reasonably priced – few tickets cost more than £30.

It's also worth visiting outside of the festival season, however: there are excellent regular concerts and lunchtime recitals in the autumn and winter months, and the surrounding coastline looks gorgeous on a sunny winter's day.

Even if classical music doesn't pluck your strings, Snape Maltings has plenty to offer. It's the ideal base from which to appreciate East Anglia's big skies, with walks along the waterways and Suffolk's romantic Heritage Coast (www.visit-suffolk.org.uk).

The Maltings also makes a fantastic spot for a relaxed day out. There's browsing potential galore in the form of craft shops, galleries and the new Home & Garden shop – a gargantuan and exhaustively stocked emporium of swanky furniture and interiors. It also boasts a Heritage Bay, with restored maltings instruments, and a neat history of the complex. The Metfield Café hosts a bread market every Saturday (01728 688303), but even more enticing is the farmers' market held on the first Saturday of each month.

The last few days of September see the Aldeburgh Food & Drink Festival (www.aldeburghfoodanddrink.co.uk). Previous attendees have included Mark Hix, Fergus Henderson, Tom Parker Bowles, Rose Prince and Sheila Dillon from BBC Radio 4's *Food Programme*. Wash down the fruits of your foodie indulgence at the Plough & Sail, a bar and restaurant occupying a site that in the 16th century was a smugglers' inn (Snape Bridge, 01728 688413, www.debeninns.co.uk).

The surrounding area is spot on for a post-prandial stroll, though do note that this is a tidal estuary – local advice should be sought, to avoid getting stranded by rising tides. The area is also renowned by birdwatchers. The Royal Society for the Protection of Birds (www.rspb.org.uk) hosts guided walks on the first Saturday of each month (to coincide with the farmers' market), setting out from the Team Room at 11am.

If you've come by car, there's plenty of village-hopping potential here too. Minsmere nature reserve (01728 648281, www.rspb.org.uk/reserves) offers more back-to-nature birdwatching with hides, trails and a tearoom, while Dunwich is known locally for its fantastic fish and chips – the Flora Tea Rooms comes highly recommended (the Beach Car Park, 01728 668625). Beer fans will find Adnams on draft in almost every local hostelry and fanatics can visit the brewer's HQ in nearby Southwold (www.adnams.co.uk). The town is known for its galleries, as is Woodbridge (*see p31*).

CULTURE

ALDEBURGH

Aldeburgh is the most obvious spot to choose to extend your day out, however. It's brimming with mercantile naval history. In the 16th century, it was a major port and ship-building centre – Sir Francis Drake's *Golden Hind* was built there.

Take a walk along the shingly beach to observe the dozens of local fishermen (who will sell you their catch around lunchtime) and you'll feel much more than 100 miles away from London. Walk a couple of miles north and you reach otherworldly Thorpeness, with Sizewell nuclear power station looming in the background. There are also dozens of opportunities to eat freshly caught fish and chips (try the Golden Galleon, 137 High Street, 01728 454685), and cosy pubs aplenty. Simply wending in and out of the narrow streets and lanes is a pleasure too – we've never seen quite so many sundials in one town. You can also pay homage to Britten and Pears with a visit to the churchyard of St Peter & St Paul. The 450-year-old timber-framed Moot Hall hosts the town's museum (01728 454666, www.aldeburgh museum.org.uk) and is also worth a look.

One of the town's more striking monuments is Maggi Hambling's controversial stainless steel four-metre scallop – a tribute to Britten. It's frequently vandalised, and not just by those who resent such a whopping man-made object planted on a natural setting; it also galvanises the split in affection in which Britten and Pears are held in the area. They left Britain for America during World War II, and in 1942 successfully applied for conscientious objector status. Britten's solid place in Britain's musical heritage is assured, but some locals, it seems, believe that his patriotism was compromised by his political leanings.

Snape Maltings
Nr Aldeburgh, Suffolk IP17 1SR (01728 688303, www.snapemaltings.co.uk).

Cass Sculpture Foundation

Cass Sculpture Foundation
Opening each April, Goodwood's rolling acres are the setting for more than 70 monumental sculptures. It's an ever-evolving collection but works currently on display include Steve Dilworth's monstrous black granite *Claw* (2007) and Antony Gormley's wry *Bollards* (2001). *Cass Sculpture Foundation, Sculpture Estate, Goodwood, nr Chichester, West Sussex PO18 0QP (01243 538499, www.sculpture.org.uk).*

Hannah Peschar Sculpture Garden
This ten-acre garden is a dreamlike place, dotted with thought-provoking sculptures handpicked by owner-curator Peschar.

Each work, whether crafted from glass, plastic or bronze, is positioned to harmonise with the natural surroundings. Represented artists change seasonally. *Hannah Peschar Sculpture Garden, Black and White Cottage, Standon Lane, Ockley, Surrey RH5 5QR (01306 627269, www.hannahpescharsculpture.com).*

Henry Moore Foundation
The atmospheric complex at Perry Green encompasses Hoglands – Moore's timber-framed farmhouse that has been meticulously restored. Also returned to its former glory are the gardens, once tended by Moore's wife Irina, and now dotted with 24 of the artist's finest works,

including *King and Queen 1952-3*, *Family Group 1948-49* and *Large Figure in a Shelter 1985-86*.
Henry Moore Foundation, Dane Tree House, Perry Green, Much Hadham, Hertfordshire SG10 6EE (01279 843333, www.henry-moore-fdn.co.uk).

Jerwood Sculpture
If 18th-century Ragley Hall's perfect symmetry isn't enough of an excuse for a visit here, then factor in the grounds – 400 acres of picturesque parkland landscaped by Capability Brown, and featuring 20th- and 21st-century sculptures from the Jerwood Foundation's collection. Follow the 2.5-mile sculpture trail to see the changing works, by artists such as Antony Gormley and Kenneth Armitage.

Jerwood Sculpture, Ragley Hall, Alcester, Warwickshire B49 5NJ (01789 762090, www.jerwoodsculpture.org).

NewArtCentre Sculpture Park & Gallery
Representing the estates of artists such as Barbara Hepworth, Kenneth Armitage and Ian Stephenson, the NewArtCentre made the 19th-century Roche Court its home in 1994, after relocating from London's Sloane Street. As well as the permanent works, a changing roster of exhibitions is displayed both in the building and the grounds, and all works are for sale.
Roche Court, East Winterslow, Salisbury, Wiltshire SP5 1BG (01980 862244, www.sculpture.uk.com).

Henry Moore Foundation

CULTURE

Sport/Active

Goodwood 164

Polo 167

A Round of Golf 169

Harrison's Rocks 171

FIVE Learn to… 174

FIVE Spectator sports 175

SNO!zone Milton Keynes 177

FIVE Places to fly a kite 178

FIVE Days at the races 180

Goodwood

Sports, spas, steaks, sparks… and speeeeeeed.

Sport has always been the passion of the Richmond family, so it seems perfectly natural that its family seat of Goodwood has become a mecca for the more sophisticated sport junkie. The 12,000-acre grounds that surround the impressive 18th-century Goodwood House boast two beautifully landscaped 18-hole golf courses, a racecourse perched atop one of the glorious rolling hills (with spectacular views over the Sussex Downs), and a motor circuit where 16-time Formula One Grand Prix winner Stirling Moss used to go for a spin.

The beauty of Goodwood lies in the fact that a visit here can take in a number of additional activities too; a tour of the house (complete with its Canalettos and sumptuous Regency interior), say, or walks through the peaceful grounds. You can pick up an organic steak from the estate's Farm Shop, or luxuriate in a facial at the hotel's spa – and then, of course, there are the special events that draw the crowds and that have earned Goodwood its reputation for an exciting, fun and unforgettable day out.

THE CARS

First up in the calendar is the awesome Festival of Speed, running over the first weekend in July. This sees the usually tranquil grounds that fall away from the house transformed into a carnival of cars. Based on an idea sparked by Freddie March, grandfather of the current earl, who decided to brighten up a quiet afternoon in 1934 by driving up the park road like a bat out of hell, the same road becomes a track for not just one but hundreds of fabulous cars, from vintage racing cars to modern supercars, revving their engines and whizzing past open-mouthed crowds. Against the backdrop of the imposing house, it's a grand – and very English – scene, and one that thrills not only ardent petrolheads but those whose understanding of cars is limited to how to open the passenger door; copious amounts of champagne help get them revved up to the sounds of the cars doing likewise. If the racing itself doesn't thrill you, you can't help but be bowled over by the incredible array of shiny cars to ogle. Here are Formula One, Nascar, MotoGP and the most complete collection of supercars in the world, not to mention cars like tin cans that your grandpa would dream about polishing, and teeny-tiny sports cars.

Each day over the weekend has something different to offer visitors. Friday sees the first runs up the hillclimb, along with the opportunity to drink in the amazing amount of engine action on show and goggle over the prices at the Bonhams Auction that takes place throughout the afternoon. Saturday is the official practice day, where 200 of the rarest cars and motorbikes go for broke to get the feel of the track, and on Sunday they go for times and battle for class and individual awards. Overhead, aircraft from the neighbouring airfield draw circles in the sky with their acrobatics.

Referred to as the 'theatre on the track' and loved by the driving professionals, whom you may very well be standing next to as you cheer the little green MG up the hillclimb, the Festival of Speed is three days of buzzing excitement that will leave you with a strong desire to start paying more attention to the Grand Prix – and with the faint smell of rubber in your hair. Car parks open at 7am throughout the weekend, with food and drink being served from 8am. The cars start running from 10am on Friday and 9am on Saturday and Sunday, until 6pm.

THE HORSES

The glamour of the Festival of Speed is matched – and arguably surpassed – by the glamorous Glorious Goodwood Festival at the racecourse. One of the current duke's major passions, racing has always been part of Goodwood and the racecourse itself has been up on the hill for over 200 years. The duke redeveloped the course grandstands just under ten years ago to reflect the pivotal standing that Goodwood has in the racing calendar. The result is a trio of spacious and smart stands with excellent bars and restaurants, and those aforementioned stunning views – which means that even if your horse is so far behind the rest that you could probably outrun it if you tried, you could still find a little bit of cheer in a chilled glass of champers and an appreciative, leisurely spot of gazing into the distance. If it's clear, your eyes could take you as far as the Isle of Wight.

The festival is just one part of a race season that starts in May and runs until October, but it is without question the calendar's highlight – five days of racing heaven in July where champagne is served alongside the glitter of the fashionable and fun. Goodwood's edge is its unique relaxed atmosphere. Where other racing events call for a strict dress code, the vibe here is very much panamas and linen suits, and while everyone makes an effort, ladies don't have to wear hats, even on Ladies' Day.

During the season, Glorious Goodwood is most definitely considered *the* place to be and be seen, which means you're likely to bump into many a celeb here for a flutter. But there's a whole lot more going on – like strawberries and cream, delicious, organic food from the Farm Shop, all that alcohol, and the races themselves, which fill the stands with giddy excitement.

The racecourse is open from 11am and racing starts at 2.15pm each day, apart from Saturday when it's 2.05pm (2.15pm during the festival and 6.15pm on evenings in June). Seven races are scheduled each day, with the course closing an hour after the last races – for the festival, it's usually all over by about 7pm.

If you're thinking of driving the 60 or so miles to Goodwood, think twice; it's through lovely countryside, but do you really want to forego all that lovely champagne for miles of traffic jams, when a free shuttle bus from Chichester station (90 minutes from London) runs throughout the season? (If you do choose to bring your car, parking is easy and extensive.)

THE FROCKS

As bright summer days give way to autumn hues, Goodwood trips down its own colourful memory lane with the Goodwood Revival weekend, fast becoming one of the UK's most talked-about events. If you like your fashion vintage-style, its period theme of 1950s and '60s is the perfect place to show off your bobby socks

Festival of Speed

SPORT/ACTIVE

and fedora. And obviously lots of people do: thousands flock to Goodwood for the weekend, dressed to the nines in stunning period outfits.

The track is based around the site of the old RAF Westhampnett airfield (where you can still fly in a vintage Harvard training plane on one of Goodwood's Track Days; *see below*) and was reopened in 1948. When the current earl was growing up, he spent his childhood watching drivers like Stirling Moss and Jackie Stewart racing around the track, dazzling onlookers with their derring-do, and it very clearly left an impression; when he took over the estate, the earl decided to create an event that mirrored its birth, an event that was about the glory days when fast cars and glamour went hand in hand.

Attention to detail for both Revival-goers and the Revival itself is meticulous. As the gates open, the be-hatted (boys) and red-lipsticked (girls) crowd swells through the entrance tunnel as cars roar across the track overhead. And then it's into the heart of the site: period banners adorn white picket fences, leather-clad airmen wander past on their way to perform some aerial acrobatics in the vintage aircraft on display on the airfield, a jive band provides period music and there's the flash of bright underskirts as a couple twirl beside it. Chips are served in vintage newspaper and Marilyn Monroe has just pinched one of yours but you don't care. And through it all the air is tangy with the smell of 4 Star petrol, shiny bonnets of old-time race-cars flash past, and you cling to the barrier cheering them on.

Friday is the official practice day, when you can watch the drivers put the foot to the floor in an attempt to get the best time possible: it's all about the grid position, baby. Saturday is Ladies' Day, where there's a prize for the best dressed and fashion almost overshadows the cars. We say almost because part of the all-day racing action includes the legendary St Mary's saloon car race, where famous faces are obscured by helmet visors as they rumble past on their way round the two-mile track. Sunday features the one-hour, two-driver, star-studded Royal Automobile Club TT celebration for '60s GT cars, which is a staple in any petrolhead's diary, as well as another round of the St Mary's saloon car race and Grand Prix cars.

Starting from 9am on Friday and 10am on Saturday and Sunday, races run until around 6pm and there's the added bonus of the free shuttle bus from Chichester station. Tickets sell out fast, though, so book early.

If all the action makes you yearn to have a go yourself, you can. Track Days have become increasingly popular and can be purchased via the Goodwood website or the Motor Circuit Team, and tailored specifically for you or your loved one. Here you can develop your own kind of thrill, be it in your own car, a classic Aston Martin or a brand new Ferrari. Or, if you need even more edge-of-the-seat action, have a crack at some vintage flying in the Harvard warbird, where you can experience the combat skills young pilots would have learned such as steep turns, barrel rolls, loops and sequences. Aerobatics are part of the deal too, so make sure you have a strong stomach – real pilots don't hurl. Back on the Motor Circuit, if you and your friends have got some hot wheels, you can book a timeslot on the track to take them out for a spin, something car clubs make regular use of.

Goodwood House
Goodwood, Chichester, West Sussex PO18 0PX (01243 755000, www.goodwood.co.uk).

Eating & Drinking

Richmond Arms at the Goodwood Hotel
Goodwood Estate, PO18 0QB (01243 520167, www.goodwood.co.uk). Open noon-2.30pm, 6-10.30pm Mon-Sat; noon-2.30pm, 6-10pm Sun.
Round off your day, or even make it a long lunch, at the light-filled former coaching inn the Richmond Arms. The estate has its own executive chef, Tim Powell, previously of Le Pont de la Tour, who looks after all the menus and food, and all food is seasonal and locally produced where possible, most likely on the estate's farm. The hotel itself has an excellent spa if you really want to spoil yourself.

Other Attractions

If adrenalin's not your bag and you just fancy a relaxing day out in the country, there's a whole lot more to explore. For a spot of culture, what could be finer than losing yourself among the bluebells of the estate's Cass Sculpture Park (*see p160*)? Its 24 acres of ancient woodland feature work from artists such as Tony Cragg, Andy Goldsworthy and David Mach.

Golf is also very much at the heart of Goodwood, with the excellent Downs Course, designed by legendary course designer James Braid in 1914. In 2009, non-members will be able to play here for the first time. Running from the Goodwood Hotel, you can Pay & Play for a game across the Park Course, against the dramatic backdrop of the house. Visit www.goodwood.co.uk for more details.

Polo

The 'sport of kings' isn't just for royalty.

Polo is a crucial feature of that quintessentially British concept, 'The Season'. In a large field somewhere in the stockbroker belt, high-society types quaff champers in the company of faded rock stars and hedge-fund managers, while the players indulge in an afternoon of pukka chukkas. During breaks in play, everyone adds to the Jilly Cooper atmosphere by strolling around the playing area replacing the turf dug up by the horses' hooves before retiring for more liquid refreshment.

It's an easy sport to satirise. After all, the entrance fee at the exclusive Guards club in Windsor Great Park (01784 434212, www.guardspoloclub.com) is £17,000 plus £5,450 per season. This, of course, is the venue for the Cartier International in July, the sport's annual showpiece event, usually graced by sundry HRHs and plenty of binoculars.

Guards Polo

In contrast, many other clubs are making an effort to broaden polo's social mix, seeking to attract spectators and participants from outside the upper echelons.

The first ever polo match in Britain was played in 1871, between regimental teams of the Royal Horse Guards and the Tenth Hussars on Hounslow Heath. You'd be hard-pressed to find any trace of polo in Hounslow today, but a club survives not too far away, in Ham. Here, you can watch for just £2 per person or £10 per car, and you're positively encouraged to take a picnic (8334 0000, www.hampoloclub.com).

There are competitive but relaxed inter-club and charity tournaments every Sunday from May to September, starting at 2pm. If you then want to thwack a few balls about, a lesson costs £95 – and you don't need to provide your own pony (details from 07766 222111).

Most polo clubs are to the west of London, amid the leafy acres of Surrey and Berkshire. Yet the sport seems ideally suited to Essex, a county with a unique blend of rural tradition and, around its metropolitan fringes, lairy ostentation. At the Duke of Essex Polo Trophy (0871 226 2690, www.dukeofessexpolo.com) on the Gaynes Park Estate near Epping each July, the programme asks, 'Are you part of the Essex glitterati?' and actually sets aside half an hour for 'celebrity helicopter arrivals'.

But if it's the feel of several tonnes of pony between your thighs that you're after, the place to head for is the Ascot Park Polo Club near Chobham in Surrey (01276 858545,

www.polo.co.uk). Here, 80 per cent of those attending two-hour 'Discover Polo' sessions have little or no previous riding experience.

The session starts with a milk crate in the club's indoor arena – you stand on it to practise the four main shots. In ascending degree of difficulty, there's the offside forehand shot, the offside tail shot, the nearside backhand shot and the nearside tail shot. Polo is the only sport you have to play right-handed, so in this final move you're leaning across yourself to hit forward from the left-hand side of the milk crate/pony – which is almost as difficult to explain as to execute.

Then it's into the marquee to learn the sport's most important rule of all – the 'right of way'. A player following the ball on its exact line has right of way over all others, and anyone who crosses a player on the right of way in a dangerous manner commits a foul. Given the fact that large animals as well as comparatively frail humans are involved, it all seems eminently sensible. Other than that, a 'chukka' lasts seven minutes, it's four a side and the aim is to smack the ball into the goal.

Finally, note that, lest the impression be given that polo is a solely male pursuit, Ascot Park is also home to the International Women's Polo Association. Half the students on courses and 35 per cent of the club members are female. Every August, the best compete in the IWPA National Tournament, the largest women's event in the world.

Sylvester Stallone once likened the game to 'trying to play golf during an earthquake'.

Guards Polo

A Round of Golf

Know your irons from your woods.

Most sports clubs have their thrashers and thwackers, people who are in love with a particular game but utterly hopeless at playing it. Golf is an exception. To join a club, you will almost certainly require a handicap certificate as a guarantee of basic competence and an understanding of golf's rules of dress and etiquette – and you're unlikely to be allowed to play as a guest at any private club without that certificate.

A handicap is the figure used to calculate a 'net' score from the number of strokes you actually play. The lower your handicap, the better golfer you are. This all raises one of those tricky catch-22 questions: how do you get a handicap certificate if you can't get out there to practise and improve?

The best solution is to book lessons with a qualified coach. The Cranfield Golf Academy (8529 6961, www.cga-golf.com) has five venues around the capital and promises to get a total beginner successfully hitting that irritatingly small white ball within 90 minutes. Better still, claims founder Scott Cranfield, 'you really will be ready to play a game of golf after four weeks' – sufficient time to understand the fundamentals of swing and putting. Having paid £57-£71 to learn the basics, there's a driving range and putting green to groove those techniques. After that, it's just a question of how many hours you've got spare.

So you've learnt how to hit the ball, and even how to putt and drive a bit, but what next? Richmond Park Golf Club (74 Corringway, London, W5 3AD, 8876 3205, www.richmond parkgolfclub.org.uk) welcomes novice players to try for membership and that all-important handicap certificate by completing three rounds over the full 18 holes within six months.

Your card must be marked by a golfer already holding a handicap, and at least one round must be to a handicap of no worse than 28 for men and 36 for women. This means a man must go round the course in no more than 96 strokes, and a woman in no more than 108. Manage this, remember not to turn up in denim shorts and a Metallica T-shirt, avoid embarrassing yourself at the 19th hole – and you're in.

Did we mention women there? In many clubs they're still called 'ladies'. Although some clubs persist with men-only bars and patronising attitudes, the sport's infamous pomposity and stuffiness are being knocked out with every new wave of golfers. Clubs need new players to survive, the retired brigadiers are dying off, the social profile is broadening – and, let's face it, many women are excellent players. Media

SPORT/ACTIVE

coverage of the women's game is improving too, although the likes of Europe's 2009 Solheim Cup captain Alison Nicholas still receive far fewer column inches than Padraig Harrington, Ernie Els or Sergio Garcia.

For proof of the quality of the women's game, why not make a trip to a major tournament? Sadly, many British events on the professional Ladies' European Tour are far beyond a day's outing from London., but you can check out the current programme by calling 0121 456 2088 or visiting www.englishwomensgolf.org. The really big names usually play in Britain around half-a-dozen times each year at events such as the PGA Championship every May at Wentworth in Surrey, and the European Open at the London Golf Club in Kent, also in May. The big prize, however, is the Open Championship, which moves around the country. Full details of each event can be found at www.europeantour.com. The Senior Tour is for players aged over 50 and, with

events at Sunningdale in Berkshire and Woburn in Bedfordshire, makes for an enjoyable day out; golf is a game in which skill counts for more than athleticism, and the standard remains very high among older players.

Out on the course, you can opt to find a decent viewpoint at a single hole and watch everyone playing through, or, more tiring but rewarding if you're a fan, follow a particular player all the way round. There are plenty of food and drink outlets if you choose not to take a picnic, and spectators are generally courteous towards each other and the players – it'll be busy, but not like a football match.

Will you learn anything from close study of the stars? Some coaches believe it has value, others insist the technique of the top players is just too far divorced from the average hacker's style. One thing's for certain, though. Watching someone five above par at the ninth go on to win a Major certainly makes those dreams of doing it yourself more realistic.

Harrison's Rocks

Scale new heights at Kent's sandstone crag.

There is no typical sort of person who comes to climb Harrison's Rocks, a sandstone outcrop in a forest several miles south of Tunbridge Wells. (If travelling by train, the nearest station is Eridge, a 55-minute journey from London Bridge.) Families, expert climbers, outdoorsy types wanting to try something new and even stag groups have climbed them.

Although the rocks are only nine metres high, there are more than 330 different climbs along the crag, covering most grades of difficulty, which helps to explain why Harrison's is one of the best known and most popular climbing spots in the south of England. (It's also a playground for scrambling and, occasionally, caving.) Taster sessions for the uninitiated are run by Nuts 4 Climbing (01892 860670, www.rockclimbingclasses.co.uk), where you'll learn the basic climbing techniques and use of equipment, and where you'll get an insight into the exhilarating, strength-building – and occasionally perilous and elitist – world of rock climbing.

The rocks' popularity, coupled with the fragility of the sandstone, has meant, however, that they have been subject to erosion. To prevent further damage, the British Mountaineering Council (BMC), which owns Harrison's Rocks, has put into place protective measures: all routes are bolted so that running ropes are not in contact with the rock; abseiling is strictly banned; and the wearing of soft-soled shoes is enforced.

SPORT/ACTIVE

Dangling upside down in a cave, with only a large muddy puddle between your hands and terra firma, is not how most climbing expeditions begin, but at Nuts 4 Climbing taster sessions, things are a little different. 'It's an excuse to be a big kid,' climbing instructor Sarah Cullen says. 'Everyone enjoys clambering across boulders and through caves, and getting a bit muddy. It helps people to get used to the feel of the rocks before climbing them. And it's really good fun,' she adds.

Climbs in the UK are graded between one and nine, and further split into a, b and c. Despite their diminutive height, Harrison's Rocks cover every grade from a 1a scramble up to a frankly terrifying 6c, with overhangs and sheer walls – although a 7b can be found at nearby High Rocks (*see below*). New climbs are frequently claimed, and each is given a name by the first person to climb it. Monikers such as Goats do Roam, Mr Spaceman and Rhapsody Inside a Satsuma suggest that climbers are a rather loony bunch (something that might not come as a surprise to those for whom the very concept of rock climbing could appear a little crazy).

Complete beginners normally start on a 2a or 2b climb, such as Tame Variant. Granted, its name doesn't sound too exciting, but when you're clinging on to the slippery face by little more than fingernails and toes, several metres off the ground, your senses are certainly heightened. Yet harnessed and supported by a constantly taught rope, any vertiginous feelings normally dissipate; there is no chance you would fall more than a couple of inches. Training is on the wall face, and Sarah continuously shouts out instructions: 'left foot on that ledge', 'reach up to the grip on the right', 'shift your weight', 'come on, nearly there', she encourages. With 20 years' worth of experience of climbing these walls, she knows every nook and cranny.

Climbing is something of a problem-solving exercise, comparable to a game of chess; figuring out what your next move will be, and how that will affect the move after that is one of the skills you start to develop. It's as much a test of intellectual mettle as it is of physical strength. Most important, however – and the reason it's so popular for team-building sessions – is developing the confidence to make the next step. Once you overcome that mental barrier, you'll suddenly find yourself at the top, exhilarated, cheering and, quite likely, addicted to rock climbing. A high percentage of people return for an introduction course (run over two intensive days or across six weekends), after which you're free to climb unaccompanied.

After tackling a couple of trickier climbs and learning some basic knots, the beginners' group is dragged away from the rock face and through the door of the nearby Huntsman (Eridge Road, Eridge Green, Tunbridge Wells, Kent TN3 9LE, 01892 864258), for an excellent, locally sourced pub lunch.

During the afternoon there's time for some less energetic exercise around High Rocks, another popular climbing spot a mile away towards Tunbridge Wells, which is generally used by more experienced climbers. Unlike Harrison's Rocks, which is owned and maintained by the BMC for the sole use of climbers, High Rocks is a privately owned area that charges climbers £5 and non-climbers £2 (payable at the High Rocks restaurant, 01892 515532) to explore the

picturesque destination. As well as offering
a variety of climbs, it's also a lovely spot for a
leisurely walk, especially if there are children
in tow. The Spa Valley Railway (www.spa
valleyrailway.co.uk) also goes through – and
stops at – High Rocks. The steam engine runs
three and a half miles (although it is due to be
extended) between nearby Groombridge and
the historic town of Tunbridge Wells, from
where you can take a train back to London.
It's an excellent way to unwind at the end of
a hard day's climb. As you shunt through the
Kent and Sussex Weald, the soothing smell of a
stream train in your nostrils, and the satisfying
ache of physical exercise in your muscles, you'll
feel a strong sense of achievement.

FIVE Learn to...

Fly a glider

You need good thermals for gliding. Yes, it can get chilly, but we don't mean that sort. We mean the upward currents of warm air that enable these aircraft to soar without the aid of engines and propellers. The Essex Gliding Club offers a trial flight with a qualified instructor, during which you get to try the controls yourself. If you decide to join the club afterwards, the cost of the trial is refunded.
Essex Gliding Club, Ridgewell Airfield, Ashen, Sudbury, Suffolk CO10 8JU (01992 522222, www.essexgliding.com).

Handle a bird of prey

The IBPC runs a breeding programme, and rescues wild birds of prey, as well as operating training days. There are separate one-day courses featuring hawks, owls and falcons. On the falcon day you're taught how to tie a falconer's knot, pick up the birds and – most excitingly – fly them to your fist. Visitors also get the chance to hold the largest bird on duty that day, perhaps a bald eagle, for example.
International Birds of Prey Centre, Newent, Gloucestershire GL18 1JJ (01531 820286, www.icbp.org).

Play real tennis

Real tennis is the oldest racket sport in the world, and the forerunner of modern lawn tennis. The ball skids rather than bounces, the racket is slightly lopsided and the court has unique features such as a sloping-roofed 'penthouse' and galleries designed to represent the layout of monastery cloisters. The Hatfield House club offers a free introductory lesson and courses for new players.
Hatfield House Tennis Club, Hatfield House, Old Hatfield, Herts AL9 5NF (01707 273391, www.hatfieldhouserealtennis.com).

Sail a boat

The reservoir at Queen Mary Sailing Club is a great place for getting to grips with a boat. The club is an accredited Royal Yachting Association training centre and its one-day 'Try Sailing' course combines theory and practice on 700 acres of water – as well as comprising the first half of the RYA's Level 1 qualification.
Queen Mary Sailing Club & Sailsports, Ashford Road, Ashford, Middlesex TW15 1UA (01784 248881, www.queenmary.org.uk).

Shoot a clay pigeon

The sport of shooting has been tarnished by association with gun crime. The A1 Shooting Ground is the place to discover how enjoyable the activity is, and the rigorous safety policies that accompany it. Clay discs skitter from traps in various trajectories, mimicking the flight patterns of game birds. The satisfaction gained when a direct hit shatters the clay is immense. Don't be squeamish – they don't look anything like the real thing.
A1 Barnet Shooting Ground, nr Rowley Green, Herts, EN5 3HW (020 8441 9986, www.a1sg.co.uk).

International Birds of Prey Centre

Basketball: Guildford Heat

Guildford Heat only joined the British
Basketball League in 2005 but have
been among its top teams ever since.
Home court is the Spectrum Leisure
Centre, nicknamed 'The Furnace' by
fans, and game nights feature music,
lights, lots of crowd noise, cheerleaders
and interactive events during time-outs
led by mascot Scorcher.
*Guildford Spectrum, Parkway, Guildford,
Surrey GU1 1UP (01483 443333,
www.guildfordheat.com).*

Cricket: Kent County Cricket Club

There are few more attractive venues
in which to watch county cricket than
the St Lawrence Ground in Canterbury.
A lime tree more than 200 years old
actually stood inside the boundary rope
until it was blown over in a gale in 2005.
This was merely the end of an era, not
of a tradition – a new oak has been
planted in its place.
*St Lawrence Ground, Old Dover Road,
Canterbury, Kent CT1 3NZ (01227 456886,
www.kent-ccc.co.uk).*

Hockey: Surbiton Hockey Club

Hockey has long been thought of as
a sport that's better to play than
to watch. However, new-generation
water-based pitches have made the
game quicker and more dynamic than
ever before. Surbiton works hard to
attract spectators, staging some
National League matches – featuring
players from the GB Olympic squad
– in the early evening under floodlights.
*Sugden Road, Long Ditton, Surrey
KT7 0AE (020 8398 2401,
www.surbitonhc.com).*

Ice Hockey: Bracknell Bees

The world's fastest team game is big in
Bracknell. The Bees are ace exponents
of nifty stickwork and speedy skating,
and more than capable of looking
after themselves when things get
rough. The toughened safety glass
surrounding the rink lets spectators
get right up close to the action, where
you can really appreciate the players'
lightning reflexes and tactical awareness.

*John Nike Leisuresport Complex, John
Nike Way, Bracknell, Berkshire RG12 8TN
(01344 789000, www.bracknell-bees.org).*

Rugby Union: London Irish

When the oval-ball game turned
professional in 1995, many leading clubs
shifted from their homely but cramped
grounds to football stadia that held bigger
crowds. London Irish have made a
particular success of their move to share
Reading's 24,000-seat Madejski Stadium,
retaining the unique atmosphere of their
former home in Sunbury while creating
a family-friendly match-day experience.
*Madejski Stadium, M4 Junction 11, Reading,
Berkshire RG2 0FL (01932 783034,
www.london-irish.com).*

SPORT/ACTIVE

SNO!zone Milton Keynes

Slope off to a 'real snow' ski centre.

SNO!zone (we'll forgive the corny name because it's so much fun) consists of a giant freezer of ski slopes at the Xscape leisure park in Milton Keynes. Here, at any time of the year, you can come and play in 1,500 tonnes of real snow. With no melting, no poor coverage and guaranteed powder, a trip to Europe's slopes is no longer the only option for practising your '360' in 'real' conditions. And if you can't afford the airfare to Val d'Isère, you can console youself with the fact that you can now hop on the train from Euston and be on the slopes within the hour.

A day on the main 558-foot-long (170-metre) slope really gets the adrenalin going; this is as close to the real thing as it gets, in contrast to dry ski slopes that feel like sliding down sandpaper with combs stuck to your feet. SNO!zone makes 14 tonnes of the white stuff every night, for slopes set to a constant temperature of -5 degrees, so you really are skiing on freshly laid snow (albeit in an indoor dome).

It's worth arriving with plenty of time to get kitted up before your session, especially on weekends and evenings, when the slopes are at their busiest.

Head straight to the main slope if it's not your first time on piste (sessions are booked by the hour). Here you can either go it alone or improve your skills with an advanced lesson from the experienced instructors. Those who want to show off some moves should look out for the freestyle parks constructed twice a week, where you can practise and perform tricks on rails and boxes.

In addition to the main slope, there's a gentler learners' slope for the uninitiated, where one-to-one tuition is available, as well as children's classes. Skiing lessons start at a reasonable £27 for one hour and also cover intensive day sessions and snowboarding classes – perfect for getting your confidence up pre-holiday. Equipment is included in the entrance price and ski suits can be hired, but wrap yourself up warm as you'll feel the cold whizzing downhill.

Skiing and snowboarding aren't the only ways to enjoy the indoor winter wonderland. The Ice Slide, a carved-out ice run on which to glide through on a rubber ring, is also great fun. But for the ultimate thrill, opt for tobogganing. Night sessions for both activities are held on weekend evenings (for over-16s).

A day on the slopes wouldn't be complete without the après-ski experience; the lounge area is the place to head for a warming hot chocolate, while the upstairs bar provides something a little stronger. Parties and club nights are held regularly with DJs and bands for those looking to recreate the complete ski holiday vibe.

An alternative day trip option is available in the form of Hemel Hempstead's Snow Centre (www.thesnowcentre.com), opening in 2009. With drag lifts to maximise your time going downhill, it's set to become one of the UK's premier ski practice spots and will bring the snow experience even closer to London.

Unlike at Chamonix and Val d'Isère, the snow at these centres poses no threat of an avalanche, is guaranteed year round, and can easily be fitted into a day-trip. And nagging doubts relating to the environmental impact (it takes a huge amount of energy to keep those slopes at such a cool temperature) can perhaps be assuaged by the fact that you won't be taking a flight to reach the slopes.

SNO!zone Milton Keynes
Xscape Leisure Centre, 602 Marlborough Gate, Central Milton Keynes, Buckinghamshire MK9 3XS (0871 222 5670, www.snozoneuk.com). Open Oct-Apr 9am-11pm daily. May-Sept 9am-11pm Wed-Sat. Admission from £21.

SPORT/ACTIVE

FIVE Places to fly a kite

Dunstable Downs
The area at the top of the Downs has outstanding views over the Vale of Aylesbury and is the highest point in the east of England. The wide open space makes it perfect for kites, but gliders and paragliders can also often be spotted. The Chilterns Gateway Centre offers information, facilities and refreshments. *Dunstable Downs, Dunstable Road, Whipsnade, Bedfordshire LU6 2GY (01582 500920).*

Epsom Downs Racecourse
When the horses aren't racing, an area of land near the Tattenham Corner turn is a prime kiteflying spot. The Downs is an extensive area of chalk land and the wide skies and lack of tree cover make it a popular spot, but there are restrictions, and kiteflying is only allowed after midday. *Epsom Downs Racecourse, Epsom Downs, Epsom, Surrey KT18 5LQ (01372 470047, www.epsomderby.co.uk).*

RHS Garden Hyde Hall
Perched on a hilltop, this sumptuous Royal Horticultural Society garden provides a stunning backdrop for kiteflying. There are two organised kite weekends at Hyde Hall each year, in spring and high summer, where the public can watch flying demonstrations, buggy rides and kids' kite-making workshops.

Bring your own kite and join in (you have to pay the standard admisson price). *Kite Weekends, RHS Garden Hyde Hall, Buckhatch Lane, Rettendon, Essex CM3 8ET (01245 400256, www.rhs.org.uk/hydehall).*

Southsea Common

Home of the Portsmouth International Kite Festival on August bank holiday, the waterfront expanse of Southsea Common is the place to spot kites of all shapes, sizes and colours all year round. During the festival, however, the skies are positively packed with entries from some of the best kite-makers in the world. Kite stalls and workshops are on site during the festival.

Portsmouth International Kite Festival, Southsea Common, Clarence Esplanade, Southsea, Portsmouth, Hampshire PO5 3PB (02392 826722, www.visitportsmouth.co.uk).

Uffington White Horse

The hill made famous by the 3,000-year-old figure of the horse carved into its side is located halfway between Wantage and Swindon. It has magnificent views across the Vale of White Horse, and is blustery enough to make it an exhilarating spot for kiting. Uffington Castle, Dragon Hill and Wayland Smithy nearby make it an area rich in historical interest too. *See also p48. Uffington White Horse, Uffington, Oxfordshire.*

Ascot

Ascot

The Royal Meeting in June is Ascot's traditional highlight, although many racegoers lament its decline into little more than a fashion show, with 'Ladies Day' a source of particular derision. Ascot is perhaps better enjoyed when the atmosphere is less fraught. This historic course – it was founded in 1711 – stages a further 20 flat and jumps race-days throughout the year; the family friendly Ascot Festival in September is a notable draw.
Ascot Racecourse, High Street, Ascot, Berkshire SL5 7JX (0870 727 1234, www.ascot.co.uk).

Epsom Downs

The Derby, racing's supreme test of speed and stamina, is the centrepiece of Epsom's early June meeting, attracting around 150,000 people to one of the great occasions in Britain's sporting and social calendar. The course stages 12 further race days each year, including a series of Epsom Live! party nights on Thursdays in July, each with live music. The impressive Queen's Stand and Grandstand Enclosure both offer fine viewing, while the grassy Lonsdale Enclosure is ideal for a picnic and offers close-up views of the action.
Epsom Downs Racecourse, Racecourse Paddock, Epsom, Surrey SW1E 6LB (01372 726311, www.epsomderby.co.uk).

Kempton Park

Kempton will never win awards for its scenery, but it's an excellent course in every other respect. It's a busy place too with jump racing from October to April and afternoon and evening flat racing all year round. A particular highlight is the Christmas Festival, featuring the King

George VI Chase on Boxing Day. Summer themed nights – 'Australia', 'Irish', 'Best of British', for example – and family days, with plenty happening on and off the track, are justly popular. *Kempton Park Racecourse, Staines Road East, Sunbury-on-Thames, Middlesex TW16 5AQ (01932 782292, www.kempton.co.uk).*

Sandown Park

Sandown is attractively sited in a natural amphitheatre and winner of several 'Racecourse of the Year' awards. Racing takes place all year round, with April's Gold Cup the highlight of the jumping season and the Coral-Eclipse Stakes in July the main feature of the flat programme – both pushing horses to the limit on Sandown's infamous hill finish. There's also a run of summer evening meetings, most with live music. Families are welcome; a free crèche is available for under-fives on Saturdays, and there's a dedicated picnic area during the summer months. *Sandown Park Racecourse, Esher Station Road, Esher, Surrey KT10 9AJ (01372 464348, www.sandown.co.uk).*

Windsor

Windsor takes full advantage of its picturesque setting on the banks of the Thames, and you can travel to meetings courtesy of a riverbus service from Barry Avenue Promenade in the town centre (£5.50 return, details from 01753 851900, www.boat-trips.co.uk). There's a relaxed feel about the place, which is at its best during the summer Monday evening fixtures from April to August. These attract large crowds to the course's plentiful bars and the Castle Restaurant overlooking the winning post. *Windsor Racecourse, Maidenhead Road, Windsor, Berkshire SL4 5JJ (01753 498400, www.windsor-racecourse.co.uk).*

SPORT/ACTIVE

Epsom Downs

Relaxation

Sequoia at the Grove   185
Bath Thermae Spa   188
The Haybarn   190
The Spa at Pennyhill Park Hotel   192
The Vineyard Spa   195
FIVE Soothing sunsets   198
Calcot Manor   200

1000 songs, films and books to change your life

1000 Films to change your life

timeOut

THE MOVIES THAT MOVE US, BY

Monica Bellucci | Nick Broomfield | Jonathan Demme | Atom Egoyan
Holly Hunter | Terry Jones | Takeshi Kitano | Ken Loach | Michael Mann
Samantha Morton | Christopher Nolan | Roman Polanski
Isabella Rossellini | Steven Soderbergh
and many more

1000 **Films** to change your life

1000 **Songs** to change your life

1000 **Books** to change your life

Sequoia at the Grove

Chill out in grand style.

Hertfordshire ladies who lunch have sensibly kept this sweet secret to themselves, but no more we say. Set in 300 acres of park and woodland, the Sequoia spa at the Grove Hotel offers a wholly enticing range of treatments and packages guaranteed to make you feel a million dollars – for nowhere near that kind of money. It's true that there are packages here that would buy you a weekend in Paris, but they're the top end of the range (and are often for two people so the cost is halved); it's easy to come along for a few hours, have a couple of treatments, relax in the black-tiled mosaic pool, hang out in a fluffy robe and slippers and feel like you've been away for weeks before heading back to the big smoke, all for less than £200.

The range of treatments is impressive, and likely to have you poring over the online brochure for hours. From ten facials, choose skin brighteners, a repairing and restoring superfacial or an advanced age defyer facial. Body treatments are equally wide-ranging, and include a number of hot-stone and Ayurvedic-influenced treatments – the Dosha specific hot-stone massage and body wrap (two hours, £160) looks particularly satisfying.

Hands, feet, face, head and pretty much every other body part are dealt with through the various options available, but if it's all too much, a range of day packages means you don't have to make any decisions at all; the Sequoia Time Ritual, for example, involves an initial confab with a therapist who then charts out a two-hour minimum package of treatments, while the Ayurvedic Influence enables you to select a range of massage treatments lasting at least two

RELAXATION

hours and 20 minutes. Top of the range is a his
and hers relaxation package that lasts more than
four hours – and that's not including the two-
course lunch that's part of all the day packages.

Why come here though rather than a top-notch
central London spa? Because the treatments are
first class, because you get to relax in a really
beautiful part of the country that's just 16 miles
from London, and because a whole range of
other facilities makes it unique for a UK spa.
You can run or cycle on the numerous trails
that criss-cross the parkland and woodland
using complimentary bikes and trail maps. Or
lounge on the beach (yes, the beach) and swim
in the outdoor pool in the walled garden. Or
play croquet. Or do a Pilates class in an exercise
studio filled with natural light – when was the
last time you were able to find one of those in
London? Last year the spa was voted Favourite
UK Hotel Spa at the Condé Nast Traveller
Reader Awards, and the hotel Best Leisure
Hotel – after a day sampling the delights of
both, it's easy to see why.

Sequoia at the Grove

*Chandler's Cross, Hertfordshire WD3 4TG
(01923 807807, www.thegrove.co.uk). Rates
from £195 full day, including 2-course lunch.*

Bath Thermae Spa

Hot springs and history lessons.

Forget sightseeing buses and back-to-back guided walks, the most relaxing way to soak up the beauty of Bath is from the Thermae Spa's stunning, open-air rooftop pool. Head straight to the top of Nicholas Grimshaw's slick glass cube and submerge yourself in the warm, mineral-rich jets for an effortless tour of the city skyline, Bath Abbey and the hills beyond. The views are impressive at any time of day but an evening visit is particularly magical – think well-considered lighting, twinkling streetlights and steam rising off the water's surface as you recline high above the city.

Should you manage to drag yourself away from the cityscape, there are plenty of additional watery pursuits to relax mind, body and soul here. Drift away on the gentle currents and whirlpool jets of the lower floor's curvaceous Minerva bath or submit to plumes of steam and relaxing essential oils (peppermint, lavender, frankincense) in one of the four circular glass aroma steam rooms. Or why not kick your slippers off for a relaxing foot bath? Or just stand under the huge, waterfall shower until you can no longer think of a reason why you shouldn't install one at home. To take the de-stressing up another notch, book in for one of the spa's excellent treatments – everything from hot-stone massage to caviar facials to Watsu therapy (a unique combination of acupressure, massage and stretching in water) is on offer.

RELAXATION

Alternatively, wrap up in your robe and head to the stylishly minimal restaurant for a reviving salad, soup or hearty dish of the day (a fragrant seafood paella, perhaps) – all can be washed down with a decent glass of red.

Not only is there no pressure to abstain from life's more indulgent pleasures here (coffee and cakes are offered alongside the fruit smoothies), you can leave any etiquette anxiety at the door too. Spontaneous visits are encouraged (advance booking is only available for groups of six or more), prices are accessible (you can even bring your own towel and robe to save cash if you choose), and there are plenty of discreet instructions on everything from where to find the loos to what you should be wearing where. What Bath Thermae Spa lacks in complimentary wheatgrass shots and gold-plated incense burners it makes up for tenfold in its egalitarian ethos, relaxed atmosphere and affordable sense of style. One look at the clientele and it's clear the concept is working – yes, there are mother and daughter gossip sessions galore in the steam rooms, but this is also somewhere men, couples, even minor celebrities (we spotted *Mock the Week*'s Russell Howard hanging out with a couple of mates in the bubble jets) feel comfortable relaxing.

Two-hour, four-hour and full-day sessions are available, as are an array of packages including treatments and refreshments (an Entrée package combines a two-hour spa session with a back, neck and shoulder massage and either a Reviver facial or a foot massage for £65). For the ideal top-off to a day's shopping (*see p41*) or more traditional sightseeing day in the city, the bargain Twilight Package (£35) is worth checking out. Sessions are available from 4pm (last entry 6.30pm), on any day but Saturday, and include three hours' spa time for the price of two, complimentary use of towels, robes and slippers and a meal and drink in the restaurant. A finer end to a day in Britain's most elegant spa town we can't imagine.

Bath Thermae Spa
Hot Bath Street, Bath, Somerset BA1 1SJ (0844 8880844, www.thermaebathspa.com). Open 9am-10pm daily. Admission from £22 (2hr session).

The Haybarn

Go Ayurvedic at Daylesford Organic's Gloucestershire estate.

If you're seeking inner peace, you can probably find it at a spiritual retreat or achieve monkish serenity through good deeds and sacrifice. Or, you could book yourself in for a day session at the Haybarn, where inner peace comes enveloped in divine aromatics, the walls are painted a just-so chalky white and the calming staff seem to float slightly above the ground as they lead you to your treatment room. You want style, class and attention to detail? You got it – with impeccable ethics (this is one of several noble green enterprises by Daylesford Organic) thrown in for good measure.

Located on the lush Daylesford estate near Kingham in the Cotswolds, the Haybarn is perfect for a spot of rural relaxation. The site is a shade over an hour from London – by train from Paddington to Kingham, then taxi (01608 843808) – but offers everything you need to fill a day with health, luxury and indulgence. Wander through the perfectly manicured gardens, pop into the farm shop for organic bread, fruit and cheese, relax in the fabulous café or admire luxe homeware, clothes and garden equipment, before making your way to the tranquil barn for some serious self-restoration.

RELAXATION

It's impossible not to feel relaxed as you sit in the small waiting area here, with a pot of herbal tea, contemplating the beautiful ceramic light fittings and tastefully ethereal decor. We were joined by a gaggle of glamorous young mothers celebrating a friend's impending new baby – excitable chatter about maternity nannies was replaced with silent contemplation in about five seconds flat. Yep, this place is supremely relaxing.

The Haybarn specialises in all things Ayurvedic and health-giving – think massage, yoga and meditation rather than caviar facials, jacuzzis and chocolate mud baths. There are regular group yoga, meditation and Pilates sessions, and private classes (individual or one-to-two) are also available.

We opted for a one-hour private yoga class with one of the resident experts. Sessions take place in a huge, airy upstairs yoga studio (complete with sprung floors and atmospheric countryside views) and the one-on-one attention was a revelation. Any Londoner who's struggled to keep pace at a busy pre-work or lunchtime class, or tried to wrestle out of an asana without whacking their too-close-for-comfort neighbour in the face, will appreciate the extra space and time. Having a session tailored to your own specific needs (pregnancy, injuries or a desire to perfect your shoulder stands can all be taken

into account) and undertaken at your own pace is fantastically invigorating – our hour felt like more like two as far as our stretched and relaxed muscles were concerned.

It would be wrong to leave the building without also sampling one of the Haybarn's holistic treatments, which take place in lovely rooms furnished using luxurious natural materials. On offer is an array of massages (deep tissue, Thai, aromatherapy, pregnancy and Ayurvedic included) as well as REN facials, holistic lifestyle consultations, Ayurvedic rituals, stone therapy and reflexology. We sampled the Indian head massage, which relieved what little tension we had left with calm efficiency. The Bamford body treatment (a full-body massage combined with a foot bath, shiatsu energy work, reflexology and Indian head massage; £100 for 90 minutes) also comes highly recommended.

Back in the relaxation area post-treatment, all that remains to be done is to sit back, sip virtuous-tasting teas and browse the fantastic Bamford Body range (stylishly packaged organic and botanic products) and yoga gear displayed on the neat white shelves. A lazy wander round the rest of the site before leaving completes this ideal day-long rural retreat.

Haybarn Daylesford
Nr Kingham, Gloucestershire, GL56 0YG (01608 731703, www.daylesfordorganic.com). Open 9am-5pm Mon-Sat; 10am-4pm Sun. Call for rates of individual classes and sessions.

► For Daylesford Organic Farm Shop, see p209.

The Spa at Pennyhill Park Hotel

Steam away your aches and anxieties.

A day at Pennyhill may not be long enough to dip your toe into every pool, hot tub and steam room that this deluxe spa offers. And that's before considering the gym, the relaxation areas (one of which is full of black leather massage loungers) and the myriad treatments available. Even the changing rooms are special – spacious and swanky, with big lockers and plenty of lotions, towels and hairdryers. What's more, the staff are friendly and helpful, much more so than in many smart spas.

The Spa is located down a long drive, just behind the Pennyhill Park Hotel complex, in 120 acres of Surrey parkland, and offers an adults-only, no-expense-spared day of total relaxation. Unless you've come to work out, of course, in which case there's 3,000 square feet of gymnasium to keep you happy, stocked with all the latest cardiovascular and resistance equipment (with individual entertainment systems) and a free weights area.

RELAXATION

There are 21 treatment rooms, and a long list of possible treatments, from facials and manicures to 'the Dreaming', an all-encompassing three-hour session. The 60-minute Kodo massage claims to leave your body 'laughing with joy' – we didn't quite achieve this state of nirvana, but it was an excellent massage given by a skilled practitioner. There are treatments specially tailored for men, couples and pregnant women; for various bits of the body (the 30-minute scalp massage, for example); and beauty salon extras such as St Tropez spray tanning.

Usually, the 'spa day' package deals include a treatment, but there's plenty to do even without

one. The saunas and steam rooms make up what Pennyhill Spa describes as 'thermal heaven', a sequence of herbal saunas, aromatic laconium (cooler than a traditional Scandinavian sauna), tepidarium, ice cave and steam room – our favourite was the blissfully scented herbal sauna, but there's no denying it's an alluring and good-looking sequence, and one that encourages you to slow down and take things easy.

Also eye-catching is the biggest of the pools, the 'crystal blue ballroom' swimming pool, an indoor bathing area complete with underwater music, and a lovely big jacuzzi on one side overlooking the outdoor (heated) pools. This room is full of natural light and it's a great place in which to lie on one of the loungers and read (though do remember to bring your own books and magazines with you – lack of glossy mags is the Spa's one failing, and you don't want to be stuck with the *Daily Mail*). One final tip: shop around for a day package that includes lunch because the café prices reflect the well-heeled clientele (smoked salmon bagel, £10.50; coffee and biscuits, £4.50).

The Spa at Pennyhill Park Hotel
London Road, Bagshot, Surrey GU19 5EU (01276 486100, www.thespa.uk.com). Rates from £175 full day.

The Vineyard Spa

A day of delicious pampering, by grape, bean or truffle.

Although just a hop, skip and jump from the busy A34, and less than an hour from hectic Paddington station, the five-star Vineyard at Stockcross hotel and spa near Newbury is perfect for a day of luxurious peace and quiet.

Surrounded by its own golf course, the Vineyard has five treatment rooms (one of them specifically designed for couples), as well as a sauna, spa bath, steam room, swimming pool and poolside restaurant. If you're here for a day of total pampering, you can't go far wrong with the Ultimate Spa Day (£250), 'the ultimate in relaxation and bliss'.

Upon arrival (as early as possible to make the most of your day), a gentle giant of a doorman greets you with the kind of welcome usually reserved for A-list stars, ushering you in to the seductive silence of the pool area. Once cosied up in your white towelling bathrobe, slippers on your feet, you can lounge – perhaps with a book and a mint tea – beneath the domed ceiling that crowns the circular pool. Lulled by the distant bubbling of the pool-side spa-bath, you'll struggle not to relax here.

The three Ultimate Spa Day treatments last for 85 minutes, 55 minutes and 25 minutes, and the range of options you can choose from is impressive. You might fancy something restorative for your hair from ghd, such as the 40-minute Age Defying Treatment, or you can opt, say, for a 55-minute ESPA Lifesaving Back Treatment. The most popular choices are the Vineyard's signature treatments, in particular the 85-minute Balinese Journey, which seeks to unblock energy channels and bring balance and vitality back to your body through rhythmic body brushing, hot mitts infused with lime and traditional Balinese massage.

The ISHI treatments are another popular option. These consist of three elements: ChocoTherapy, VinoTherapy and TruffleTherapy. And yes, they're exactly what you think. Chocolate-lovers might well find the sensation of the sweet stuff running across their cheeks during the 85-minute ChocoFacial is as delicious as eating it. Designed to improve skin tone by stimulating natural drainage, the chocolate-based products nourish your skin and, apparently, reduce signs of ageing. They smell wonderful. A back, neck and shoulder massage is part of the treatment, and accompanying edible chocolates made by the hotel's Michelin-starred executive chef John Campbell are also included, as they are for the TruffleTherapy – a facial that's designed to ease tension and calm and lighten the skin.

VinoTherapy also mixes exterior products with devourable goodies, taking advantage of the natural minerals and antioxidants contained in grapes to detoxify and rebalance the skin; this time, your massage is finished off with a soothing glass of fine wine. Both the ChocoTherapy and VinoTherapy treatments have the option of a 115-minute Body Treatment, which is supposed to fight cellulite through a process that involves cocooning you in white chocolate mousse or thermal mud.

After lunch, why not have a snooze on your lounger while waiting for the next treatments. Perhaps this time you'll have the Vineyard's signature Hot Stone Therapy, which uses aromatic oils selected according to your mood, followed by the Vineyard Hand & Foot Ritual as your final treatment, giving your tootsies and digits the attention they really deserve.

The Ultimate Spa Day is the most luxurious package available, but all purse-sizes can exercise their right to relax here. A Deluxe Spa Day costs £190 and affords you two 55-minute treatments, while the Luxury Spa Day (£150) includes a 55-minute and a 25-minute treatment. If you want to focus on saunas and steam rooms, then the Spa Experience Day (£120), which grants you full access to the spa, plus two 25-minute treatments, or Spa Taster Day (£90) – a 25-minute treatment and all-day access to the facilities – might do more to fulfil your relaxation yearnings. And if your busy lifestyle doesn't leave enough time for a full-day escape, then you can opt for the Spa Evenings, which for £70 give you a 25-minute treatment prior to a relax in the spa.

You can also book a single treatment rather than buying a tailored package – a good gift option. Or, if you're up for pampering in a pair, there's the Couples Treatment option, where you can experience the signature treatments side-by-side. The Vineyard also offers specific

RELAXATION

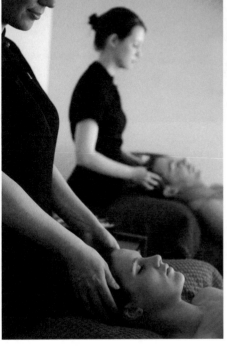

mum-to-be treatments such as an enjoyable Deluxe Pedicure (£50), and for something ultra-indulgent, the spa offers Spa Break packages; starting at around £400 per room per night, these include a 25-minute treatment, full use of the spa, an à la carte dinner prepared by Campbell in the destination restaurant, and a full breakfast.

However you choose to experience the Vineyard Spa, you'll float back to town with your skin glowing, a beatific smile on your face and your troubles (at least temporarily) banished from mind.

The Vineyard Spa
Stockcross, Newbury, Berkshire RG20 8JU (01635 589415, www.the-vineyard.co.uk). Open 7am-9pm Mon-Fri; 8am-8pm Sat, Sun.

RELAXATION

Avebury

The ancient ring of stones at Avebury, a UNESCO World Heritage Site in the care of the National Trust, has plenty of atmosphere on a sunny day. But at sunset, they're electrifying. And, unlike its more famous counterpart at Stonehenge, this megalithic monument can be walked up to and touched.
Avebury, nr Marlborough, Wiltshire SN8 1RF (01672 539250, www.national trust.org.uk).

Devil's Dyke

Once the site of an Iron Age hill fort, Devil's Dyke in Sussex enjoys commanding views of the South Downs, the Weald and, on a clear day, even the Isle of Wight. Enormously popular with Victorian tourists, the Dyke once had a fairground, funicular railway and cable car. Now, come for the blazing sunsets – John Constable rated this view, so who are we to argue?
Devil's Dyke, north of Brighton, South Downs, West Sussex *(www.national trust.org.uk).*

Holkham Beach

North Norfolk is rightly lauded for its vast beaches, where the sun sets on your left and transforms the huge sky into a hundred

shades of orange and pink. The sands of Holkham found disguised fame in *Shakespeare in Love* – when Gwyneth Paltrow emerges from a shipwreck, supposedly in the New World, she's actually here. Visit off-season, and appreciate the view without the crowds. *Holkham Beach, nr Wells-next-the-Sea, Norfolk (www.holkham.co.uk).*

Ivinghoe Beacon

High up in the Chilterns, Ivinghoe Beacon is the easternmost point of the Ridgeway, 87 miles of ancient chalk ridge trail that extends to Wiltshire and is thought to be Britain's oldest road. Late on a winter afternoon, when the wind begins to bite, you might well have the sunset to yourself. *Ivinghoe Beacon, Buckinghamshire (www.nationaltrail.co.uk).*

Malvern Hills

The Malvern Hills dramatically divide Worcestershire and Herefordshire, rising out of the landscape to provide England with some of its finest views. Head up North Hill and face west as the sun sinks below the craggy Black Mountains of Wales, where the clinging clouds create unforgettable skies. *Malvern, Worcestershire (www.malvernhillsaonb.org.uk).*

Calcot Manor

Unwind in style in the chocolate-box Cotswolds.

This part of Gloucestershire truly is chocolate-box country – assuming, of course, those chocolates are of the classy variety rather than toffee pennies. On days when a flawless blue sky arches over the patchwork green fields, and the sun lingers on cottages and churches hewn out of golden stone, even the most grit-worshipping urbanite feels like breaking into a hearty rendition of 'Jerusalem'. Until, that is, an enormous shiny Range Rover with three perfect blonde children in the back forces you off the road and into a hedge.

It's this kind of money that funds the area's sophisticated restaurants, hotels, gastropubs (natch) and spas. There seem to be more exquisitely run small hotels here than in any other British county, and in recent years some of the best have had the foresight to add a luxury spa.

Calcot Manor is one of the finest examples. It's just a few miles from Tetbury or ten miles from Kemble (an hour and a half from Paddington station), situated just beyond the village of Beverstone and its miniature 13th-century castle. A sprawling farmhouse with converted barns and stables, it was built in the 14th century by Cistercian monks, and now nestles in 220 acres of gently rolling Cotswold countryside, through which a three-mile 'trim track' winds, perfect for a jog or bike ride (if you can't bring your own, you can always borrow one here).

Unusually for a luxury spa hotel in such an effortlessly romantic location, Calcot is notably child-friendly: ten of the hotel's 35 rooms and suites are specifically designated as family rooms and housed in a separate barn, there's an all-day crèche, and the spa has a shallow, slip-proof pool for little ones. That's not to say the pool area is child-centric, for those worried about their sense of serenity being punctured, since kids are only allowed in a few hours each day.

The spa is housed in its own building, constructed around a central courtyard.

At the heart of this is a large hot tub where staff will serve you a glass of champagne, as well as keep the outdoor fire stoked with fragrant logs. It's open throughout the year and there can be few more welcoming treats for a jaded, just-arrived guest on a winter's day than this: steam rising from the tub, the roar of the fire and a glass of bubbles in hand.

Inside, the decor is understated but stylish, with plenty of soft olive and biscuit shades. Comfy sofas and chairs with squashy cushions are everywhere, and the relaxation room, with views of the surrounding fields and a restfully tinkling water feature, has plenty of beds to lounge on. Thoughtful touches such as chair arms big enough to stand a drink safely on and jugs of citrus- or cucumber-flavoured water make it even more cocoon-like.

As well as a sauna and steam room, there's a comprehensive treatment menu over which to deliberate; even teens get their own mini-menu. The products used include Guinot, Cornish-made Spieza Organic Products and Aromatherapy Associates. The three 'Luxury Treatments' are aptly named. The most indulgent of these is simply called 'Bliss', and costs a reasonable £98 for almost two hours. A head-to-toe massage is followed by a full facial using Aromatherapy Associates languor-inducing oils (you get to choose which scents you like at the beginning).

Tired tresses get a look in too, with pioneering hair spa treatments from ghd (yes, ghd of ceramic irons ubiquity) available. The 40-minute 'Age Defying Treatment' (£44) replenishes stressed locks with a mineral-rich mud mask, while the 'Men's Experience' exfoliates the scalp using extracts of tea tree and grapefruit (£34.50 for 25 minutes).

For those guests who relax by letting off their own steam, the gym is well stocked with Technogym cardiovascular and resistance equipment. Log in at the beginning of your workout and the machines keep track of how many calories have been burned. The spacious fitness studio holds from two to six classes a day, including Pilates and adult ballet.

Whether lying prone with a copy of *Tatler* in hand or bouncing about in the gym, you'll need to refuel at some point. The food is delicious. Lunch can be pre-ordered and includes luscious soups with own-made bread, Mediterranean-influenced salads and open sandwiches. Mid-afternoon (or morning) hunger pangs are easily assuaged with slabs of cake and tall glasses of thick hot chocolate.

All in all, it's hard not to love Calcot Manor, with its restful interior, glorious surroundings and friendly and helpful staff.

Calcot Manor Hotel & Spa
Nr Tetbury, Gloucestershire GL8 8YJ (01666 890391, www.calcotmanor.co.uk). Rates £68 Twilight package, £97 half day; £127.50 full day.

RELAXATION

Food & Drink

Middle Farm, Glynde 205
Daylesford Organic Farm Shop 209
FIVE Farm shops 211
Novelli's Academy 212
TEN Food markets 215
Mrs Tee's Wild Mushrooms 220
Pick Your Own 222
FIVE PYO farms 223
FIVE Seasonal food events 224

Get the local experience

Over 50 of the world's top destinations available.

Middle Farm, Glynde

Sample England's finest cider… in Sussex.

It's a rare thing these days for consumers to directly connect the four-legged thing in the field with the gourmet delight on the counter, now that a weekly shop typically involves an often-stressful slog around a halogen-lit soulless supermarket. But a visit to Middle Farm helps you do just that: turn the weekly grocery grind into a day of simple country pleasures.

Between the picturesque Sussex towns of Firle and Lewes – easily reached by train (Victoria to Lewes in just over an hour, then a ten-minute train to Glynde, from whence it's a 15-minute walk) – lies Middle Farm, a land of epicurean delights where family-run farming and low-priced activities for children go hand in hand. What began as fifth-generation farmer John Pile selling marmalade, eggs and bread from his kitchen door has gradually expanded to encompass the National Collection of Cider & Perry, a snug assembly of 100 casked and 150 bottled varieties of the nation's finest brews; an acclaimed farm shop overflowing with home-made goodies and artisan produce from 1,000 British suppliers; and a pretty little garden centre, gift shop and restaurant thrown in to boot, all situated within 625 acres of glorious countryside.

If you arrive in need of some grown-up refreshment, head straight for the stable-block. Bolstered by the vogue for all things traditional, cider and perry (the pear version) are making an extraordinary comeback – both the dry, deep flavours of real West Country scrumpy, and the clear Sussex ciders derived from culinary and dessert apples are now popular again. We visited the National Collection building on a chilly autumn morning, when the sharp smell and satisfying scrunch of apples being hand-pressed made for a deliciously appropriate overture. Once inside, co-founder Rod Marsh pointed to a photograph of Harold and Frank Naish, octogenarian cider brewers with a 200-year-old family business. They might have played stand-ins for *Last of the Summer Wine*'s Compo and Foggy; life, you assume, had not been kind. 'Actually they became millionaires,' says Rod. Harold died in 2005, shovelling apples into the traditional crusher until he was 84, and reputedly disgusted when 81-year-old Frank bought a state-of-the-art machine to save his back. 'He was furious. Wouldn't have anything to do with it,' chuckles Rod.

Their story is typical of the ethos of many 'real' cider brewers, who speak vehemently about widespread adulteration by sugar, additives and corporate values. Proper cider is made by using only pear or apple juice – adjusting only the length of ripening, the blend of apples or the depth of filter to alter a naturally tannin-rich, astringent beverage that's dark,

FOOD & DRINK

cloudy and strong. It was this home-brewed cider that historically powered farm-workers through the harvest, sometimes even forming part of their wage. The process was simple – a 'cheese' of loft-ripened, milled fruit would be pressed through layers of straw, horsehair or muslin, then left to ferment over the winter in oak 'pipes'. And with more than 6,000 varieties of British apples (glorying in names like Ten Commandments or Hoary Morning), anyone could in theory have a go with whatever apples they had to hand, creating plenty of local variations. Many producers still restrict their business to the farm gate or local pubs. 'It's difficult to describe,' enthuses Rod, 'but it's about what the French call the *terroir*: your own relationship to the soil and what you can draw out of it. And the ultimate goal of any cidermaker is to preserve that unique taste of the apple within the beverage.'

Appreciating the different results is easy. Just take a taster cup and work your way merrily around the casks. With a potency of up to eight per cent – names like Double Vision and Wiscombe Suicider should speak for themselves

where they can peep at the new calves, kept separate from their mothers so we can drink their milk. Unpasteurised, naturally. 'We have people coming from London just for that,' laughs Sue, the farm's dairy expert. What's so special about it? 'The idea is it retains the taste of whatever the cow has eaten. And some believe it's better for you.'

Sue presides over more than 50 cheeses, from 17th-century favourites like Lord of the Hundreds to modern, fancier versions with cumin, cloves or beer, all with a story and a geography, many available to sample before you buy. There are also three on-site butchers specialising in custom cuts of Middle Farm's own pork, lamb and beef (Jersey and Aberdeen Angus cross-breeds) with free-range Sussex poultry and local game. There are so many different types of sausage that there's a weekly rota (try wild boar and apple, or venison and red wine). Squeezing your way past a plentiful supply of fruit and veg, you'll find baskets overflowing with fresh bread, trays of cakes and scones, and plenty in the freezer too: bread puddings, raspberry cheesecakes and Yorkshire pork pies the size of footballs. Crammed on to shelves are row upon row of blackberry jams, pomegranate jellies and date and walnut chutneys, and the usual supplies of syrups, vinegars and colourful pastas. It's a challenge to take it all in, and at weekends requires plenty of time to browse.

Any kids in tow will be amply entertained while you shop, however, by the shire horses, rabbits and guinea pigs, patrolling geese and noisy peacocks. Call ahead in the school holidays to find out about special activities like pig-feeding or Pat-a-Pet. Adults have their own programme – a traditional Christmas Fair, a raucous Apple Festival with 20 local bands, and even courses on keeping your own poultry. Meanwhile, the local area contains plenty to keep you occupied for a whole day – a stroll up Firle Beacon or over the Downs, a trip to the antique shops of Lewes (see p35; it makes for a popular walk from Glynde) or a visit to the opera at Glyndeborne. Then there's the fantastic selection of local pubs. Try the Trevor Arms at Glynde (01273 858208) or the wonderful Cricketers Arms at nearby Alciston (01323 870469, www.cricketersberwick.co.uk), for a homely atmosphere and hearty food to see you home.

– it's best to get some tips from Rod or wife Helen first. Connoisseurs might head for single variety brews like Kingston Black, brave souls might opt for the Naish brothers' Honest To Goodness, while all should sample the house cider/perry blend, Little Red Rooster. Once you decide on a purchase, just fill up your selected vessel and take it to the counter. And if you don't like cider, a tempting array of fresh apple juices, sloe gin, country wines and Sussex ales ensures there's something for everyone.

Having quenched the thirst, it's time to address the stomach. Fortunately, the farm shop and adjacent restaurant are a short stumble away. High animal-welfare and environmental standards are central to Middle Farm's ethos; nonetheless, managing director Helen is keen to stress the relationship between what takes place on the farm and what ends up in the shop. 'We're unsentimental about our animals,' she says. 'Some of the pigs the children see are pets – the rest will end up in our sausages. We don't try and pretend otherwise.' That's visible in the milking shed, where kids can watch the daily routine at 3pm, and in the children's haybarn,

Middle Farm, Glynde

Firle, Lewes, East Sussex BN8 6LJ (01323 811411, www.middlefarm.com). Open 9.30am-5.30pm daily.

Daylesford Organic Farm Shop

Stock up on the chic.

Seconds into a visit to the Bamford family's neat, green Daylesford estate, it becomes clear that this may well be a farm shop – but not as we know it. It starts as you park your rust-bucket of a car (you'll soon come to think of it that way) between shiny 4x4s and Bentleys, continues as you join the browsing glossy haired locals placing prettily wrapped jars of chutney into artisan-made wicker baskets, and ends as the impeccably polite and well turned out staff bid you farewell as you depart. There are no grubby fingernails proffering crinkly old Tesco bags full of mud-caked carrots here.

What you will find at the spick and span Daylesford Organic Farm Shop are exquisite, organic, seasonal vegetables (from the on-site kitchen garden), award-winning cheeses (from the creamery), towers of freshly baked baguettes, sourdoughs, cakes and pastries (from the bakery), pre-cooked meals that make your usual microwave curries seem about as nutritious as a plateful of crack, organic meat (including farmed venison from the family's other estate in Staffordshire) and endless sauces, chutneys and preserves. It's food shopping grown up, gone green and just back from finishing school – you could spend hours (and hundreds of pounds) here.

Whether you have the weekly shop or just a spot of decadent browsing in mind, we recommend you take time (make sure you book ahead) to enjoy brunch or lunch at the shop's fabulous café. Take a seat on the mezzanine level for fantastic views of how the other half live, as you tuck into enormous – and reasonably priced – plates of butternut and parsley risotto or venison casserole. A finer, heartier luncheon we can't imagine – and from the gregarious glass-clinking bonhomie we witnessed on our recent visit, nor can anyone else in a 20-mile radius. There's a fabulous courtyard for summer alfresco eating too.

Even when you're done with food, there's plenty more to discover here. Head for the Haybarn (*see p190*) for yoga, treatments and Bamford beauty products, the Bamford Barn for luxurious clothing, crafts produced by local artisans and swanky but sustainable homewares, and the garden shop for kitchen diaries, fancy plant pots and trowels with handles made from antlers (by-products of the venison, naturally). There are regular events held throughout the year too, including cookery demonstrations, food and wine matching sessions and seasonal events for adults and children such as festive wreathmaking and meet Father Christmas afternoons. A damned fine place to escape the city and indulge your inner high-class eco-warrior.

Daylesford Organic Farm Shop
Daylesford, nr Kingham, Gloucestershire GL56 0YG (01608 731700, www.daylesfordorganic. com). Open 9am-5pm Mon-Sat; 9am-4pm Sun.

FOOD & DRINK

▶ For Daylesford's Haybarn Ayurvedic centre, see p190.

Daylesford Farm Shop

FIVE Farm shops

Better Food
This small but busy shop and café sells its own locally grown fruit and veg, fresh bread, organic store cupboard essentials, eco-friendly beauty products and more. The café serves breakfasts, Sunday roasts and satisfying wedges of cake. *Proving House, Sevier Street, St Werburghs, Bristol BS2 9QS (0117 935 1725, www.betterfood.co.uk).*

Farmcafé & Foodmarket
Unassumingly located beside the A12, this Suffolk venture takes the roadside caff concept up a notch – and then some. A shop, added in 2007, sells great breads, cakes, meat, fruit and veg. Don't leave without sampling the full English. *Main Road, Marlesford, Woodbridge, Suffolk IP13 0AG (01728 747717, www.farmcafe.co.uk).*

Macknade Fine Foods
As well as shelves stacked with everything from pasta to preserves, you'll find a huge array of cheeses, high-quality meat, a fishmonger, local crafts, a coffee shop, an adjacent garden centre and a regular weekend farmers' market. *Selling Road, Faversham, Kent ME13 8XF (01795 534497, www.macknade.com).*

Organic Farm Shop
Farm-fresh fruit, veg, meat and dairy products as well as farm tours, child-friendly walking trails, cookery classes and courses galore. Everything is organic and as local as possible. Try before you buy with lunch in the café. *Burford Road, Cirencester, Gloucestershire GL7 5HF (01285 640441, www.theorganic farmshop.co.uk).*

Windsor Farm Shop
This refined farm shop's location outside the town centre is a blissful escape from the camera-wielding masses. Quality fruit, veg, cakes, soups, pies and ales awaits, with lots of locally sourced produce (meat and dairy come from the royal farms). There's an adjacent café too. *Datchet Road, Old Windsor, Berkshire SL4 2RP (01753 623800, www.windsor farmshop.co.uk).*

FOOD & DRINK

Novelli's Academy

A taste sensation in Hertfordshire.

Although it's just a short taxi ride from Luton Airport Parkway station and the surrounding industrial complex, the drive to the Novelli Academy takes you along beautiful tree-lined country lanes, winding up outside the 14th-century farmhouse that houses Jean-Christophe Novelli's cookery school.

The Academy's Tasting & Demonstration day makes for a perfect foodie day-trip from London, but is just one of a range of courses run here; more intensive (and expensive) one-day masterclasses with the famous French chef himself are also on offer, as well as seafood, food and wine, seasonal and Indian food courses run by various host chefs.

Sitting in the homely demonstration kitchen, London feels a long way away. We're listening to Steven Kitchen, Novelli's resident executive chef, as he prepares us for the top dog's appearance. 'Jean's always very intense, because he's so passionate about what he does,' explains Kitchen. 'I know he's going to inspire you, because even when I'm working with him, I'll be like "Oh, that's good".'

We sit at one of four marble counter tops. Above the bottles of condiments and bowls of shiny vegetables hang watercolours of cows, a metal figurine clutching the legend 'The original Hell's Kitchen' and a floor-length painting of the Michelin-star winner. What with this and Kitchen's 'warming up' of the crowd in preparation for the forthcoming appearance, it's a little like waiting for the entrance of an international statesman.

And Novelli's entrance doesn't disappoint. With the click of a door latch, he enters the building and tours the room, shaking hands with a finger-crushing grip. Attendees are asked to introduce themselves and explain what they'd like to learn from the day. It transpires that most of the participants have been given the session as a birthday present, and that professions and cooking ability vary widely (although the group is weighted towards the novice, this being an introductory course).

There's a call for a round of champagne, and Novelli explains the interplay between himself and Kitchen ('We're like a double act: I slice the onion, he cries'), before we're ushered to our feet to gather around the stove in preparation for the eight-course menu that's about to be rustled up.

'It's not supposed to be complicated. It's not meant to be so hard that you don't

want to attempt it. It's the simplicity of the dishes, and the combination of the flavours,' explains Kitchen, as Novelli starts to produce ingredients. Given that the day's dishes include creations like garden-pea cappuccino soup with foie gras, black pudding and pancetta, you could be forgiven for a little scepticism, but as the ingredients start to hit the pan, the truth of Kitchen's statement soon becomes obvious.

Novelli drops a slab of pork belly into a hefty frying pan, muttering something about any decent cut of meat losing 30 per cent of its weight through water loss, as he starts frying. Seasoning goes into the pan, along with some honey and cider, and soon the room is filled with a tastebud-awakening scent.

The pan is passed under the noses of all participants so they can smell each new ingredient as it's added, with Novelli teasing the flavour of the sauce first one way, then the next. 'I could stand here and change the taste of this for hours,' chuckles the chef, 'but I'm crazy like that.' First he throws in some cream for richness, then a squeeze of lemon juice for sharpness. Spoons are proffered and we're encouraged to taste at every stage so we can see how each addition has affected the dish. To Novelli, the pork's smell is 'dramatic' and the quality of the cream 'powerful'; his hyperbole is infectious.

Amid the murmurs of appreciation, it's explained that it's the intimate feel of a small group that is the beauty of these courses, and so we should feel free to ask questions. The queries flow thick and fast, with Novelli responding enthusiastically. 'What if you don't have a pan like that?' – 'Then you'll have to make sandwiches'. 'Aren't you meant to use only best quality wine when cooking?'

– 'Who told you that? A wine merchant? Cooking with it changes its flavour. It'd be like feeding caviar to a pig. We use £2.50 bottles of merlot.' 'Is it best to make your own puff pastry?' – 'There's no need. Ready-made's consistently good. Making your own's like taking a bucket to the seaside, and getting some water to make your own sea salt.'

More champagne is issued, and a variety of dishes, including dark-chocolate cocoa pots with whisky, and Shetland blue shell mussels in a coconut-scented broth, are demonstrated. We're shown how to prepare a tomato sauce so intensely rich it's hard to believe its only two ingredients are garlic and tomatoes simmered until they've lost all wateriness. Tips fly thick and fast. Don't fancy paying exorbitant prices so that you can procure balsamic vinegar that doesn't taste like it'd take the paint off doors? Easy, just reduce cheap balsamic with sugar, so it's a syrup. Fed up of spending time chopping garlic? Don't bother. Just hit it with your hand and throw it in. After all, for Novelli, 'The less you do, the better you are at cooking.'

Finally, it's time to taste the finished creations. Glasses of wine are poured as the food is dished up and Novelli takes a seat among the group to eat and chat about how intimate courses such as this are now his life rather than the boiler room of a restaurant kitchen ('You want people to come close to you and see how you really are. The last thing I want to do is impress. That's what's great about the cookery school: people leave and they're shocked at how much they've learnt'), as well as throwing in snippets of gossip about his celebrity contemporaries. All of the various courses are delicious. And there's just time for the Frenchman to demonstrate how to make his signature caramel swirls, and pose for photos before it's all over, albeit a couple of hours later than intended.

We make to leave, congratulating the chef on his energy. 'Actually, you know what? I'm not on top form today. I've been really ill, this is the sixth class I've done in six days, and last night I was doing a demonstration in Surrey in the evening. I'm absolutely knackered.' If that's the man when he's low on energy, we can't imagine what he's like on form.

Novelli Academy
Crouchmoor Farm, Tea Green, Hertfordshire LU2 8PS (01582 454070, www.jean christophenovelli.com/cookery+school). Cost from £350 (with Jean-Christophe).

TEN Food markets

A market in full swing is a joyous, exuberant event, an antidote to the uniformity of supermarket shopping. In England, there's a marked split between farmers' markets and most general street markets – some might call it social apartheid. Farmers' markets attract well-to-do foodies and wannabe Domestic Goddesses or Hugh Fearnley-Whittingstalls, while general markets draw canny bargain hunters, buy-in-bulkers and elderly wielders of tartan shopping baskets. Both types, though, provide bags of local flavour. Markets are constantly changing, so some stalls may turn up one week, but not the next, and many pack up early in bad weather.

Street Markets

Alton
Steam trains of the Mid Hants Railway's Watercress Line stop at Alton, which suggests what to buy from the market's costermonger (two locally grown bunches, £1.50). Stalls pack the little high street of this fetching market town, with classy food to the fore. Grab a focaccia from the Italian baker's stall, slip a sole into your bag at the fish van, buy beef from Glen Davies ('the honest butcher') or Melton pork pies from the deli stall. Mr Pickle's hot chilli sauces come in heat-grades from three to an eye-watering nine, and the New Forest Pannage Pork trader sells sausages alongside wild venison. Fill up with excellent fried noodles at the 'Chinese healthy food' van.
High Street, Alton, Hampshire GU34 2BW (www.smtcmarkets.co.uk). Open 9am-4pm Tue.

Hitchin
There are beautiful old streets off Hitchin's handsome market square, but in 1973 the council shifted traders from here to land behind the Churchgate shopping precinct, where stalls cower under corrugated metal roofing. Head for the packaged food seller for cut-price jars of capers and tins of anchovies. Or peruse the Asian and Afro-Caribbean food kiosk, with its fresh yams, jars of hot pepper sauce and tins of ackee. Nearby, a miked-up meat trader roars

FOOD & DRINK

about sirloin while a fishmonger proffers whelks and live mussels. If you're lucky, Jackie of Ware will be selling her pies and cakes; buy a brownie to eat by the duck-speckled river a few steps away. *Biggin Lane, Hitchin, Hertfordshire SG5 1DN (01462 456202, www.hitchin markets.co.uk). Open 9am-4pm Tue, Fri (including antiques market), Sat.*

Olney

Olney, with its pleasing old stone buildings, is most famous for a pancake race, which starts from the market place every Shrove Tuesday and dates back over 500 years, but it also hosts a cracking little market every Thursday. As well as three fruit and veg stands and a couple of meat traders (selling everything from tripe to hulking great pork joints) there are several specialist stalls. Buy lapsang souchong or freshly ground monsoon malabar from the tea and coffee stall, Harborough curd cakes from the baker, or four cheeses for a fiver from the cheese van. Around the market's perimeter you'll find several enticing independent food and wine stores. *Market Place, Olney, Buckinghamshire MK46 4AJ (01234 711679, www.olneytowncouncil. co.uk/market.php). Open 9am-4pm Thur.*

Romford

Coach parties travel from as far as Norfolk to reach Romford's rumbustious market. Around 270 stalls fill the huge Market Place, and a couple of dozen more occupy permanent cubicles in the spanking new Shopping Hall. There's a strong flavour of the East End here, with five seafood and fish stalls selling pickled whelks, cockles, roll-mops, vast bowlfuls of jellied eels (£27), and a 'lovely bit of conger, to make yer live longer'. Otherwise, dine on stewed eels at McDowell's pie shop in the Shopping Hall, where you'll also find organic meat, game, Asian foods and lahmacun (Turkish pizza). Outside, a burger van sells toast and marg for 30p among its 'Best of British' delicacies. *St Edwards Way, Market Place, Romford, Essex RM1 3ER (www.havering.gov.uk). Open 8.30am-4.30pm Wed, Fri; 8.30am-5pm Sat.*

Thame

Tuesday has been market day in Thame for over 800 years, and the attractive town is still transformed by the weekly display. Regular pitches include three fruit and veg stands, Eadles meat stall (sausages, bacon and chitterling from own-reared pork), Chilli the Fish (salmon, fresh squid) and a cheese stall (oxford blue, stinking bishop). At the far

end is the Country Market stall, where capable Women's Institute ladies sell fresh herbs, cakes, quiches and pies, plus rarities such as quince in season. On the second Tuesday of each month, the farmers' market gets its own section to sell meat, trout, apples, goat's cheese and pies. Look out for squirrel fillets. *Upper High Street, Thame, Oxfordshire OX9 2DW (07973 520140, www.thametown council.gov.uk). Open 8.30am-4.30pm Tue.*

Farmers' Markets

Brentwood Farmers' Market
One of the busiest and best-attended of Essex's farmers' markets, this monthly shindig takes place amid the kerfuffle of Saturday on the high street. There's a decent spread of food on the stalls, including organic breads and flours from Greenwich's Flour Power City bakery, rare-breed pork and sausages from Rhyne Park Farm in Suffolk, and fruit and meat pies from Farm 2 Kitchen, near Arlington in East Sussex. These are joined by seasonal produce such as soft fruit, apple and pear juices from Core Fruit Products (keep a look out for Hard Core Cider), and venison from Godmersham Game.

High Street, Brentwood, Essex CM14 4RR (01277 362414, www.essexfarmers markets. co.uk). Open 9am-3pm 1st Sat of mth.

Guildford Farmers' Market
Guildford's quaint cobbled high street makes an apt setting for this corker of a farmers' market. Around 50 stalls are attracted every month, with produce ranging from soft fruit in summer to winter root crops, via springtime asparagus. Norbury blue cheese (from Dorking), beer (from Hog's Back Brewery), fish, meat and eggs are brought to market by local producers, and you'll also encounter baked goods, pickles, chutneys and herbs. Several events are run through the year, including regular live-animal displays, a St George's Day market and a strawberry market in June. Guildford also holds a street market on North Street every Friday and Saturday. *High Street, Guildford, Surrey GU1 3JL (01483 444401, www.guildford.gov.uk). Open 10.30am-3.30pm 1st Tue of mth (except Jan).*

Henley Farmers' Market
The photogenic town-centre site and a plentiful supply of affluent customers ensure that producers are keen to take

FOOD & DRINK

The biggest and the best Sunday Market in England. Bargains galore, acres of parking, fantastic food court delights.
Wembley Market open Sundays.

WEMBLEY SUNDAY MARKET

Directions: Wembley Park tube or follow brown signs to Wembley Stadium
wembleymarket.co.uk   01895 632221
Closed for major stadium events check for details

a pitch in Henley. Pathfinder Ostrich Farm is a regular, selling steaks, pâté, and quiches made from whopping great ostrich eggs. Other highlights include Oxfordshire Black smoked gammon from the Acorn Herd stall, Little Whittenham lamb, fidget pie from Harvest Foods, 21-day-aged Dexter steak from Challow Hill Meats, freshly boiled crayfish from Brookleas Trout Farm, and Anila's Indian Chutneys (snap up some of the methi curry sauce). There are cheeses, cakes and preserves too. Don't miss Gabriel Machin's shop at 7 Market Place: a traditional butcher's, fishmonger's and smokery.
Market Place, Henley-on-Thames, Oxfordshire RG9 2AA (www.henleytown council.gov.uk). Open 8.30am-1.30pm 4th Thur of mth.

Whitfield Farmers' Market
Situated just off the A2 near Dover, Whitfield Farmers' Market has a Women's Institute vibe by dint of its location in the village hall. Some 300 customers are attracted each week to cluster round trestle tables laden with local produce. Sue's Fresh Fish is hauled off her husband's boat and the catch might include crabs, lobsters and scallops. Ashmore Kentish cheese, made

near Faversham, along with eggs, home-made cakes, jams, chutneys and pickles, fruit and meat pies, fudge and Indian ready-meals are all equally tempting. In the kitchen, local ladies serve bacon butties, tea and coffee. Bucolic bliss.
Whitfield Village Hall, Sandwich Road, Whitfield, Kent CT16 3LY (01304 853174, www.kentfarmersmarkets.org.uk). Open 9am-noon Thur.

Windsor Farmers' Market
Over the past three years, Thames Valley Farmers' Markets has successfully created traditional street-market bustle in Windsor. St Leonard's Road is an ideal thoroughfare: near the town centre, lined with local shops and with a neighbourly buzz. Cheese-makers from Shepton Mallet travel here, cheddar in tow, and Mr Whitehead makes the journey from the New Forest to sell strong dry cider (try the two together). There are plenty of meat producers, including the Complete Pig; try the coarse pâté and pork pies. For dessert, there's fudge made from Homefield House goat's milk, or the much healthier option of soft fruit from Haynes Horticulture.
St Leonard's Road, Windsor, Berkshire SL4 3BL (07973 155574, www.tvfm.org.uk). Open 9am-1pm 1st Sat of mth.

Mrs Tee's Wild Mushrooms

Foraging for fungi in the New Forest.

We're sitting agog around the dining room table of a wonderfully homely B&B, clasping large mugs of steaming tea, and being told that puffballs are good but anything with white gills is bad.

This is the home of Mrs Brigitte Tee, one of the world's foremost authorities on mushrooms, and we're attending one of her seminars where we're going to learn how to identify edible mushrooms, eat a fabulous lunch and then go and forage for our own bag of goodies in the beautiful nearby New Forest.

FOOD & DRINK

The eccentric Mrs Tee started her journey in the world of mushrooms at the age of three when her grandmother would take her out picking. Since then she's become one of the biggest mushroom distributors in the UK, providing chefs and restaurants in London and the Southeast with tasty morsels from both nearby fields and woodland and via import from Europe.

She started her seminars 12 years ago to provide novice fungi fans with a thorough grounding in how to pick, where to pick and when to pick. The seminars proved to be hugely popular and are now held throughout the year, their content tailored around the seasons: in May to December the focus is on practical experience, where a morning class is followed by an afternoon of foraging in the New Forest, whereas the January to April sessions focus on gourmet cooking with Mrs Tee and an informative walk.

At 10am, we arrive at Mrs Tee's Edwardian B&B hidden down a back lane near Lymington, Hampshire (two hours from Waterloo to Brockenhurst and ten minutes in a taxi). Mrs Tee herself opens the door in an apron and Jimi Hendrix T-shirt, and bustles us past the heavenly smelling kitchen into the dining room, where 12 other mushroom fans are seated in front of Jackie, the seminar leader.

Jackie has been picking all her life (and has the stories to prove it), and what she doesn't know about mushrooms ain't worth knowing.

The first part of the seminar is dedicated to the most important part of mushrooming: what *not* to pick. We listen nervously to tragic tales of uneducated pickers, and some of us begin to wonder if we'll ever eat mushrooms again. Happily, we move on to what *won't* kill us and it becomes apparent that, actually, if you stick to the rules, the likelihood of losing your dinner-party guests shortly after serving up your risotto is pretty slim.

Our fellow mushroomers are a mixed crew. Some view it as a great way to get to know the

New Forest, others want to learn how to make the most of their woodland walks, while one has received the seminar as a gift. The rest are confirmed foodies who are barely able to contain themselves when lunch is served. After a light salad starter with a chilled glass of rosé, a hearty mushroom risotto is served alongside a huge cream-laden mushroom omelette prepared by Mrs Tee herself. It's nothing short of delicious, and a perfect internal hot-water bottle to prepare us for the foraging ahead.

After lunch is cleared away, we head off in convoy; it's a beautiful drive into the New Forest, with wild ponies nonchalantly grazing on the roadside and sublime views.

Once parked and in the forest, Jackie explains very clearly what we're looking for – the winter chanterelle – and we begin the forage, a long row of slightly nervous mushroomers walking very slowly, scouring the ground like extras in a scene from *CSI*. We all clamour with excitement when the first specimen is spotted, and everyone crowds in to see. It's not a chanterelle: 'It's one of the 3,000,' Jackie says, referring to the 3,000 unidentified and untried mushrooms that exist and should be left well alone. 'Try again,' she says. It's not long before a clutch is found, and then another, and then our confidence is up and we start to get a bit competitive: following each other or sneaking in behind a recent find to bag the rest. An hour later and our plastic bags are bulging with winter chanterelles and the sun is beginning to set.

Back at the cars, all mushrooms are checked and inedible ones discarded before we're presented with a pound of Mrs Tee's wild mushrooms to take home alongside our own foraged booty.

Mrs Tee's Wild Mushrooms
Sway Road, Lymington, Hampshire SO41 8LR (01590 673354, www.wildmushrooms.co.uk). Seminars £95.

FOOD & DRINK

Pick Your Own

Jam with the best of them.

FOOD & DRINK

Pick-your-own farms aren't new; as far back as the 1950s fruit farmers were establishing PYO operations. But it wasn't until the 1970s and the arrival of big domestic freezers that the trend really took off, when the numbers grew to an estimated 10,000 farms. Most of them were wiped out in the '80s with the arrival of supermarkets buying in bulk from centralised suppliers and selling seasonal produce all year, but the last decade has seen a resurgence, driven by a need for independent farmers to find the means to survive and the middle class's desire to rediscover the idyllic rural England of their youth – as well as fresh, cheap produce easily and enjoyably harvested by all.

PYO can be done with no preparation – most farms will supply baskets and punnets, and friendly ones may even give you free jars if you ask nicely – but planning ahead does no harm. If you decide to make a day of it, pack a coolbox for a picnic of strawberries and cream, or be adventurous and throw in some meringues for a DIY soft-fruit pavlova. But most of all, think about your group and what will suit them. At some PYOs, fruit is planted in growbags on tables so you don't even need to bend down, which is heavenly for arthritic knees, but for a

proper day of PYO, you need to feel the wonder of the plants growing in the earth, and that means getting down and dusty. With berries, there's no bending, so these are great PYO crops for all ages; little ones can pick the fruit nearer the ground while grown-ups keep a watchful eye from above as they bag the hard-to-reach fruit.

Most of the 1,000 or so PYO farms in England are open from May to October and offer a wide range of produce. At Allens Farm in Plaxtol, near Sevenoaks, Kent (01732 812215, www.cob nuts.co.uk), you can pick your own cobnuts along

with the cherries and plums, but most offer soft fruit and climbing vegetables in the summer months, and root vegetables and orchard fruits in the autumn. The soft fruits are the ones we're all drawn to, but don't overlook the veggies; you can pick delicious peas and young runner beans from June, but freshly picked baby broad beans start ripening even earlier, are impossible to find in shops and taste like heaven on earth. And as the season progresses and the autumn days shorten, a day spent picking raspberries, plums, apples and root vegetables really does revive the spirits.

Top picking tips include: arriving early at the weekend for the best pickings; wearing long sleeves (there are now many thorn-free varieties of berries, but where there aren't you'll be glad of arm cover); not picking overripe fruit unless you're planning to eat it on the way home; and bringing a hat and sunscreen and wearing old clothes. And tempting as it may be to munch your way around the field, don't be too greedy: at least one PYO has shut up shop because gluttonous visitors were eating all the fruit without paying for it (others have survived by growing sour fruits to avoid this problem). However, it's fine to taste frequently – in fact, the only way to discover how good the produce is, is by sampling it. Also, it's worth remembering that slightly under-ripe fruit is best for jam-making, and that raspberries freeze well but strawberries don't.

FIVE PYO farms

The Farmers Retail & Markets Association (www.farma.org.uk) and www.pickyour own.info have lists of PYO farms.

Crockford Bridge Farm, Surrey
The selection here includes asparagus (Apr-June), mangetout (June-July), sweetcorn (Aug-Sept) and Christmas trees (Nov-Dec), as well as soft fruits, marrows, courgettes, peas and rhubarb. Thorpe Park is nearby. *New Haw Road, Addlestone, near Weybridge, Surrey KT15 2BU (01932 853886, www.crockfordbridgefarm.co.uk).*

Garsons Fruit Farm, Surrey
One of Britain's oldest PYO farms has up to 40 crops: courgettes, cauliflowers, kohlrabi and flowers, as well as plums and orchard fruits. There are regular petting days, a garden centre, restaurant and farm shop. *Winterdown Road, Esher, Surrey KT10 8LS (01372 464389, www.garsons.co.uk).*

Grove Farm, Bedfordshire
More than 30 different fruits and veg are available including spinach and garlic. Baskets are provided to make harvesting easier. The play area has picnic tables. *Ivinghoe, Leighton Buzzard, Bedfordshire LU7 9DZ (01296 668175, www.grovefarmpyo.co.uk).*

Sharnfold Farm, East Sussex
Blackberries, strawberries, tomatoes, sweetcorn and root veg are available through to October. It has a play area, picnic area, fishing lake and farm trail, as well as farmyard animals and 300,000 plants. Pevensey beach is nearby. *Hailsham Road, Stone Cross, Pevensey, East Sussex BN24 5BU (01323 768490, www.sharnfoldfarm.co.uk).*

Spencers Farm Shop, Essex
Pick asparagus from April at this long-standing PYO, where a range of soft fruits includes loganberries and tayberries. Spencers also offers strawberries, and 18 varieties of apple, until November. *Wickham Fruit Farm, Wickham St Pauls, Halstead, Essex CO9 2PX (01787 269476, www.spencersfarmshop.co.uk).*

FOOD & DRINK

Rye Bay Scallop Festival

activities like boat trips and RSPB-guided walks. In the wider area, look out for mushroom-spotting, food safaris and guided walks round farms.
Snape Maltings, Snape, Suffolk IP17 1SR (01473 734017, www.aldeburgh foodanddrink.co.uk).

Apple Week
The Brogdale Collection in Faversham, Kent, home to Britain's most extensive orchards, boasts more than 2,000 types of apple (and 500 of pear) among its 4,000 varieties of fruit. Each October it celebrates this fact with Apple Week, when it holds apple displays and tastings, (as well as wine and cider events) when rare and unsual varieties can be sampled and purchased. And it doesn't stop at fruit: does anything go better with apple that crispy pork? Find out with a hog roast and apple sauce roll while watching one of the live bands. Guided walks through the orchards enable you to pick your own apples and learn about the varieties, and there's even a little railway to enjoy.
Brogdale Road, Faversham, Kent ME13 8XZ (01795 536250, www.brogdale collections.co.uk).

Dorset Nettle Eating Championships
No excuses are needed to spend a day in this beautiful part of Dorset, but watching hundreds of contestants from as far afield as Australia chomp their way through as many stinging nettles as they can in an hour surely adds to the draw. Now in its 23rd year, the contest, which takes place in mid June, evolved from an argument between two farmers about the length of their nettles and now encompasses a beer festival, bands, a medieval fayre and, for those not into nettles, a barbecue. All this takes place around a perfect olde-worlde English country pub, the Bottle Inn, which has its own campsite.
Bottle Inn, Marshwood, nr Bridport, Dorset DT6 5QJ (01297 678254, www.thebottleinn.co.uk/nettlespage.htm).

Rye Bay Scallop Festival
If you've ever slit your thumb shucking an oyster or torn a nail wresting a scallop from its shell, help is at hand at the Rye

Aldeburgh Food & Drink Festival
Now in its fourth year, the Aldeburgh Festival sees a number of towns and villages in the area participate in a wide range of events over nine days, but the centrepiece event is a two-day festival at Snape Maltings (*see p156*) over the last weekend of September. In 2008, more than 70 local producers offered tastings, alongside workshops and cookery demonstrations from some of the UK's top celebrity chefs. Little ones are catered for too with a range of child-friendly

Totally Tomato Show

Bay Scallop Festival, held every February. Scallops are joined by a tempting range of other in-season shellfish, along with scallop-cutting lessons and tasting and cookery demonstrations. If the thought of a cold February day leaves you shivering in your cockles, however, then hold out for the annual Whitstable Oyster Fair. Held in July around the feast day of St James of Compostella (the patron saint of oysters), the opening includes the Landing of the Oyster Ceremony and the Oyster Parade, as well as walks around the old town (For more on Whitstable, see p82.) *Rye Bay Scallop Festival, various venues Rye, East Sussex (www.ryebayscallops.co.uk); Whitstable Oyster Festival, various venues Whitstable, Kent (01227 862048, www.whitstableoysterfestival.co.uk).*

Totally Tomato Show

Look hard enough and you'll probably find a festival celebrating every kind of fruit and veg in Britain, but we particularly like the sound of the Totally Tomato Show, held in the first weekend of September. More than 150 varieties of tomato are displayed, judged, tasted and cooked in West Dean's walled kitchen garden, where tomato-growing tips and tomato recipe demonstrations are all part of the fun. West Dean Estate is 6,000-acres housing a college, gardens, gallery and tapestry studio, where artists and craftspeople, conservators and restorers work alongside gardeners, farmers, foresters and builders. So you can fill up on culture and nature as well as tomatoes. *West Dean Gardens, West Dean, Chichester, West Sussex PO18 0QZ (01243 818210, www.westdean.org.uk).*

Apple Week

Journeys

FIVE Transport rentals   229
The Bluebell Railway   230
FIVE Scenic drives   233
FIVE Boat trips   234
Blackdown Farm's Rural Rides   235
FIVE Bike rides   239
Beachy Head   243
Hot-air ballooning   246

Camper Vans

Bedfordshire outfit Snail Trail offers new VW Camper Vans shipped in from Brazil, so they're all shiny and smart. Starting at £500 for a week's hire they're equipped with pretty much everything you'll need (even Scrabble!) for a grand road trip, and once you've met Betty, or Pearl, or Matilda, we bet you'll be smitten. *Snail Trail, Edworth, Biggleswade, Bedfordshire SG18 9TJ (01767 600440, www.snailtrail.co.uk).*

Cycling in the New Forest

With more than a 100 miles of traffic-free cycle paths, the New Forest is a terrific place to spend a day on wheels. Brockenhurst, the most central point from which to start a trip, is the base of Cycle Experience, which has tandems (as well as regular bikes, kids trikes, trailers and tag-alongs) for hire at £20 a day. *Cycle Experience, Brookley Road, Brockenhurst, Hampshire SO42 7RR (01590 624204, www.cyclex.co.uk).*

Narrowboats

If Camper Vans and bikes are just too darned speedy, consider the leisurely narrowboat. Lee Valley Boats has a great selection of gorgeous canal and narrowboats for short breaks (2-3 days) or longer, though if you just want to spend a sunny day splashing about on the Thames, *Mr Badger* the day boat might be just the thing. *Lee Valley Boat Centre, Old Nazeing Road, Broxbourne, Hertfordshire EN10 6LX (01992 462085, www.leevalleyboats.co.uk).*

Harley-Davidsons... and other classic bipeds

Renting the ultimate hairy biker wheels costs around £150 a day, but there is life beyond the Harley, particularly at Classic Bike Hire in Surrey, where old-school design fans will love the vintage British bike range. Or why not remake *Quadrophenia* with a Vespa by the sea? At Brighton-based Vroom By The Sea you can rent a classic Vespa from £33 a day. *Classic Bike Hire, c/o FCL Motorcycles, Telford House, Little Mead Industrial Estate, Alford Road, Cranleigh, Surrey GU6 8ND*

(01483 275868, www.classicbikehire.com); Vroom By The Sea, 3A Queens Place, Hove, East Sussex BN3 2LT (01273 772222, www.vroombythesea.com).

Vintage sportscars

The 75 miles you'll have to drive in your own motor to get to Dream Car Hire will make the thrill of the Lamborghini Gallardo Spider or Aston Martin you'll be temporarily swapping it for even greater. These are luxury super cars to live out your James Bond fantasy in, and they don't come cheap; at the lower end of the fantastic range, £350 will buy you a day in a Maserati Gran Turismo. *Dream Car Hire UK, Whitehorse Business Park, Stanford-in-the-Vale, Oxfordshire SN7 8NY (0844 800 0195, 01367 710507, www.dreamcarhire.com).*

JOURNEYS

The Bluebell Railway

Spend a nostalgic day on a toot sweet steam train.

The gently swaying railway carriage. The heartbeat of the wheels (clickety-clack, clickety-clack). The clouds of white steam, puffing past the window. The rattle of teacups in saucers and the oversweet allure of a french fancy. A white-jacketed waiter proffers a laden silver platter before tonging two triangles of crust-free cheese sandwich on to the empty bottom tier of your cake stand.

You could be excused for expecting a flapper in pearls to come bursting through the carriage door, crying 'There's been a murder!', and Poirot himself to suddenly pop up, smoothing the crumbs from his waxed moustache and calling on his 'leetle grey cells'.

But *Murder on the Orient Express* this is not. This is afternoon tea on the Bluebell Railway, a Heritage Steam Railway that pays such close attention to vintage detail (1880 to 1955) that the atmosphere is soaked in the buzz of railway's glory days – a time when your holiday really did start the minute you stepped on the train. From the adverts on the platform to the kind of stuffing in your seat, everything has been researched and finished with OCD levels of attention.

Running along nine miles of restored track between Sheffield Park and Kingscote in Sussex (midway between London and the south coast), on what was once the East Grinstead to Lewes line, the Bluebell Railway (01825 720825, www.bluebell-railway.co.uk) has been providing railway enthusiasts and pleasure-seekers with steam journeys since 1960. Its collection of 30-plus steam 'locos' (as they're affectionately known), many of which are available for viewing in the engine shed, is considered second only to the National Railway Museum itself. (Find out which trains will be running from the website or by phoning the 24-hour timetable information line.)

The railway is run largely by volunteers, and it's these enthusiasts who really make the place special. They're not only dressed for the part, but also full of knowledge: ask them anything about the railway, the train, even your carriage, and they'll gleefully fill you in. Greeting you in the ticket hall is one of the cheerful ticket inspectors, head-to-toe in the traditional uniform of black suit and cap, and white shirt.

And once on the platform, you're no longer in this century: train drivers and firemen in blue, oily overalls shout over the sound of the steam as they top their engine up with water; guards give timetable advice, their silver buttons glittering. And the trains themselves are spectacular – from the gleaming paintwork and shining brass, these are gorgeous feats of engineering and beautiful objects to boot.

The reason for the line's original closure by British Rail back in the 1950s is partly what makes the Bluebell Railway's journey so special: it ran through underpopulated countryside and the route has remained relatively untouched. This means you're travelling through the gently rolling hills of the Weald, through woods and open farmland, past elegant houses and twee cottages, enjoying the same views as people enjoyed more than 100 years ago. Autumn is especially beautiful, partly because of the orange and gold tree canopies along the route and partly because twilight comes earlier, which is especially cosy if you're in one of the fancier carriages. Bluebell season is in May, when you can catch the glorious carpets of blue in woodland glades.

What kind of journey you should take (there are several options) depends on when you come. You can just ride the train (from either Kingscote or Sheffield Park) and enjoy hidden pockets of rural life that can't be seen from anywhere else. Or choose to take elevenses in classic comfort in a meticulously restored Lounge Car, have a cream tea for Mothers' Day or join in on a Family Fun Weekend in June. For the Victorian Christmas service, which runs from Horsted Keynes to Kingscote, you get your own compartment with a hamper and a visit from Santa, and all the stations are clad in wonderfully festive lights. September sees the Victorian Picnic Evening, complete with a music hall show.

The afternoon tea – served at 3pm on weekends through designated months – is enduringly popular. One of the carriages used is the newly restored 1955 First Class 3064 car, with its honey-coloured wood interior; it was once part of the Ocean Liner Express. When you get on board, you'll find yourself ensconced in luxuriously deep, winged seats decorated with a Festival of Britain pattern, and with fresh flowers on the table. The atmosphere isn't at all stuffy or geeky: everyone's relaxed, chatty and friendly, pleased to be out for the day doing something different and memorable.

With a whistle, the train will slowly pull out of the station and the faint smell of steam will

fill your carriage. Everyone on the platform will wave as you leave. And then you're out in open country.

There really is nothing quite like eating a delicate sandwich triangle of ham and mustard while chocolate-box views slide past the window at no more than 25mph. Especially when those sandwiches are served on such a laden cake stand: sandwiches below, stacks of mini-cakes above. By the time you pull into your station, you'll be stuffed and ready for 20 minutes' strolling round the station. Now you can chat to the volunteers and watch as the engine is turned around and the carriages rejoined to take you back down the line.

During the return journey, daylight will fade and your carriage take on a luminous glow. You need do no more than gaze out of the window, imagining a simpler time. And then have another mini-raspberry cream puff.

Even more glamorous are lunch or dinner on the Golden Arrow Pullman Service. For these, the food is served at tables lit by little lamps – perfect for special occasions that require a bit of old-time luxury, perhaps a Valentine's treat or even a wedding reception (Sheffield Park and Horsted Keynes both hold marriage licences). You can even do a breakfast trip at special times of the year. In fact, the Bluebell Railway runs different special events all through the year, from Vintage Buses to Lounge Car Weekenders, so ask them what's happening – and book well in advance.

Getting to the Bluebell Railway can be a bit of an adventure too – take the train to East Grinstead and jump on the 473 bus to Kingscote station. If it's a bank holiday or you're coming on a Special Event weekend, the 473 becomes the Grenested Rambler, which means you can stop off at Standen, a National Trust property just outside East Grinstead. Built in the Arts and Crafts style by William Morris's friend Philip Webb, and decorated throughout by Morris himself, the house has a beautiful hillside garden with lovely walks. Those with their own wheels head for the main Sheffield Park station (Kingscote's inaccessible to cars) and, while there, can take in gorgeous Sheffield Park, renowned for its Capability Brown landscaping.

And if you always dreamed of being a train driver, volunteers are always welcome. You can work your way from Cleaner through the grades to Fireman, then Passed Fireman, to finally become a fully fledged Driver. How about that to add to your CV?

FIVE Steam railways

Bredgar & Wormshill Light Railway
Privately owned and run by a group of friends since 1970, Bredgar & Wormshill is now open to the public on the first Sunday of each month during the summer. Running from Warren Wood station near Sittingbourne, Kent to Wormshill, the railway threads through delightful woodland.
01622 884254, www.bwlr.co.uk.

Chinnor & Princes Risborough Railway
This 1870s line takes you on a picturesque seven-mile journey through the Chiltern Hills and the Vale of Aylesbury between April and October. Families get involved when, among other special events, Thomas makes an appearance.
01844 353535, www.cprra.co.uk.

Epping & Ongar Railway
Built as part of the Great Eastern Railway in 1865, Epping & Ongar Railway now runs through six miles of Essex countryside, alongside the beautiful Essex Way. The line is easily accessible by Central Line tube to Epping, followed by a Vintage Bus Link (operating only when special events are on).
01277 365200, www.eorailway.co.uk.

Lavender Line
At just a mile long and open only on Sundays and bank holidays, the Lavender Line offers an endearing 15-minute journey to Little Horsted in East Sussex. It's only half an hour's drive from the Bluebell line, and there's a decent pub next door to the departure station.
01825 750515, www.lavender-line.co.uk.

Romney, Hythe & Dymchurch Railway
Even though its scale engines are only a third the size of your average steam loco, the miniature RHDR covers a hefty 13.5 miles of narrow-gauge line between Hythe and Dungeness (*see p73*) in Kent. The line has been in operation since 1927.
01797 362353, www.rhdr.org.uk.

FIVE Scenic drives

Chiltern Hills

Let the A40 sweep you out of London to journey north through the Chiltern Hills. Exit for the market town of Wendover (A413) near the Prime Minister's country residence, Chequers. Heading to Dunstable, cruise past cyclists tackling some of the South East's most challenging peaks as you relax behind four wheels on winding country roads (B4009 then B489). Dunstable itself is a market town with an Augustinian priory church of St Peter founded by Henry I in 1131 (only the original nave remains). It was here, in 1533, that the annulment of Henry VIII's marriage to Catherine of Aragon was announced and, in the subsequent separation of the Church of England from the Roman Catholic Church, and the Dissolution of the Monasteries, the Augustinians were evicted.
Dunstable via Wendover 1 hour, 30 minutes, 50 miles.

Dungeness

Appledore, Snargate, Brenzett – no, this isn't the road to the home of Bilbo Baggins, but the delightful country route (B2080) through the garden of England to Dungeness (*see p73*). Tiny villages with duck ponds and post offices you want to fight for dot the journey through swathes of Kent farmland. The drive ends on a huge, desolate, shingle beach housing Derek Jarman's eerily beautiful garden (*see p73 and p151 Five Works of art*). Dungeness Point didn't exist 1,000 years ago but, over the years, longshore drift has built up banks of flint shingle (57 feet deep in places) that stretch miles out to sea in a unique promontory on which a lighthouse offers superb views for those prepared to climb the 169 steps.
Dungeness 2 hours, 77 miles.

North Kent coast

With few roads hugging the North Kent coast, the local ones connecting Whitstable, Herne Bay and Reculver are a real treat. The stretch out of the coastal fishing town of Whitstable (*see p82*) offers expansive sea views. On your way out of Whitstable, don't miss the tiny turning for Reculver; here history meets modernity – a Roman fort, built around 180 AD, looks out to offshore wind farms. The Reculver coastline is also where Barnes Wallis secretly tested his famous 'bouncing bomb' (as immortalised in the film *The Dambusters*). Stop off at Herne Bay to admire the world's first freestanding clocktower, erected in 1837.
Reculver 1 hour, 35 minutes, 67 miles.

South Downs

Head to Ditchling Beacon in East Sussex (A23), where you can drive up and over one of the South Downs' highest points. Ditchling Beacon is along the South Downs Way – a 100-mile-long trail from Winchester, as far as Eastbourne, which follows the old routes along the chalk escarpment. The hill fort site takes its name as one of the places where beacons were set and ready to light as a warning of imminent invasion. A narrow, winding country lane off a blink-and-you-miss-it turning (Beacon Road off B2112) makes for an exhilarating, steep drive ascending the chalk hill as the splendour of the Downs are revealed below. In the summer, the chalky grassland of the Downs is rich with flora and fauna, including the chalkhill blue butterfly.
Ditchling Beacon 1 hour, 20 minutes, 50 miles.

Surrey Hills

For a jaunt through the breathtaking Surrey Hills – designated an Area of Outstanding Natural Beauty – take the A3 (exit Ripley). Drive through Clandon and down over Newlands Corner to enjoy the serene countryside of rolling chalk downs, flower-covered grass- and heathland, and dense woodlands full of yew and box. Descend to Silent Pool, spotting kingfishers in the blue-green spring water. Carry on to the picture-perfect village of Shere to finish with a lemonade (for the designated driver) or a pint of real ale in the 15th-century White Horse (Middle Street). For further information on attractions, details of pretty villages and suggestions for itineraries, see the Visit Surrey website (www.visitsurrey.com).
Shere 1 hour, 32 miles.

JOURNEYS

FIVE Boat trips

Hire a launch at Henley

Get your straw boater and blazer out and join the toffs on Regatta day for a duck's eye view of the action. Or just cruise down the reach in your Edwardian-style motor-launch and admire some of the best real estate in the country. *Also see p58.*
Hobbs of Henley, Station Road, Henley-on-Thames, Oxfordshire RG9 1AZ (01491 572035, www.hobbs-of-henley.com).

Join the crew of the Leopard 3 racing yacht

Feel the wind in your hair and the salt on your skin during a breathtaking high-speed race on board the *Leopard 3*. Be prepared for a serious adrenalin rush – this is one of the most technologically advanced yachts on the water.
Leopard 3, Ocean Village Marina, 2 Channel Way, Southampton, Hampshire SO14 3TG (0238 022 0388, www.leopard3.com).

Punt in Stratford-upon-Avon

Arm yourself with a copy of the sonnets and a picnic and head off past the Royal Shakespeare Theatre, the church that contains Shakespeare's tomb and some beautiful parks and gardens. Stop for lunch beneath the willows on the grassy banks and let the Bard do the rest.
Avon Boating, The Boathouse, Swan's Nest Lane, Stratford-upon-Avon, Warwickshire CV37 7LS (01789 267073, www.avon-boating.co.uk).

See the White Cliffs of Dover at sea

A great trip for kids, who are allowed to take the helm and steer this 70-seater passenger boat themselves (under the captain's supervision). There are stunning views of the port, the castle and cliffs, and the commentary fills you in on the colourful history of one of Britain's busiest shipping ports.
Dover White Cliffs Tours, 3 Lawrence Close, Folkstone, Kent CT19 4BA (01303 271388, www.doverwhiteclifftours.com).

Take a narrowboat to Hungerford, returning from Hilperton

Worried about your carbon footprint? Hiring a canal boat is one of the greenest

Leopard 3 racing yacht

holidays out there, and it's a fun option for families or groups. Sit back with a glass of wine and cruise through the lush Wiltshire countryside with nothing but the sound of the ducks to disturb you. Pass by the Savernake Forest, an ancient woodland mentioned in the Domesday Book.
UK Boat Hire, PO Box 232, Worcester WR1 2SD (0845 126 4098, www.ukboathire.com).

Blackdown Farm's Rural Rides

Saddle up in the Sussex countryside.

Few activities can banish city blues faster than a day's horseriding, inhaling the pastoral perfume of leather, sweet hay and friendly beasts. Riding in London, however, tends to be of the jump-on, jump-off variety and full of repetitive circuits. Even outside the city, riding schools are often limited to taking clients out on whatever land they may own due to the insurance premiums involved in taking riders out on the roads. Blackdown Farm Riding Club (50 minutes from Waterloo, then a short taxi ride) is unusual in being able to offer riders plenty of off-road hacking, so that you get all the exhilaration of charging about the countryside, but with someone else doing the legwork.

Situated on an 800-acre farm near the Sussex village of Fernhurst, on the wooded slopes of the Western Weald, the club offers unrivalled access to two of the region's highlights: the National Trust land belonging to the beautiful ruins of the Cowdray Estate, and nearby Blackdown, the second highest point in the South East. On a clear day, views stretch 40 miles across Ashdown Forest, the South Downs and, if you know where to look, the sea. No wonder Tennyson built a house at its windswept peak.

JOURNEYS

The club encourages riders to arrive early to groom, tack up and become acquainted with their steeds, during which time keen endurance rider and club founder Joyce Whatley can explain how she runs the show. Fully approved by the British Horse Society, Blackdown doesn't generally offer lessons, instead taking keen riders out along the Sussex Border Path on weekly one- to three-hour hacks (costing from £30/hr), or full-day summer rides with a picnic or pub lunch en route. Activities for total novices are run on an ad hoc basis, and groups can arrange to perhaps combine a lesson with an hour's hack, but, with some seriously fit ex-competitors of both the horse and human variety, Blackdown is geared to those with at least some experience of riding – and frequently

those returning to riding after a break. 'It seems to have become something of a speciality for us,' says Whatley's daughter Clare. 'Some of our clients are mothers who no longer have the time or the money to have their own horse, others rode as teenagers but now live in the city; they just jump on the 8am train from London.'

Safety is the number one priority, so forget hanging on and hoping for the best – this isn't a sport for blaggers. New riders must sign a form clearly outlining their level of competence. 'We have people who come with a "can do" attitude, ticking every box on the sheet, and within five minutes it's obvious they can't even do a rising trot,' sighs Joyce. Be upfront and they'll do their best to match you with people of the same level.

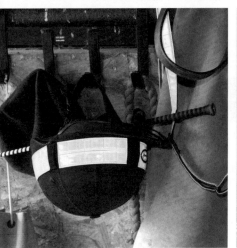

Boxes ticked and steed mounted, this is an unbeatable way to experience the local scenery. Our hack took us along a little path around a lake, skirted a field of crops, then set off at a smart trot uphill and on to the woodland bridleway, flush with oaks and chestnuts in glorious autumnal technicolour. The crisp air and the smell of hoof-churned leaves and mud was an invigorating combination and we managed a decent climb from which we took in fabulous views of our progress.

'You should see this wood in summer,' a fellow rider commented. 'It's a sea of bluebells – absolutely beautiful.' Then with a squeeze of the heels, we were off at a bracing canter, dodging low-hanging branches as we go. The thrill banishes London stresses in seconds.

For some post-riding refreshment, head to Fernhurst's friendly, low-beamed Red Lion (The Green, GU27 3HY, 01428 643112) or the cosy Royal Oak in nearby Critchmere (Critchmere Hill, GU27 1LS, 01428 642328).

And for a full day's activity without the exertion of a full day's ride, try out some of the area's nearby attractions after your hack. The pretty town of Midhurst or the baronial Tudor ruins of Cowdray are both worth a look, and there are plenty of proper country pubs where you can stretch out those aching thighs.

Blackdown Farm Riding Club
Lower House Farm, Ropes Lane, Fernhurst, West Sussex GU27 3JD (01428 654106, www.ruralridesuk.co.uk).

Discover the city from your back pocket

Essential for your weekend break, 25 top cities available.

POCKET SIZED *from* £6.99

FIVE Bike rides

Lewes to Alfriston

This 17-mile circular route follows the windswept spine of the South Downs into the charming village of Alfriston, and back along the Old Coach Road, taking in some lovely country pubs along the way. It's a thrilling ride of two halves. It starts off serenely enough as you meander along deserted country roads out of the ancient town of Lewes (see p35; Romans were there long before its famous castle was built in 1087), and onwards through sheep pastures and corn fields, until, jutting steeply out of the gently rippling landscape, is Firle Beacon – and everything changes. After a calf-crunching ascent of the chalk scarp, there are challenging singletracks, jarring open Downland, twisting downhills, killer uphills and technical side trips. It's a hoot.

To get to the start, hop on a train from London Victoria (one hour) then turn left out of Lewes Station. Turn immediately right on to Priory Street, past Anne of Cleves house, bearing left until you cross a bridge over the A27. The lanes through Ilford and Rodmell are usually deserted. At the Southease crossroads turn left and cross the River Ouse and a railway line.

Follow the signs for the South Downs Way up a strenuous ascent to Itford Hill and on to Firle Beacon. The views across the tumbling South Downs, and the English Channel on the southern horizon, are outstanding. It's fairly flat up here, but remember chalk is like ice when wet and you'll need a mountain bike or very sturdy hybrid. At the second car park at Bostal Hill, head south and fork left. Here the fun really starts with the endless descent into Alfriston, zig-zagging across open chalkland, jumping warrens and skipping around sheep, before flying into a jolting singletrack through the gnarly woods and into the quaint village of Alfriston. Stop for a snack on the green in front of the 14th-century Clergy House, or a pint in Ye Olde Smugglers Inne (Waterloo Square, 01323 870241), a former hide-out of the Stanton Collins smuggling gang (they also stole the Red Lion head from a ship that now stands outside the Star Inn).

At the market cross, bear left and continue up a narrowing lane and the beginning of the Old Coach Road. Although the road is largely paved, it's in disrepair and can be very muddy in places – water-filled potholes have claimed a few casualties. It's a thrilling, fast and undulating ride to Firle's Ram Inn (The Street, 01273 858222), a 16th-century coaching inn, with excellent food. Head back to Lewes, briefly along the busy A27, before turning right into Glynde, and left along Ranscombe Lane to Lewes. There are plenty of great pubs there, but the bohemian Snow Drop Inn (South Street, 01273 471018) is fairly used to hungry mud-splattered cyclists popping in – and, yes, you will be mud-splattered.

Chalk & Channel Way
This excellent four-mile route, created by sustainable transport charity Sustrans (www.sustrans.org.uk), runs along the cliff tops between Dover and Folkestone and can be completed either way round. We recommend catching the Charing Cross train to Dover and starting here where the sharp incline – as you leave the town and head for the hill – is marginally less

challenging than starting from Folkestone. Even so, many a cyclist has found there's no shame in hailing a black cab to ferry them and their bikes to Crete Road East to start there; from here the terrain is dirt track for most of the way. Watch for the occasional headwind as you follow the foot and cycle path westward. On a clear day you can see France shimmering in the distance. Enjoy the stunning views over tea and cakes at the Cliff Top Café (Old Dover Road, 01303 255588) before joining the North Downs Way footpath.

Take the signposted detour down to Samphire Hoe where you dismount and pass through a tunnel to reach arguably the youngest patch of English soil, a nature reserve tucked against the white cliffs created out of fill from the Channel Tunnel excavations. Along the route watch out for the open-air sculptures that are part of the Art & Travelling Landscape permanent exhibition commissioned by Sustrans. Most stunning is John Easterby and Pippa Taylor's *Samphire Tower* – a 33-foot oak and larch structure reminiscent of a wood-panelled lighthouse. Sound installations complement the artwork – dial the access number supplied and listen on your mobile to Ros Barber's poems about the area. Joining the road as you pass Capel le Ferne you then head towards Folkestone. Freewheel down the hill into town and don't stop until you reach the creative quarter near the harbour. Check out the Whole World Café (41 The Old High Street, 01303 246999) for organic pizza and chocolate cake before catching the train from Folkstone back to Charing Cross. See the Sustrans website for more information.

Along the River Lea

This laid-back Sunday afternoon ride takes you along the River Lea's towpath between Lea Bridge lock heading north-east to the Waltham Town Lock out towards Enfield. It's one of Greater London's more bucolic waterways, with a surprising variety of changing countryside and urbanscape. Flat and quiet for most of the way, its 13 miles make a ride that's ideal for a family with older children.

Your ride starts in beautiful Springfield Park, east London's hidden gem of Victorian landscaping. Test your mettle against the sharp but short incline up to Spark Café (www.sparkcafe.co.uk, no phone) and bolster yourself with a hearty breakfast before setting off.

Head to the far north-east entrance to the park and cross the bridge over the river to reach the towpath. The River Lea is one of the Thames' major tributaries – even once used by Vikings – and various acts of parliament have ensured its usability via the installation of locks. Bordered to the east by the Lee Valley reservoir and nature estate, the river is as much a thoroughfare for the abundance of wildlife as the canal boats on moorings lining the water's edge. As well as moorhens, swans and ducks, you're likely to see gaggles of geese, bitterns and even the odd kingfisher if you're lucky.

The cycling surface is largely smooth but past Tottenham Lock loose gravel can make it somewhat skiddy, especially if you're on road tyres rather than mountain bike tyres. Once past Tottenham Lock you head through a bit of an industrial wasteland, characterised by gas works and the backside of the Edmonton IKEA, but about a mile past here the grey buildings fade into the distance and you're soon streaming past sheep grazing on the steep bank of the William Girling Reservoir.

Past Enfield Lock the towpath crosses over to the left bank and the track becomes a fairly rough dirt track. Crossing back over at the Hazlemere Bridge you come to a long boat club – though you technically need to be a member, a winning smile might bag you a cold pint on a hot summer's day. Once that's downed you can turn tail and head home.

Tonbridge Castle to Penshurst Place

Less than an hour out of London, this fairytale-esque five-mile ride, taking in castles, forests and lakes, will have you questioning why you've left it so long to take your bike out of the capital. Created by Sustrans, the route is well signposted with blue Regional Cycle Route 12 signs and follows cycle paths and tracks for the majority of the way.

Catch the train from Charing Cross to Tonbridge train station, then head left from here along the high street to reach Tonbridge Castle (01732 770929, www.tonbridgecastle.org) on Castle Road. You can take an hour or so to explore this medieval motte and bailey castle, or head straight on with the journey. At the outer reaches of town the ride starts to blossom into countryside as you pass playing fields and head into the Haysden Country Park. This expansive nature reserve is brimming with waterfowl clustered around the two lakes and wildflowers, with a few great picnic areas thrown in for good measure. The best is yet to come, though. Once you've passed beneath the A12, you turn right then left to cycle into a magical wood filled with coppiced trees, butterflies and various species of bird. Those who visit in springtime will also be rewarded with a carpet of pink and yellow stitchwort, clover and buttercups.

Cycling on beyond here following the River Medway's broad flank, you reach the ride's only real climb, which comes between the bridge over the River Medway and Well Place Farm. Adult cyclists will conquer this with ease, younger ones might want to get off and walk. Pause at the summit to admire the surrounding countryside before freewheeling down past two lakes to arrive at Penshurst Place (01892 870307, www.penshurstplace.com). There's £1 off the entrance fee for anyone arriving by bike to this rather splendid medieval mansion and grounds. You can picnic here or head a couple of minutes up the road into Penshurst itself and have a well-earned pint at the Leicester Arms (High Street, 01892 870551, www.leicesterarmspenshurst. co.uk). Those up for more action can press on to the Penshurst Off Road Cycling Centre (01892 870136) in Viceroys Wood nearby; everyone else can catch the train back to Charing Cross from Penshurst station. See www.sustrans. org.uk for further information and maps.

A day on the B184

The A13, linking the city to Southend and immortalised in song by Billy Bragg, is often considered the archetypal Essex road: flat, featureless and unremittingly grey. Such a belief, however, is merely to confirm the stereotype of this much-maligned county. Away from its metropolitan fringe, Essex is largely agricultural and surprisingly picturesque. And cycling along the B184 is a great way to discover its unseen character. The road runs from High Ongar, just beyond the M25, to Great Chesterford on the Cambridgeshire border, a distance of 32 miles. If you can't manage the full distance in a day, there are two options.

One option is to take your bike on the overground stretch of the tube to Epping and connect to the Epping Ongar Railway (www.eorailway.co.uk), which chugs for six miles along a single-track line. From Ongar it's an easy ride into the Rodings – Abbess, Aythorpe, Beauchamp, Berners, High, Leaden, Margaret and White: eight hamlets and villages, all with unassuming churches to mooch around and, at Aythorpe Roding, an 18th-century windmill open on the last Sunday of each month from April to September. There's usually tea and cakes available in the village hall, or if you need something a bit more sustaining, the nearby 17th-century Axe & Compasses (Dunmow Road, 01279 876648, www.theaxeandcompasses.co.uk) was voted best traditional pub at the 2008 Essex Food & Drink Awards.

Alternatively, catch the train from Liverpool Street to Great Chesterford, and pedal into Saffron Walden. The conservation area in this unspoilt market town boasts every style of architecture from the 12th century onwards. There's also the largest turf maze in England, plenty of boutique-style shopping, and the Fry Art Gallery (Castle Street, 01799 513779, www.fryartgallery.org) featuring many of the artists who were part of the community that flourished in and around the nearby village of Great Bardfield before and after World War II.

A short ride away is the English Heritage-owned Audley End House (see p129), a spectacular Jacobean mansion boasting sumptuous Adam interiors and Capability Brown-designed grounds.

Head on to Thaxted and enjoy its 600-year-old guildhall, opulent parish church, windmill and almshouses. This lovely village is the home of the Thaxted Morris Men (www.thaxtedmorris.org), founded in 1911 as part of the reawakening interest in ancient folk customs and the oldest 'side' in England.

The other major cultural contribution to come from Thaxted is the annual music festival (19 June-12 July, 2009; 01371 831421, www.thaxtedfestival.org.uk). Started in 1916 by Gustav Holst – who composed 'The Planets Suite' while living in a cottage in Monk Street – it attracts leading classical performers. With plenty of pubs and tearooms to choose from, Thaxted makes an ideal stopping point on this two-wheeled tour of unexpected Essex.

JOURNEYS

Beachy Head

A walk that's as beautiful as it is precipitous.

Geography lessons are three-dimensional for the children of Eastbourne. Within seven miles of the town are Britain's highest chalk cliff, meandering rivers, woodland and, yes, even longshore drift and ox-bow lakes. History comes alive for them here too. On field trips to the South Downs, they can see 3,000-year-old burial sites, known as tumuli, and Iron Age farmsteads, and hear stories about smugglers. Even without the local history, though, there's interest and amusement to be had from nearby places with names like Crapham Bottom and Butt's Brow, which are in turn surrounded by plants with names like squinancywort and bastard toadflax.

The rolling chalk cliffs of the Seven Sisters and Beachy Head are the finest examples of chalk downland in Britain, and make a wonderful day excursion across some of the loveliest landscape in the country. Strictly speaking, the Seven Sisters stretch west from Birling Gap to the Cuckmere Haven, but it would be a shame to miss the charming seaside town of Eastbourne (a scenic 90-minute journey from London Victoria) and, especially, Beachy Head.

This nine-mile hike passes Beachy Head and its candy-striped lighthouse, continues along the chalk tops of the Seven Sisters to the meandering river of Cuckmere Haven at Exceat, and goes on, through Friston Forest, past a fine country pub. From here, regular buses run back to the starting point of Eastbourne station. The whole walk takes around three to four hours, but it can be easily shortened if time is tight or you get waylaid in a pub.

Approaching Eastbourne by train, the South Downs rise sharply out of the gentle green waves of the Weald. On leaving the station, turn left and follow Terminus Road until you hit the sea. To the east is the pier and to the west the foot of the Downs. Walk along the upper path of the promenade, passing the Victorian hotels and Napoleonic Wish Tower, as far as St Bede's School. Here the Downs begin in dramatic form with a steep 460-foot climb – take care if it's been raining, since chalk can be like ice when it's wet. During the summer, adults often trudge up the hill, while children enthusiastically run up and roll down, again and again and again. Still, once you've toiled to the top, you can take a well-earned breather. As you do, turn around and enjoy the magnificent view of Eastbourne, Bexhill, Hastings and, on a clear day, Dungeness. All manner of vessels can be seen to the south in the English Channel and to the west you can see the chalk grasslands of Beachy Head and the Seven Sisters. Climb on towards a communication tower by the pub at the hill's brow.

From here on, ash, hawthorn and gorse are permanently doubled at right angles because of the continuous south-westerly wind that ravages the Downs. Few solitary trees are able to survive the storms that hit the coast, but below knee-height is robust flora such as round-headed rampion and the rainbow colours of milkwort, which bloom during summer and attract silver-spotted skippers and adonis blue butterflies. As autumn approaches, the blackberry and raspberry bushes are laden. More than 20 types of orchid have also been found in the area.

Beachy Head is the most crowded part of the walk. During summer, holidaymakers fly kites, bring picnic hampers and get precariously close to the 530-foot drop into the English Channel, while thrillseekers throw themselves off the cliff with hang-gliders tied to their backs. This landmark has also attracted such illustrious visitors as George Orwell, Claude Debussy, Karl Marx and Friedrich Engels; the latter loved the place so much that he requested his ashes be tipped over Beachy Head. You might recognise the area from scenes in *Atonement*, *Harry Potter & the Goblet of Fire* and *Quadrophenia*. It's most famous, however, as a suicide spot, hence the sombre sign for the Samaritans next to the phone box. Take extreme care here: every year several people are either blown off the top or fall when a soft chalk overhang crumbles beneath their feet. The ledge is receding at about 16 inches a year (in Bronze Age times the edge would have been more than a mile closer to France) and the council gave up replacing most fences years ago, so keep children and dogs close.

From Beachy Head, wander down to Birling Gap, where there's an unremarkable pub and tearoom (and a car park). Skip them and follow the white path from Belle Tout lighthouse, walking to East Dean and the Tiger Inn, an 11th-century pub on a village green that serves good food and well-kept Harveys, a local beer. (If the pub proves more alluring than the rest of the walk, a regular bus heads through the village back to Eastbourne.)

FIVE Interesting walks

Cambridge
If you've always wanted to explore the architecture of this university city, go online first for a selection of interesting options. Shape Walks has a range of themed podcasts and MP3 guides to take you round the city, as well as maps to print off marked with all the places of interest. The themes include 'contemporary architecture', 'historic highlights', 'green spaces' and more esoteric delights like 'clocks and sundials'. *www.stridedesign.com/projects.html.*

Clacton-on-Sea to Walton-on-the-Naze, Essex
Seven gentle and pretty miles of coastline, with plenty of swimming and picnicking opportunities, a lovely peninsula at the Naze and a hearty lunch stop at the Oakwood Inn (175 Frinton Road, 01255 812209), about three miles from the start of the walk. Download a PDF with walk instructions and details from the Walking Club website. *www.walkingclub.org.uk/book_3/walk_52/index.shtml.*

Hastings to Rye
Take in one Cinque port and two ancient towns on this six-hour, 12-mile walk. A strenuous start, heading east from Hastings along the coastal path, brings you to Pett Level. From there, the going gets a lot easier for a few miles before the ascent to Winchelsea, a picture-postcard tea stop. Continuing east, you'll be rewarded with terrific views over Romney Marsh and the Kent Downs, before descending for an easy stroll to Rye. This is just one of many walks in volumes one and two of *Time Out Country Walks*. *www.walkingclub.org.uk/book_2/walk_29/index.shtml.*

Ivinghoe Beacon, Bucks
At more than 800 feet above sea level, Ivinghoe Beacon makes for a strenuous but exhilarating three- or four-hour walk in the Chiltern Hills, along the end of the Ridgeway Path. Watch out for low-flying aircraft: keen model-makers flock here to 'slope soar' elaborate aeroplanes from the top. Park in the pretty village of Aldbury, then make your breathless way up to the Beacon through the lovely Ashridge Estate, stopping to admire the Vale of Aylesbury spread out below. *For more details, see Duncan Unsworth's Walking in the Chilterns.*

White Cliffs of Dover
A walk of four miles along the spectacular cliffs of the Kent coast, starting at the Langdown Cliffs and ending at the historic South Foreland Lighthouse, built in 1843 and the site of the first international radio broadcast. As well as providing stunning views across the English Channel, this walk is great for wildlife: in summer it's easy to spot Exmoor ponies grazing on the grass and hundreds of butterflies. Less easy to spot, but thrilling for plant fans, is the rare early spider orchid, which appears in spring only on the south coast. *Download the walk, part of the Neptune series of coastal walks, from www.nationaltrust.org.uk.*

Up the path to the right of the Birling Gap Hotel you'll enter Crowlink, and head up to the first of the Seven Sisters. This designated Area of Outstanding Natural Beauty is the only protected coastline along the south-east coast. The seven peaks and troughs here were first named in the 1588 Mariners Mirrour, the first set of charts engraved in England. The seven are Went Hill Brow, Baily's Hill, Flagstaff Point, Brass Point, Rough Brow, Short Brow and Haven Brow. Occasionally, the subtle Flat Hill is recognised – but the Eight Sisters obviously didn't have the same ring to it.

On the eastern slope of Baily's Hill is an obelisk built by WA Robertson, who donated the land to the National Trust in memory of his brothers who died in the Somme. A more ancient reminder can also be made out here: an unnatural mound at the top of Baily's Hill is one of the thousands of tumuli that dot the South Downs and its Ordnance Survey maps. Although the South Downs have been inhabited for more than 6,000 years, these burial sites were first used around 2,000 BC, when the first agricultural farmsteads were built. This was also when sheep farming (still the main form of agriculture in the area) led to the decimation of the forest, creating the scrub and chalkland we see today. Continuing over the undulating grassland, kittiwakes and jackdaws can often be seen flitting around their cliffside nests, while skylarks, wheatear and the lovely meadow pipits choose to make their home among the shrubs. Kestrels hover in the air before they swoop down on some unsuspecting field mouse, and sparrowhawks and peregrine falcons can often be seen hunting small birds.

Climbing over the final hill – Haven Brow, with splendid 360° views – the habitat changes dramatically. The Cuckmere Haven is a shallow tidal estuary that attracts waders such as ringed plover and dunlin, as well as oystercatchers, kingfishers and geese. A canal, cut in 1847, can be seen on the far side of the valley, while the meandering 'river' is actually a lake, preserved in its original shape. (There are plans to flood the valley again, returning it to its natural saltmarsh.)

From the top of Haven Brow, follow the gentle slope inland until you reach an easy-access trail (good for wheelchairs, pushchairs and bikes) that leads along the river, across a road, and into the visitors' centre (open daily April to October, weekends only November to March). A welcome café serves cream teas and, across the bridge, the Golden Galleon pub is popular with coach parties in summer. From here, buses back to Eastbourne pass four times an hour, but we suggest a further walk in Friston Forest, through the village of Westdean to Litlington. From the duck pond in Westdean (a village that's almost cringeworthily quaint) you can follow the signs to Jevington if you fancy walking the four hours back to Eastbourne. If you don't, follow the South Downs Way through the dense forest for a mile and a half. Past Charleston Manor, you'll see a White Horse carved into the chalk valley opposite. Then it's straight through the door of the Plough & Harrow (01323 870632) in Litlington, where you can order a pint of Harveys and a ploughman's, sit down and reflect on a great day out.

Hot-air ballooning

Floating baskets and champagne landings.

You've walked in it, driven around it, and taken the train through it; now try sailing over it. A flight in a hot-air balloon over the Home Counties' countryside is a unique way to reconnect with the scenery of the South East. The tranquillity of floating along, suspended from a brightly coloured silk balloon, is disturbed only by the occasional dragon's roar and whoosh of the flame that keeps you afloat. While you drift, there's nothing to do but take in the view as the wind decides your course.

A stately ascent over Kent affords stunning coastal views, not only of the county itself but north to Essex and east to Sussex. On a clear day, France and the distant beacon of Canary Wharf can also be seen. Dozens of companies are ready to whisk you skywards – though to avoid adverse weather conditions and ensure vehicles don't get stuck in soggy fields, most companies only fly from April to October.

One of our favourite operators is Kent Ballooning, run by a husband and wife team. Of its seven launch sites across the county (which the pilot chooses from on the day, according to the wind), possibly the most coveted is the centre of Canterbury, where you ascend over the cathedral and soar above the historical World Heritage Site. If you have your own sufficiently sizeable patch of land, it may even be possible to set off from your back garden.

The Kent countryside changes dramatically with the seasons. In May, yellow fields of rapeseed spread out beneath you in a bright patchwork; in September, autumn leaves form great swathes of red and gold. Any time of year is great for trying to spot wildlife from a bird's eye view.

Subject to weather conditions, most flights take place at sunset and sunrise, when winds are most calm. For early risers a morning flight is a delight, as you see the model village-like world below slowly waking up – but if you're driving down from London and prefer a later start, descending through the colour-washed sunset sky is unforgettable.

When the pilot finds a suitable landing spot and you come back down to earth, you'll toast your sail with a glass of champagne – a tradition dating from the Montgolfier brothers' first balloon flight in the late 18th century. A Land Rover then picks you up and returns you to the launch site.

Flight vouchers are available for regular flights (£125-£150); chartered flights for larger groups can also be arranged. The VIP package for a flight for two (£550) is popular with couples about to pop the question.

MORE FLIGHTS

If you fancy heading west, HOT Balloons (01491 574101, www.henleyballoons.com) flies from Henley-on-Thames, offering views down the river, and from Oxford, where you float over the dreaming spires. Balloon Safaris (0800 700007, www.balloonsafaris.co.uk) also flies from nine sites near London, all just ten minutes by car from a train station, with the most popular being over the Sussex Downs. But whichever county you choose, flying high and without wings will be the most serene way to see it.

Kent Ballooning

Yew Trees Studio, Stanford North, Ashford, Kent TN25 6DH (0800 032 5060, www.kent ballooning.com). Open Apr-Oct sunrise-sunset.

Children

TEN Theme parks and adventure playgrounds	251
Hayling Island	255
Hollycombe Steam Fair	256
FIVE Animal adventures	258
Roald Dahl Museum & Story Centre	260
FIVE Model villages	262
The Lodge	264
FIVE Mazes	266
The Living Rainforest	267

Make the most of London life

Canterbury Tales

Chaucer's characters are alive and well and living in animatronic form in the Canterbury Tales attraction in – where else – Canterbury. You first meet the pilgrims at the Tabard Inn, where, clad in the requisite wimples and cloaks, they prepare for their journey to the tomb of 'hooly blissful martyr' Thomas à Becket in Canterbury Cathedral. On the road you hear several of their lively tales, accompanied by suitable sounds, smells and special effects (the bum out the window effect for the Miller's Tale is particularly popular with younger visitors), before finally reaching your destination: a reconstruction of the shrine of St Thomas. (For information on shopping in Canterbury, see p42.)

St Margaret's Church, St Margaret's Street, Canterbury, Kent CT1 2TG (01227 479227, www.canterburytales.org.uk). Open 10am-5pm daily except 25-26 Dec & 1 Jan. Admission £5.75-£7.75.

Chessington World of Adventures & Zoo

Chessington seems to work on the Ben & Jerry's theory of production – cram as many different treats into one pot and come up with a winning formula. So, as the name suggests, Chessington World of Adventures & Zoo is not just an interactive zoo, but also incorporates four levels of adventure rides, from Beanoland to the Forbidden Kingdom, plus a spanking new Sealife centre with a 250,000-litre aquarium stocked with shrimps, clownfish, sharks and stingrays. The Trail of the Kings is a zoological highlight, with Asiatic lions, binturongs, gorillas and Sumatran tigers, though smaller kids might prefer petting the skunks and pygmy goats in the children's zoo.

Leatherhead Road, Chessington, Surrey KT9 2NE (0870 999 0045, www.chessington.com). Open Phone or see website for details. Admission £7.50-£12.

Thorpe Park. See p254.

CHILDREN

**Chessington World of
Adventures & Zoo. See p251.**

Dickens World

It seems strange that it took until 2007 for Dickens World to come into existence – the author's characters and novels are so perfect for a theme park you'd think it would have been dreamed up long ago. Dickens World may not go so far as to re-enact the great man's most memorable scenes but it does lovingly recreate his characters and locations with animatronics and actors, complete with ramshackle clapboard buildings and peopled with a cast of pickpockets, barmaids, flower sellers, policemen and rat-catchers. Visitors can take a peek at a traditional schoolroom in the style of Dotheboys Hall, be mildly frightened by the ghosts in Ebenezer Scrooge's house and recreate Magwitch's ill-fated escape in the Great Expectations boat ride.
Leviathan Way, Chatham Maritime, Kent ME4 4LL (01634 890421, www.dickensworld.co.uk). Open 10am-5.30pm (last entry 4.30pm). Admission £6-£12.

Diggerland

Budding Bob the Builders, *Scrapheap Challenge* fans and anyone who digs diggers and dumpers take note: excavation heaven is here. Gouge enormous holes out of the ground (and fill them in again), drive construction machinery, race JCBs, or watch, bemused, as formation diggers dance to music. Kids can drive bulldozers and dumper trucks, or zoom off on the Young Driver Experience – if they're not swinging in a giant JCB scoop or digging for buried treasure. There are rides for kids as young as two but those out of short trousers needn't miss out: adults, stag (and hen) parties included, can take part in racing 8.5-ton JCBs.
Roman Way, Medway Valley Leisure Park, Strood, Kent ME2 2NU (0870 034 4437, www.diggerland.com). Open Phone or see website for details. Admission £13-£15.

Go Ape Experience

Go Ape's centres give you the chance to express your inner monkey, by swinging from tree to tree for roughly a mile through the tree canopy, using rope bridges, zip slides and Tarzan swings to take you up to the tree tops high above the forest floor. Happily, you're not expected to survive your aerial adventure by a powerful grip and monkey-like agility alone: you'll be fitted with a sturdy safety harness before

setting off. The Surrey site is set in the ancient Alice Holt forest, once adopted by William the Conqueror as a Royal Hunting Forest, while the Crown Estate woodland at Bracknell has a discovery centre with permanent science and nature exhibits. Participants must be at least ten years old.
0845 643 9215, www.goape.co.uk. Open May-Nov; see website for details and prices.

Legoland

Legoland's grounds cover 150 acres and there are over 50 rides and attractions. The best way to squeeze maximum enjoyment out of those 55 million bricks is to visit each attraction in reverse order to cut through the crowds and queues. It seems obvious, yet surprisingly few visitors do it. You'll only have a ten-minute wait for a Wave Surfer soaking. From here hit the Jungle Coaster or whiz round to Pirate Falls for more watery fun; the latter's right next to the Dragon and Dragon's Apprentice rollercoasters. For teenies, there's the Duplo Play Town, though the highlight for discerning adults is Miniland, with its scaled-down but architecturally immaculate landmarks from Europe and the US.
Windsor Park, Winkfield Road, Windsor, Berkshire SL4 4AY (0870 504 0404, www.legoland.co.uk). Open Phone or see website for details. Admission £22-£35.

Lower Leas Coastal Park

A slice of the Riviera in Folkestone, the Lower Leas clifftop promenade is lined with stairways, pathways and Mediterranean style trees and plants among which the smart Victorians and Edwardians used to amble and people-watch. During Folkestone's Victorian and Edwardian heyday as a fashionable resort, the Leas clifftop promenade was the place to see and be seen. Now it has been restored and includes a large children's adventure play area, an amphitheatre and a Sustrans cycle route. In summer this unique setting has a full programme of music, dance and drama.
Folkestone, Kent CT20 2DY (01303 850388, www.kentattractions.co.uk). Open all year. Admission free.

Port Lympne Wild Animal Park

Forget Kenya: a safari experience can be yours for a fraction of the price in Kent, at the Port Lympne Wild Animal Park. Home

to some 650 animals, including the largest breeding herd of black rhinos outside Africa, the park's most exciting option is an overnight safari package. After dinner around the communal campfire and a surprisingly cosy night under canvas (in commodious tents with proper beds), you get to accompany the rangers on a magical dawn safari, getting up close and personal with the park's free-range zebra, giraffe, antelope and wildebeest.
Lympne, nr Hythe, Kent CT21 4PD (01303 264647, www.totallywild.net). Open Summer 10am-6pm (last entry 4.30pm). Winter 10am-5pm (last entry 3.30pm). Admission £9.50-£15.

Thorpe Park
If you fancy a day out getting soaking wet and messing with your inner ear balance then Thorpe Park, with a plethora of vertigo-inducing rides, is just the place for you. Rides are divided into three categories. Extreme Thrills are offered by the Colossus, Thorpe Park's first major white-knuckle ride, which incorporates ten inversions and four corkscrew-like twists in quick succession, and the iconic Stealth – a blink-and-you'll-miss-it 14-second journey that's one of the fastest rides in the country, reaching speeds of 80mph in just two seconds. Those of a gentler disposition can take on the 'Thrilling and Fun' rides and dodge through the simulated white water on the Rumba

Rapids ride. Meanwhile, the 'Young Thrill Seekers' rides like Happy Halibuts and Sea Snakes and Ladders are aimed squarely at the kids.
Staines Road, Chertsey, Surrey KT16 8PN (0870 444 4466, www.thorpepark.co.uk). Open Phone or see website for details. Admission £16-£24.

Wildwood
Wildwood is a delightfully English take on the wildlife park: instead of lions prowling through an ersatz English savannah or monkeys tugging the windscreen wipers off your car, this unique park concentrates on past and present British wildlife all set in 40 acres of ancient Kent woodland. Owls, otters, red squirrels, beavers, wild boar and wolves make up the menagerie of indigenous beasts, and you can also check out a recreated Saxon settlement, learn about woodcraft and Viking folklore and take part in the daily feeding programmes. The park also runs various conservation projects, which are explained in daily talks and regular events. To encourage people to leave their cars at home, entrance is half price to those arriving by bus or train, free if you come by bike.
Herne Common, Herne Bay, Kent CT6 7LQ (0871 782 0081, www.wildwoodtrust.org). Open Summer 10am-6pm daily. Winter 10am-4pm daily. Admission £9.50.

Diggerland. See p253.

CHILDREN

Hayling Island

Time for some old-fashioned seaside fun.

Hayling Island certainly has the goods when it comes to child-friendly summer holiday pastimes. There's the beach, the award-winning donkeys and chips galore, yet it's all pleasingly compact and close enough to the capital to get home in time for bed.

Three miles of Blue Flag beaches are sheltered by the West Winner sandbar, which keeps out rough weather and, it seems, the 21st century too. Most of Hayling's shoreline is shingle – child-heaven for pebble collections, tower construction and stone-skimming contests – but there's no need for the bucket-and-spade brigade to stop reading, since the grassy promenade is peppered with giant sandpits. There are also plenty of climbing frames here (the one at Eastoke makes for a small but satisfyingly challenging obstacle course) and there's also a sandy shore at West Beach (follow signs to Par 3 Golf Course).

Beachlands beach is a great base for a day out on Hayling Island and is home to Funland (www.funland.info), a charmingly small and garish fairground that offers mini versions of almost every type of adult ride. There are rollercoasters, water flumes and even a pirate ship, so your toddler can have as much stomach-churning fun as you can. Prices are reasonable, queues are short and you can walk from one end of the park to the other in five minutes flat.

Opposite Funland await Ollie and Rusty – the Hayling Island Donkeys (www.haylingisland donkeys.co.uk). Ollie was this year awarded 'Most Child Friendly Donkey in the South'. (Rusty was out for snaffling sweets from people's pockets.) Most donkey handlers lead your child in a less than ceremonious ten-yard circle but, for £3, Paul Hunt takes kids on a 200-yard walk, giving them a real opportunity to bond with their steeds.

Lunch is a good time to check out the views on the tourist train to Eastoke. This tiny steam train runs from Funland and hosts regular events such as Santa specials and pirate weekends. Eastoke has a few decent shops and is home to two proper seaside cafés (*see right*). The island's pubs are largely unsatisfactory – either unwelcoming to children or totally formulaic – so enjoy a shandy at Delia's while the kids slurp ice lollies.

Further east is the Sandy Point nature reserve where a wide range of water fowl nest. Join one of the regular informative walks led by a council ranger (www.easthants.gov.uk). Sandy

Point is also home to the island's lifeboat station, which is open to the public every Sunday.

If tales of derring-do appeal, peer out to sea for the Nab Tower – a World War I defence tower, built too late and left out at sea as a lighthouse. Hayling also played a fascinating part in World War II. It kept its lights lit as an effective decoy for Portsmouth, and the mobile harbours for D-Day were built here: one that cracked as it was being towed to France still stands where it was abandoned to the far west of the island.

Visit Hayling at the end of July when the town is decorated for the Scarecrow Festival (www. haylingscarecrows.co.uk). Otherwise, head here as soon as the sun comes out for classic summer holiday fun.

Eating & Drinking

Coastguard Café
14-16 Sea Front, PO11 9HL (02392 463202, www.coastguard-cafe.co.uk). Open Summer 10am-9pm daily. Winter noon-9pm Mon-Fri; 11am-9pm Sat, Sun.
Huge portions of fish and chips followed by freshly made knickerbocker glories are the order of the day at this cosy café. Happy parents kick back with coffee and butterscotch meringues.

Delia's Diner
6-8 Rails Lane, PO11 9LL (02392 469134, www.deliasdiner.co.uk). Open Summer 6.30am-10pm daily. Winter 6.30am-7.30pm daily.
The friendliest staff in Hayling will greet you with hearty fry-ups and kids' meals of fish cakes, chips, peas and ice lollies.

▶ For other coastal day trips, *see pp65-89.*

Hollycombe Steam Fair

Take a trip back in time.

This beautiful collection of Edwardian steam-driven fairground rides is a real treat. There's a wooden helter skelter (the Lighthouse Slip), the Razzle Dazzle (a spinning, tilting device regarded as the world's first white-knuckle ride) and a big wheel. The setting is idyllic too, with great views of the Sussex Weald from some of the rides. There are also steam railways (one of them miniature) and traction engine-hauled rides, plus a farm and woodland gardens. Once you've paid the entrance fee, all rides are free. For a truly magical trip, go in the evening.

Hollycombe Steam Fair
Iron Hill, Liphook, Hampshire GU30 7LP
(01428 724900, www.hollycombe.co.uk).
Open Summer call or check website for details.
Winter closed. Admission £11 day; £9 night.

FIVE Animal adventures

Aldenham Country Park & Fishers Farm Park

Learn about rare domestic animals like Tamworth pigs and Longhorn cattle, or simply enjoy the 175 acres of Aldenham Country Park, which contains a rare-breed farm, woodland trails, lakeside walks, picnic areas and kid's playgrounds. At Fishers Farm Park there's even more to do: your little ones can bottle-feed the farm's little ones, ride ponies and horses, have a go on a Combine Harvester, take a Shire Horse Wagon Ride or watch (probably wide-eyed) goats, sheep and more pigs racing. *Aldenham Country Park, Dagger Lane, Elstree, Hertfordshire WD6 3AT (020 8953 9602, www.hertsdirect.org/aldenham). Fishers Farm Park, Newpound Lane, Wisborough Green, West Sussex RH14 0EG (01403 700063, www.fishersfarm park.co.uk).*

Ashdown Forest Llama Park

Sure, you could do a yoga retreat or spend a fortune at a day spa, but taking a gentle, dozy llama for a slow stroll though lovely East Sussex woodlands is just as relaxing and, at £30, way cheaper than pretty much any chill-out day we can think of. The 30 acres also house a herd of alpacas and three Swedish reindeer, while a farm trail, adventure play area and museum should provide enough entertainment for younger children to make a day of it. *Ashdown Forest Llama Park, Wych Cross, Forest Row, East Sussex RH18 5JN (01825 712040, www.llamapark.co.uk).*

Piglet racing at West Lodge Rural Centre

As anyone who's watched *Mary Poppins* will know, a day at the races is fun for all ages, but a day at the races in the West Lodge Rural Centre in Kettering is likely to have you rolling with laughter. Instead of dogs, horses or snails, here you get piglets pelting round the six-lane track for all they're worth in a bid to win a treat. Check out the form beforehand by watching the piggies parade around

Port Lympne Wild Animal Park

the ring, and learn more about their care and maintenance after the race. The centre is at pains to point out that the races aren't cruel, saying that the piglets need stimulation to keep them happy. *West Lodge Rural Centre, Back Lane, Desborough, Kettering, Northamptonshire NN14 2SH (01536 760552, www.west lodgeruralcentre.co.uk).*

Port Lympne Wild Animal Park
Pretend you're in Africa, with a range of safaris in 100 acres of savannah where zebra, giraffe, wildebeest and hundreds of other animals roam free. We particularly like the sound of the overnight safari, which starts with welcome drinks before a drive through the plains to comfy luxury tents (with proper beds) at the Livingstone Safari Lodge. What follows should thrill kids and grown-ups alike: a six-course African meal and the chance to watch the animals at the nearby watering hole, as well as enjoying sea views from your private veranda as the sun sets and you bed down for the night. In the early hours,

you're woken by rangers for a dawn safari, followed by breakfast and a day in the park. Animal magic! *Port Lympne Wild Animal Park, Lympne, nr Hythe, Kent CT21 4PD (01303 264647, www.totallywild.net).*

Seal-spotting boat trips
All aboard the gloriously old-style passenger sailing boat *Wildlife* for a five-hour round-trip to the sandbanks that the local herd of Herne Bay seals calls home. The excursion includes a rubber dinghy transfer ashore, a wade in your wellies and, if the weather's right, a swim with the friendly natives. There are birdwatching tours too, and prices for both are surprisingly low: a five-hour exclusive booking of the whole boat for a party of ten is just £19.50 each. Or, up to three passengers pay £23 each, four to six pay £22 each, and seven to nine passengers pay £21 each. *8 Western Esplanade, Herne Bay, Kent CT6 8RP (01227 366712, www.wildlifesailing.com).*

Roald Dahl Museum & Story Centre

Have a fantabulous day out.

The Buckinghamshire village of Great Missenden, home to author Roald Dahl for 36 years until his death in 1990, is just 40 miles from the Big Smoke, but its rural feel makes it seem much further. Hop on a train at Marylebone Station and watch the scenery change from closely packed terraces to fields full of sheep and wide expanses of uncluttered sky in just 45 minutes.

A stroll down the hill from Great Missenden Station, through picturesque narrow streets, takes you to the Roald Dahl Museum & Story Centre – a gleaming white building covered with massive Quentin Blake murals. Aimed at six- to 12-year-olds, it's a smashing little museum that succeeds in reflecting Dahl's wildly imaginative and sometimes dark genius. Visiting kids get a 'story ideas book' (just like the author's own) to fill in as they run riot through a series of interactive rooms devoted to Dahl and his stories – an idea that would surely have charmed the writer.

CHILDREN

The Boy and Going Solo galleries tell the tale of Dahl's life. Children who make it past the chocolate bar-shaped – and scented – doors can learn about the writer's World War II fighter pilot days, watch videos (including clips from films of his books) and explore archive material on touch-screen monitors before moving on to the Story Centre. The craft room (where you can display your efforts – grown-ups too – on the walls afterwards) and dressing-up box are big hits with little ones; check out Johnny Depp's Willy Wonka costume from *Charlie and the Chocolate Factory*. Older kids have a blast creating made-up words ('You filthy old frumpet!') and fridge-poetry from Gobblefunk (the BFG's mixed-up language), as well as making photo-fit story characters and stop-frame animation films; they can even sit in Dahl's chair in a mock-up of his writing hut.

At the end of the day, the room is a glorious mess, with felt-tipped fingered kids covered in bits of coloured paper. This is the sort of place where children can truly run amok around the different areas (the central courtyard is gated to keep in over-excited would-be escapees). Parents, however, can retain some semblance of sanity thanks to the organised structure of the centre.

Storytelling sessions in Miss Honey's Classroom (where Matilda terrorised the evil Mrs Trunchbull with a piece of chalk) are a big draw and tremendous fun. Parents and kids dress up and act out parts during the sessions, while Dahl's tales are read out; if it's sunny, readings take place out in the Wundercrump

courtyard (named after the BFG's exclamation of joy). Book in advance for other activities; chocolate decorating for budding Willy Wonkas, Revolting Recipes (make Lickable Wallpaper and Mr Twit's Truffles) and Paint your Own Diddly Dinner Plate are very popular, and cost from £2. Keep an eye open for special events during the annual celebration of the author's birthday on 13 September, now officially 'Roald Dahl Day'.

The award-winning museum is a genuine joy to visit, and what is often intended as 'something to do for a couple of hours as it's raining' can easily turn into an all-dayer as parents and children have a phizz-whizzing, peachy (giant, of course) time. There are plenty of places to fuel up at in the village, but you'd miss out on the scrumdiddlyumptious own-made meals and cake at the on-site Café Twit.

Great Missenden is lovely for a wander, however. The Village Trail leaflet maps places that inspired Dahl's stories, including Hobbs Hill Wood ('Beware! Beware! The Forest of Sin! None come out, but many go in!'), and everything is close by and easily walkable. If you wish to pay your respects, follow the BFG's footprints from the commemorative bench to find Dahl's gravestone in the parish church.

Roald Dahl Museum & Story Centre
81-83 High Street, Great Missenden, Buckinghamshire HP16 0AL (01494 892192, www.roalddahlmuseum.org). Open 10am-5pm Tue-Sun. Admission £5.50.

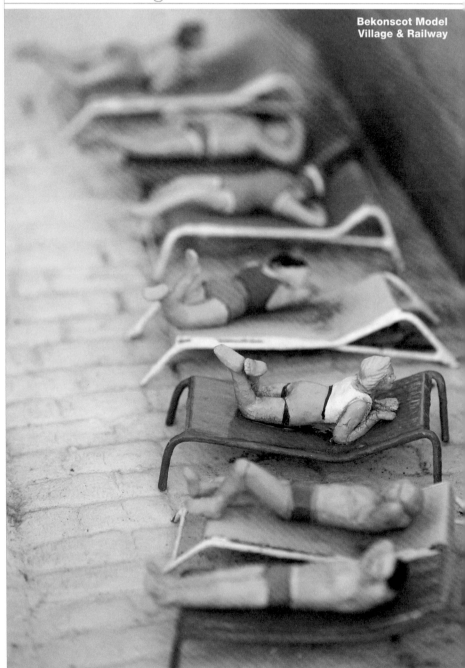

Bekonscot Model Village & Railway

Bekonscot Model Village & Railway

This Buckinghamshire treasure is a miniature window on a lost world: a 1930s vision of cricket, freely roaming children and steam trains. In short, it's Enid Blyton's England meets Lilliput. It opened in 1929, and was the inspiration for many model villages that followed. *Warwick Road, Beaconsfield, Buckinghamshire HP9 2PL (01494 672919, www.bekonscot.com).*

Corfe Castle Model Village

This picturesque little place, in deepest Dorset, got its model miniature version in 1966, though the idea had been germinating with local businessman Eddie Holland since the 1950s, the model village's golden age. Built to a scale of 1/20, it's a replica of Corfe Castle itself, complete with the tiny fort on the mount. *The Square, Corfe Castle, Dorset BH20 5EZ (01929 481234, www.corfecastle modelvillage.co.uk).*

Old New Inn Model Village

Set in the garden of the Old New Inn, in one of the Cotswolds' most famous *real* villages, this model village is one of the oldest and prettiest around; it opened

in 1937, on Coronation Day. Attention to detail is exemplified in the local stone it's built from and by the scaled-down River Windrush that runs through its heart. *Bourton-on-the-Water, Gloucestershire GL54 2AF (01451 820467, www.theoldnewinn.co.uk).*

Southsea Model Village

Southsea Model Village stands on the site of the 19th-century Lumps Fort, and was used as a military training base in World War II for the Royal Marines' Special Boat Service. A train chugs through the charming village, and the surrounding views, across the Solent towards the Isle of Wight, are lovely. *Lumps Fort, Eastney Esplanade, Southsea, Hampshire PO4 9RS (02392 294706).*

Wimborne Minster Model Town

Wimborne is not only a model town rather than a village, but each building is a tenth of the size of the *real* Wimborne Minster. The first visitors came in 1951 and it remains a 1950s idyll to this day, despite a recent refurbishment and new location. *King Street, Wimborne, Dorset BH21 1DY (01202 881924, www.wimborne-modeltown.com).*

CHILDREN

The Lodge

Take your titchy twitchers to the RSPB headquarters in Bedfordshire.

In recent years, there's been a sharp upswing in youthful awareness of our feathered friends, thanks in no small part to Bill Oddie and the BBC's *Springwatch/ Autumnwatch* nature-fests. But if sitting on the sofa worrying over nestfuls of fluffy chicks has done wonders for boosting ornithology's image among young people, there's nothing quite as inspirational as a day out in the field, face to face with the birds themselves.

At the Lodge, in Sandy (01767 680541, www.rspb.org.uk), the rural Bedfordshire headquarters of the Royal Society for the Protection of Birds, there's a year-round programme of events and activities designed to take our growing background interest in birds to a whole new level. The aim is the same at every RSPB reserve, big and small, up and down the country – as well as on the nationwide programme of smaller, quirky events designed to snare your attention in unexpected settings.

To mark the occasion of the national Feed the Birds Day in autumn, marquees are set up in the garden at the Lodge to host kids' competitions and set them off on such activities as making balls of fat for garden birds, constructing feeders, getting sneaky in heathland hides and walking the wonderful woods from the depths of an old quarry to the peak of a recently excavated Iron Age hill fort. But there's no doubt about the main attraction. Children and parents alike gather around a long trestle table set up among the marquees, peopled by RSPB ornithologists.

'Ah, a blue tit,' says the studious Dr Guy Anderson, gently extracting from a small cloth bag one of the birds caught safely on nets strung around the gardens. Holding its head between his fingers, he measures its beak and wings, and shows us how to identify the bird. Meanwhile, the tit pecks furiously at the professor's finger-ends, most indignant at being turned upside-down and popped into a film-holder for weighing.

'Eight grammes of pure anger,' the doc says of the little fellow, astonishing us with the fact that even a one pound coin weighs nine grammes. Finally, he pincers a light aluminium numbered ring on the bird's leg for identification and tracking purposes. Someone gets to stroke the tiny bird's head, to touch its powerful, outspread wing. Then it's hands up for who would like to hold the bird in their hands and set it gently

free – me! me! – from which sweaty perch it flaps straight up into the safety of the pines.

What's next? Aha, a not-so-common-or-garden nuthatch – a greenish-grey, orange-breasted 'mini-woodpecker', as Sarah Dawkins (the next expert in line) calls it; 'resident all year round, and spreading north into Scotland as the climate changes. See how its beak is shaped to wheedle out grubs from tree bark?' She explains how it can make a hole in a tree and hollow out a nest, which it lines only with oak leaves instead of the feathers and animal hair favoured by the blue tit. The nuthatch can also recycle old nestholes, expertly resizing the hole to its own minute specifications using beakfuls of hard-drying mud.

The kids take it all in, looking at the tiny talent with a whole new respect. The day started out as a walk in the great outdoors, involving fresh air and patience – but it's since become much more fun; a mixture of Pokémon and pets and football stickers, they later decide, because you get to learn the unique skills and powers of each garden beastie, how you can help look after them – and then set out to tick off the whole checklist.

'A Million Voices for Nature' – That's the RSPB's strapline. It's the number of members the charity relies on to keep spreading its message of conservation and appreciation. And events like today are how the organisation manages to enthuse so many people, by drawing attention and giving the public access to wildlife it might otherwise overlook.

Inside the Lodge, over a bowl of soup in the warm canteen, we spoke to Richard Bashford, whose very role is to set up these engagement activities all over the country. 'Connecting

▶ For the RSPB's birdwatching boat trips on the Stour Estuary, *see p108.*

People with Nature,' he says, 'That's the umbrella title of many of these events... and then there's Aren't Birds Brilliant!'

Of course, there are year-round events at all the bigger RSPB nature reserves – Rainham in Essex and Minsmere in Suffolk, to name but two – and the annual British Birdwatching Fair (held in August at Rutland Water) is a huge three-day festival that's been described as the birdwatcher's Glastonbury. But just as important to Richard are the little reserves, places that might offer just a lone information post, and those devoted primarily to single species, such as the red kite or, in North Wales, the puffin. 'Then there are the bird events that we like to set up where people least expect them, in urban areas. On the Embankment, we've been able to point out falcons from July to September, perched up on top of the Tate Modern chimney,

post-breeding!' He also explains the importance of January's Big Garden Birdwatch, which has 400,000 members joining in. 'The garden is a great place to start birdwatching, because things are always changing from season to season.'

Back at the ringing table at the Lodge, the species successfully logged by the twitchers (that is, birdwatchers who like to tick off sightings of as many different birds as possible) include a robin, chaffinch, wren, dunnock, greenfinch and goldcrest (which weighed in at just five grammes – it's Britain's smallest bird). 'A swift can stay in the air for two years,' I'm reliably informed by Frances Hammond, aged nine. 'They sleep and eat in the air.' 'And I held a greenfinch,' chips in her brother Jimmy, seven. 'He was so soft. I could feel him squiggling to get away. He weighs the same as ten smarties.'

FIVE Mazes

Hever Castle

You get two mazes for the price of one in the grounds of Hever Castle. When viewed from above the labyrinth of yew trees appears as an immaculate addition to the Italianate gardens created in 1906 by then owner William Waldorf Astor. The maze isn't a particularly large one, but it's peppered with twists and turns that delight children. It's fairly easy to negotiate thanks to the symmetrical layout, which leaves plenty of time for the kids to enjoy the far more thrilling water maze on Sixteen Acre Island. This trail of concentric stepping stone walkways sits over an expansive water feature. The object is to reach the centre without getting drenched by the water jets. Bring waterproofs and get jumping. *Also see p117.*
Hever, nr Edenbridge, Kent TN8 7NG (01732 865224, www.hevercastle.co.uk). Admission £12.

Leeds Castle

So many people get hopelessly lost in the maze that attendants sit on umpire-like chairs in the centre to help the directionally challenged. Constructed in 1988 from 2,400 yew trees, it's one of the most elaborate in existence. In tribute to the castle's nickname as the 'ladies' castle', architect Vernon Gibberd created the maze to mirror a queen's crown, a design that's visible from the raised ground in the centre. An added incentive to reach the maze's heart is the underworld grotto decorated with macabre mythical beasts by sculptor Simon Verity and shell artist Diana Reynell. To exit, make your way beneath increasingly bizarre flying fish, mythical men and a phoenix created from shells, minerals and wood. For Leeds Castle itself, *see p123. Maidstone, Kent ME17 1PL (01622 765400, www.leeds-castle.com). Admission £15.*

Legoland

They may not be in as picturesque a setting as more traditional hedge mazes, but Legoland's three mazes, in the park's Wild Woods area, should keep the kids happy for hours. The 'Celtic' willow hedge maze features a willow tunnel, glowing stones, a central pavilion, musical chimes and other interactive features; the 'Tudor' hedge maze has a walk-through waterfall, central tower, playing cards and Lego models; and the 'Nautical' fabric maze spouts foaming fountain gates. All three were designed by maze maestros Adrian Fisher and Rodney Beaumont of Gillespies, so are likely to prove entertaining as well as just the right level of difficulty. For Legoland itself, *see p253.*
Windsor Park, Winkfield Road, Windsor, Berkshire SL4 4AY (0871 222 2001, www.legoland.co.uk). Admission £28-£35.

Longleat Maze

Made up of more than 16,000 English yews, with a length of 1.69 miles if laid end to end, Longleat's spectacular hedge maze is one of the largest in the world. It takes an average of 90 minutes to get round this maze, which was first laid out in 1975 by designer Greg Bright. As an added complication, this maze is three-dimensional: six wooden bridges connect the different cells within the maze as well as giving you an elevated view over where to head to next. Should you eventually reach the centre, you can scale the observation tower and watch others battle their way through the greenery. The estate features five other mazes, ranging from the Blue Peter timber maze to the maze of mirrors. *Warminster, Wiltshire BA12 7NW (01985 844400, www.longleat.co.uk). Admission (maze only) £3.*

Maze at Hampton Court

Probably the most famous maze in the country, if not the world, the Hampton Court hedge maze is also one of the most established – as you might expect of something first planted in 1689. George London and Henry Wise, who laid out the gardens for William III of Orange, originally used hornbeam for its dense and hard properties. However, much of the half mile of paths are now lined with yews. The map legend at the maze entrances is not wholly accurate, but navigation is straightforward: always keep one hand in contact with the wall on your right and you should thread your way to the centre and back out again. *East Molesey, Surrey KT8 9AU (0844 482 7777, www.hrp.org.uk). Admission (maze only) £3.50.*

The Living Rainforest

All creatures great and small.

As you push your way through the lush vegetation, with toucans chattering in the dripping trees above you and lizards scuttling underfoot, you could almost (if you ignore the party of excited schoolchildren teasing the monkeys) be forgiven for thinking you were venturing into the heart of darkness. In reality you're nowhere near it – you're in a large greenhouse in Berkshire – but the Living Rainforest Centre does a pretty good impression of a steamy *Apocalypse Now*-style jungle.

An hour's drive from west London (traffic permitting) and very clearly signposted from the M4, this little eco-gem is at first glance rather unprepossessing. Nowhere near the scale of the Eden Project or even the Butterfly House at Kew, the centre is made up of two greenhouses with a small building attached; but while its exterior lacks the glamour of those attractions, the centre undoubtedly houses a special experience for children.

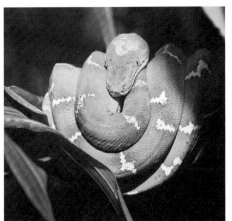 

CHILDREN

The Living Rainforest began life as a leading orchid nursery on the outskirts of the Berkshire village of Hampstead Norreys, but in 1991 philanthropist and shoe-magnate Keith Bromley led a conversion that saw it become, in 1993, a visitor centre featuring plants and animals from the world's most endangered rainforests. Over the years it has flourished, adopting more animals and birds along the way, with some, like the African chameleon, coming here after being rescued from the illegal animal trade by Heathrow Airport customs officials.

Today, the centre is a significant tourist attraction; more than 75,000 visitors come here throughout the year, including 20,000 schoolchildren on National Curriculum-linked tours. And with its laudable aims of teaching kids about humanity's impact on nature in as authentic a setting as possible, the centre's appeal is as timely as its approach is resolutely old-school – if you're after touch-screens or fairground rides you've come to the wrong place.

The eco focus is evident even before you enter the glasshouses; in wormeries and composting sites bordering the path small critters can be seen busy at work, disposing of the centre's vegetable matter and recycling nutrients. And insects are also used in active demonstrations to teach children the importance of sustainable living.

But it's the glasshouses and jungle experience that the kids are normally itching to get into. The first glasshouse, Lowland House, contains a huge variety of plant species. Children armed with activity sheets can see carnivorous pitcher plants and vanilla pods hanging from the trees, or learn how chocolate is made from the cocoa plant. But if plants don't excite them, there's also a huge bird-eating spider and a tank full of piranhas to get them in the jungle mood, and in the summer a beautiful array of butterflies comes out in force.

The second house, Amazonica, is three times the size of Lowland, and houses a wider selection of birds and animals. The centre has pushchair and wheelchair access, but the overgrown paths are great for kids and toddlers to explore; here they can spot pheasants strutting about or lizards skulking near the hot water pipes in winter. We took a four-year-old and a two-year-old who were completely charmed by the tameness of the birds and proximity of the wildlife. Tanks full of turtles and freshwater stingrays are at ground level so even the tiniest of people can get a great view of them. It's this kind of attention to detail that makes the centre such a happy place for kids. And the animals all seem quite content too. Tame touraco birds fly up and follow you around, as do the Malagasy teals (ducks to you and me) on the Amazon pool (check out the giant water lilies, big

enough to hold a baby), and little black Goeldi's monkeys swing up to the glass to make faces and throw bits of banana. If your child falls in love with one of them, £30 buys you a share in pretty much any animal you see, and the names of the owners are listed next to the enclosures.

On our midweek visit we had the whole place to ourselves, which meant a Garden of Eden-like tranquillity and a real affinity with the animals, who seemed keen to interact with us. But staff warn that at weekends and during school holidays it can be a bit of a scrum. If the mix of humidity and excited little explorers gets a bit much, you can take a break in the well-thought-out picnic area (complete with a fantastic playground), or lunch in the indoor café, which serves a selection of organic and local produce as well as a decent cappuccino (made from rainforest-friendly coffee beans, of course). Prices are reasonable (£2.50 for a baguette, or £2.90 for an organic vegetarian pasty) and where possible waste is recycled. The baby-changing and bottle-warming facilities keep up the high standards here.

After lunch the little ones might want to indulge in a spot of eco-friendly energy expenditure, easily done with a range of fun workshops and activities (running mainly during the school holidays and on weekends) that include face painting, clayplay, T-shirt painting or games like guess the tropical fruit. The Human Impact Building, which houses the shop and the Learning Zone in which these activities are held, may not be as glossy as some other kids' venues, but it's a great example of green architecture in action. Recycled newsprint insulates the walls, roof and floors, light-absorbing cells on top of the building canopy help provide electricity, and the floor coverings are made from recycled rubber.

The Living Rainforest doesn't try to compete with more commercial concerns, and is better for it. It is, after all, a charity-run conservation project as much as an attraction, and the centre hasn't lost sight of this. It's excellent value (£24.95 annual membership for two adults and two children) and children love being close to and interacting with nature, they don't need anything else. It's a lesson to other theme parks that small and simple can be beautiful. So if you're sick of queues round the block, giant gift shops and over-stimulated kids, this could be perfect. Even better, all your pleasure is guilt-free and that, surely, is worth its weight in rainforest-friendly coffee beans.

The Living Rainforest
Hampstead Norreys, Berkshire RG18 0TN (01635 202444, www.livingrainforest.org). Open 10am-5pm daily. Admission £7.95.

Counties Index

Bedfordshire
Black Horse, Woburn 53
Dunstable & Chiltern Hills 233
Dunstable Downs 178
Grove Farm, Ivinghoe 223
The Lodge, Sandy (RSPB HQ) 264-265
Snail Trail camper van hire 229
Whipsnade Tree Cathedral 94
Woburn golf events 170

Berkshire
Ascot Racecourse 180
Bracknell Bees ice hockey team 175
Cliveden 129-130
Go Ape Experience 253
Lambourn 49
Legoland, Windsor 253, 266
The Living Rainforest 267-269
London Irish rugby union matches 175
Stanley Spencer Gallery, Cookham 143
Sunningdale golf events 170
Vineyard Spa 195-197
Windsor Castle 123, 134
Windsor Farm Shop 211
Windsor Farmers' Market 219
Windsor Great Park & town 134-135, 167
Windsor Racecourse 181

Bristol
attractions 25-29, 30
Dot to Dot Festival 148
eating & drinking 29-30
shops 25, 30, 211

Buckinghamshire
Aldbury & Ashridge Estate 244
Bekonscot Model Village 263
Burnham Beeches 92-94
Chinnor & Princes Risborough
 Railway 232
Fenny Stratford cannons &
 events 43
Great Missenden 260
Hell-Fire Caves & West Wycombe 116
Ivinghoe Beacon 199, 244
Olney market & pancake race 216
Roald Dahl Museum &
 Story Centre 260-261
SNO!zone Milton Keynes 177
Stowe Landscape Gardens 100
Weighing the Mayor, High Wycombe 43
Wendover Woods 94

Cambridgeshire
All Saints' church, St Ives 43
American War Museum,
 Duxford 146
Cambridge 46, 138-141, 244
Cambridge Folk Festival 140, 148
Elton Hall 130
Grantchester 46-47

Dorset
Corfe Castle Model Village 263
Nettle Eating Championships 224
Russell-Cotes Gallery,
 Bournemouth 143
Wimborne Minster Model Town 263

Essex
Audley End House 129, 242
B184 cycle route 242
Beecroft Art Gallery,
 Westcliff-on-Sea 143
Brentwood Farmers' Market 217
Clacton to Walton coastal walk 244
Dedham 144-145
Duke of Essex Polo Trophy 168
Epping & Ongar Railway 232
Epping Forest 94
Frinton-on-Sea art deco buildings 146
Fry Art Gallery 143, 242
Hamford Water Nature Reserve 111
Kichel throwing, Harwich 43
Leigh-on-Sea 86
Manningtree & Mistley 144, 145
Mersea Island 87-89
Rainham nature reserve 265
RHS Garden Hyde Hall 178-179
Rodings 242
Romford market 216
Rossi's, Southend-On-Sea 72
Saffron Walden 143, 242
Sitooterie, Barnards Farm 151-152
Spencers Farm Shop 223
Stour Estuary 108
Thaxted 242
Walton-on-the-Naze 85

Gloucestershire
Calcot Manor Hotel & Spa 200-201
Cheltenham Literature
 Festival 154-155
Daylesford Organic Farm
 Shop 209-211
Haybarn Daylesford spa 190-191
International Birds of Prey Centre 174
Old New Inn Model Village 263
Organic Farm Shop, Cirencester 211
Snowshill Manor 133
Westonbirt National Arboretum 104-105

Hampshire
Alton market 215
Cycle Experience 229
Exbury Gardens 97
Hayling Island 255
Hollycombe Steam Fair 256-257
Leopard 3 (yacht) 234
Mrs Tee's Wild Mushrooms 220
New Forest 110, 220, 229
New Forest Otter, Owl
 & Wildlife Park 111
Sandham Memorial Chapel 151
Sir Harold Hillier Gardens 100
Southcoast Exotics, Waterlooville 19
Southsea Common 179
Southsea Model Village 263
Winchester Cathedral 152

Hertfordshire
A1 Barnet Shooting Ground 174
Aldenham Country Park 258
Ashwell 55-57
Hatfield House Tennis Club 174
Henry Moore Foundation 160-161
Hitchin market 215-216
Lee Valley Boat Centre 229
Novelli Academy 212-214

Sequoia at the Grove spa 185-187
Snow Centre, Hemel Hempstead 177
Waddesdon Manor 125

Kent
All Saints Church, Tudeley 151
Allens Farm, Plaxtol 222-223
Apple Week & Brogdale Collection 224
Botany Bay 76-78, 85
Bredgar & Wormshill
 Light Railway 232
Broadstairs 41, 72, 77-78, 81
Canterbury 42
Canterbury Tales 251
Cliftonville 81
cycle routes 78, 240-242
Dickens World, Chatham 253
Diggerland 253
Dover 240, 244
Dover Castle 122
Dover White Cliffs Tours 234
Down House 121
Dungeness & Prospect
 Cottage 73-75, 85, 151, 153, 233
Dymchurch 85
Faversham farm shops
 & events 211, 224
Folkestone 19, 241, 253
Harrison's Rocks & High Rocks 171-173
Haysden Country Park 242
Herne Bay 85, 233, 254, 259
Hever Castle 117-119, 266
Joss Bay 78
Kent Ballooning 246
Kent County Cricket Club 175
Kingsgate Bay 76
Knole 109, 130-131
Leeds Castle 122, 123, 266
London Golf Club 170
Lounge on the Farm 149
Lower Leas Coastal Park 253
Margate 78, 81
North Kent Coast 233
Penshurst Place 242
Port Lympne Wild
 Animal Park 253-254, 259
Reculver 233
Rochester Sweeps' Festival 43
Romney, Hythe & Dymchurch
 Railway 73, 74, 85, 232
RSPB Northward Hill 109-110
Samphire Hoe 85, 240
Sissinghurst Castle & Gardens 100, 132
Spa Valley Railway 173
Sportsman, Whitstable 53-54, 82
Three Chimneys, Biddenden 54
Tonbridge Castle 241
Viking Coastal Trail 78
Whitfield Farmers' Market 219
Whitstable 82-84, 85, 233
Whitstable Oyster Festival 82, 84, 225
Wildwood 254

Lincolnshire
Lincoln Whisky Shop 19

Middlesex
Kempton Park Racecourse 180-181
Queen Mary Sailing Club & Sailsports 174
River Lea cycle route 241

INDEXES

Norfolk

Holkham Beach	198-199
Thetford Forest Park	94

Northamptonshire

Coton Manor Gardens	109
King's Head, Wadenhoe	53
The Model Shop, Northampton	19
Rushton Triangular Lodge	147
Salcey Forest & Hartwell	95-96
West Lodge Rural Centre	258-259

Nottinghamshire

Dot to Dot Festival	148

Oxfordshire

Chinnor & Princes Risborough	
Railway	232
Dream Car Hire	229
Falkland Arms, Great Tew	53
Fernham	49, 50
Garsington Opera	150
Henley-on-Thames	58-61, 217-219,
	234, 246
hot-air balloon trips	246
LASSCO Three Pigeons	124-125
Oxford	20-24, 147, 246
Rousham Manor	99-100
Swan, Tetsworth	124-125
Thame market	216-217
Uffington White Horse & village	48-51, 179
Waterperry Gardens	111, 125

Somerset

Bath	41, 146-147
Bath Thermae Spa	188-189

Suffolk

Aldeburgh	72, 156-159
Aldeburgh Food & Drink Festival	158, 224
Dedham Vale	144-145
Dunwich	85, 158
East Bergholt	144
Farmcafé & Foodmarket	211
Heritage Coast	158
Latitude festival	149
Lavenham	147
Minsmere nature reserve	158, 265
Ridgewell Airfield & gliding club	174
Snape Maltings	156-159
Southwold	42, 158
Thorpeness	81, 159
Walberswick	85
Woodbridge	31-32

Surrey

Ascot Park Polo Club	168
Chessington World of Adventures	251-252
Classic Bike Hire	229
Crockford Bridge Farm	223
Epsom Downs Racecourse	178, 180
Garsons Fruit Farm	223
Gatton Park	111
Go Ape Experience	253
Guildford	42
Guildford Farmers' Market	217
Guildford Heat basketball team	175
Ham Polo Club	168
Hampton Court Maze	266
Hannah Peschar Sculpture Garden	160
Loseley Park	98
Painshill Park	99
PGA Championship, Wentworth	170
Polesden Lacey	132
Richmond Park Golf Club	169

Sandown Park Racecourse	181
Shere	233
Spa at Pennyhill Park Hotel	192-194
Surbiton Hockey Club	175
Surrey Hills	233
Surrey Hills Llamas	112-113
Thorpe Park	251, 254
Watts Cemetery Chapel, Compton	146
RHS Wisley	101-103

Sussex, East

Alciston	208
Alfriston	239-240
Beachy Head & Seven	
Sisters walk	243-245
Bluebell Railway	230-232
Brighton	13-17, 85, 147, 148-149
Camber Sands	69-72, 85
Charleston	129, 146
De La Warr Pavilion, Bexhill-on-Sea	146
Ditchling Beacon	233
Eastbourne	72, 81, 143, 243
Firle Beacon	53, 208, 239
Friston Forest to Litlington walk	245
Glynde	208, 240
Great Dixter	98
Great Escape festival	148-149
Hastings	81
Hastings to Rye walk	244
Hope Gap	85
Kensington Rocking	
Horse Company	19
Lavender Line	232
Lewes	35-39, 239
Middle Farm, Glynde	205-208
Ram Inn, Firle	53, 240
Rye	33-34, 244
Rye Bay Scallop Festival	224-225
Saltdean Lido	147
Seven Sisters Sheep Centre	110
Sharnfold Farm	223
Sheffield Park Garden	100, 111, 231, 232
South Downs Way	233, 239, 245
1066 Battle of Hastings,	
Abbey & Battlefield	126-127
Towner Gallery, Eastbourne	143
Winchelsea	72, 85, 244

Sussex, West

Ashdown Forest Llama Park	258
Blackdown Farm Riding Club	235
Bracklesham Bay	85
Cass Sculpture Foundation	160, 166
Chichester	67, 68, 151
Cowdray Estate	235, 237
Critchmere & Midhurst	237
Devil's Dyke	198
Duke of Cumberland Arms, Henley	53
Fernhurst	53, 237
Goodwood	160, 164-166
Itchenor	66-67, 68
Leonardslee Gardens	111
Lickfold Inn	53
Littlehampton	79-81
Macari's, Worthing	72
Noah's Ark Inn, Lurgashall	53
Nymans Garden	98-99
Petworth	131
Standen	146, 232
Totally Tomato Show	225
Wakehurst Place	109
West Dean Estate & Gardens	225
West Wittering	65-68, 85

Warwickshire

Avon Boating, Stratford	234
Jerwood Sculpture, Ragley Hall	161
Kenilworth Castle	122-123
Warwick Castle	123

Wiltshire

Avebury & Silbury Hill	120, 198
Bentley Wood	109
Longleat Maze	266
NewArtCentre Sculpture Park	161
Savernake Forest	94
Stonehenge	120
Vine Tree, Norton	54
West Kennett Long Barrow	120
Wilton House	133

Worcestershire

Malvern Hills	199
narrowboat trips	234

Advertisers' Index

Please refer to relevant sections for contact details.

Thematic Index

A

aircraft
fly in a vintage plane 166
gliding club 174
museum 146
ancient sites
fossils 85, 89
Iron Age hill forts 94, 198, 233, 264
long barrows 51, 120
Roman remains 122, 233
stone circles 120, 198
tumuli & farmsteads 243, 245
Uffington White Horse 48-51
animals
(see also birds; farms; horses; nature reserves; wildlife parks)
butterflies 96, 103, 105, 109, 244
deer parks 109, 131, 134
dragonflies 92, 96, 103
Dungeness rare species 73
exotic pet shop 19
five animal adventures 258-259
living rainforest 267-269
llamas 112-113, 258
otters 111
piglet racing 258-259
seal spotting 66, 78, 84, 108, 111, 259
tadpoles & newts 96
woodland habitat 92, 96, 111
architecture
contemporary 79-81, 146
experimental 74
Gothic 20
historic colleges 20, 138
historic towns 31, 37, 68, 78, 82, 146-147, 244
historic village 55-56
neo-classical 129
Palladian 133
rococo 132
ten marvels 146-147
art collections & artists
(see also sculpture)
Bloomsbury set 129
Constable country 144-145
Essex artists 242
Fitzwilliam Museum 141
five recommended galleries 143
five works of art 151-153
graffiti art 29, 30
Holman Hunt masterpiece 20
modern art collection 21
Munnings collection 144
Petworth collection 131
royal collection 134
small galleries 16, 29, 30, 37, 57, 59, 74, 158
Stanley Spencer locations 143, 151
student shows 138
studios 37, 138, 225
20th century collection 68
artistic pursuits
art courses 144
on the beach 85
in the wild 106

B

balloons, hot-air
festival 27
flights 246-247
birds
aviary 123
birds of prey centre 174
coastal habitats 68, 69, 73, 74, 79, 85, 89, 108, 158, 245, 255, 259
garden habitat 103
herons 109-110

owls 111
river habitat 241
RSPB HQ & events 264-265
woodland habitats 96, 105
boat trips & boating
birdwatching 108, 259
boat hire 60, 79
boating lake 81
Chichester Harbour 66-67, 68
five recommended trips 234
Kent coast 84, 234
Mersea ferry 89
narrowboats 229, 234
punting 21, 47, 139, 234
sailing 78, 174, 234
seal spotting 78, 84, 111, 259

C

cafés see restaurants & cafés
cars & driving
camper van hire 229
five scenic drives 233
Goodwood events 164-166
vintage sportscar hire 229
William Morris's house 59
castles
five recommended 122-123
Hastings 81
Hever 117-119, 266
Lewes 38
mazes 266
miniature 263
Tonbridge 241
Windsor 123, 134-135
cathedrals
Chichester 68, 151
Christ Church, Oxford 20, 23
made of trees 94
Winchester wood carvings 152
caves & underground secrets
hell-fire caves 116
magical grottoes 78, 266
rock-climbing caves 171
smugglers' caves 76, 78
World War II tunnels 122
chapels
art nouveau masterpiece 146
evensong at King's 139
medieval & Gothic 20, 43
children's attractions & activities
(see also farms; ice-cream parlours; kites; mazes; seaside; wildlife parks)
adventure play areas 253, 258
aerial adventures 253
amusement & theme parks 81, 85, 251-254, 255, 256-257, 266
birdwatching 265
child-friendly eating places 30, 32, 255
child-friendly hotel 200-201
conservation volunteering 106-107
craft activities 260
crazy & mini-golf 81
dolls' houses 41, 119, 123, 133
Easter treasure hunt 94
five animal adventures 258-259
food festival activities 224
garden activities 103
living rainforest 267-269
model villages 81, 262-263
nature trails & activities 92-94, 96
Roald Dahl Museum 260-261
shops 41, 42, 119
steam fair 256-257
storytelling 23, 260
trampolines 78
Warwick Castle events 123
Wind in the Willows display 60

Christmas
concerts 23
Daylesford events 209
Enchanted Wood 104
farm fair 208
llama trek & dinner 112
Mummers' Play & Sea Shanties 86
shopping for 21-22, 41
steam railway event 231
trees 223
churches
(see also cathedrals; chapels)
archetypal medieval 50
former priory 233
idiosyncratic events 43
medieval graffiti 56, 57
seafaring theme 88
towers & spires 33, 56, 144
unusual features 31, 144
courses
art 144
cookery 211, 212-214, 220
five recommended 174
foraging for mushrooms 220
gardening 125
Oxford lectures 20
cycling
five recommended routes 239-242
in the New Forest 229
paths & trails 65, 78, 186, 229, 239-242, 253
in university cities 20-21, 138

D

drink (see also pubs & bars)
breweries 38-39, 158
cider 29, 205-208, 224
festivals 89, 158, 209, 224
whisky shop 19
wine & vineyards 41, 42, 89, 99

E

ecology (see also nature reserves)
conservation volunteering 106-107
living rainforest 267-269

F

farms
cider collection 205-208
city farm 30
farm park 258
farm shops 164, 208, 209, 211, 223
guided walks 211
horse riding 235-237
organic 224
pick your own 222-223, 224
rare breeds 258
sheep centre 110
festivals & events (see also Christmas)
apples 208, 224
arts 33, 60, 140, 149
balloons 27
birdwatching 264-265
Bonfire Night 37
Brighton 13
Bristol 27
Cambridge 140
carnivals 23, 140
Cheltenham 154-155
drink 89, 158, 209, 224
Easter treasure hunt 94
eccentric 37, 43, 224, 255
film 27, 140
five recommended 148-149
flower show 103

INDEXES

folk 86, 140, 148
food 27, 60, 89, 158, 224-225
Goodwood 164-166
Henley 60
kites 27, 179
Leigh-on-Sea 86
literary 23, 78, 140, 154-155
May Day 23, 43
music 60, 86, 103, 140,
148-149, 151, 156, 242
Oxford 23
pancake race 216
regattas 58, 60, 84, 88
seafood 84, 224-225
sports 79, 164
steam railway 231, 232
Summer Solstice 57
tree 104
film
Broadstairs cinema 78, 81
celebrity homes 82, 151, 153
festivals 27, 140
locations 69, 92, 94, 111, 133, 151,
199, 244
silent movies 27
fishing
lake 223
from the seashore 73, 85
sea-fishing 79
food
(*see also* farms; restaurants & cafés;
shops)
apples 205-208, 224
cookery courses 211, 212-214, 220
cookery demos 60, 209, 224, 225
eccentric events 43, 224
festivals 27, 60, 89, 158, 224-225
foraging for mushrooms 220
markets 27, 41, 42, 60, 158, 211,
215-219
oysters & scallops 82, 84, 224-225
tomatoes 225

G

gardens
arboretums 102, 104-105
bluebells 97, 109
botanic 46, 109
castles 119, 123
Derek Jarman's 73, 151
gardening classes 125
living rainforest 267-269
rhododendrons & azaleas 97, 111
RHS gardens 101-103, 178
royal gardens 134
sculptures 160-161
snowdrops 111
stately homes 129-133
ten recommended 97-100
walled 146
gay scene
Brighton 13, 17
geology
chalk reef 76
fossils 85, 89

H

horses
polo 167-168
race meetings 164-165, 180-181
racehorse training area 49
riding 65, 69, 85, 235-237, 238
Suffolk Punch museum 31
wild ponies 110, 244
hotels & guest houses
B&B 67, 220
boutique 38, 72
glamorous 74, 129, 147, 164, 166
spas 166, 185-187, 192-194, 200-201
traditional 57, 78

I

ice-cream parlours
Brighton 15
Oxford 21
retro 72

K

kites
festivals 27, 179
flying 27, 178-179
shop 30

L

learning (*see also* courses)
libraries 20, 119, 130, 138
Oxford lectures 20
literary connections
authors' homes 33, 78, 130-131, 132
Beachy Head 244
Canterbury Tales 251
Charles Dickens 78, 253
festivals 23, 78, 140, 154-155
Grantchester 46, 47
Littlehampton 79
museums 47, 51, 78, 260
Roald Dahl 260
Tom Brown's schoolroom 51
Wind in the Willows 60

M

markets
antique & flea 14, 17, 41
art 42
Christmas 41
crafts 41, 42
farmers' 27, 42, 60, 158, 217-219
food (general &
street markets) 41, 60, 215-217
slow food 27
sundry goods 41, 84
mausoleums
Dashwood family 116
royal 134
mazes
five recommended 266
Hever Castle 119, 266
maize 97, 102
turf 242
Morris dancing
Sweeps' Festival 43
Thaxted side 242
motorbikes
classic bike hire 229
museums
animals 31, 258
art & design 141, 143
Darwin's house 121
eclectic & quirky 24, 133
jam 145
literary 47, 51, 78, 260
local history 31, 55, 57, 88, 145, 159
natural history 88
oldest village museum 55, 57
Oxford 21, 24
river & rowing 58, 60
schoolroom 51
smuggling 78
steam railway 231
war planes 146
witch trials 145
music
Aldeburgh concerts 156, 158
Cambridge venues 138, 139, 140
church venues 139, 151
festivals 60, 86, 103, 140, 148-149,
151, 156, 208, 242
folk 53, 86, 140, 148
Folkestone events 253
lunchtime concerts 138, 158
opera 150, 208
sea shanties 86

N

nature reserves
Aldenham 258
Bentley Wood 109
Burnham Beeches 92-94
Cudmore 89

Dover 240
Dungeness 73, 74
East Head 66, 68
near Grantchester 46, 47
Hamford Water 111
Hastings 81
Haysden 242
Minsmere 158, 265
Northward Hill 109-110
Rainham 265
Sandy Point 255
Stour Estuary 108
Walberswick 85

P

picnics
country parks 242, 258
on the farm 223
with llamas 112
at the opera 150
Oxford meadows 20-21
provisions 21, 30, 32, 33, 37, 41, 57
by a rainforest 269
at the seaside 65-66, 79, 244
Shakespearean 234
with stories & music 23
Victorian 231
at Wisley 103
plants & flowers, wild (*see also* gardens)
bluebells 96, 97, 104, 109, 231, 237
maritime habitats 68, 73, 111, 243
spider orchid 244
woodland habitat 92
pubs & bars
characteristics:
Adnams pubs 158
cider 29
cocktails 16-17
good food 34, 49-50, 53-54, 68,
135, 145, 172
live music 24, 138, 139
llama-trekking haven 112-113
riverside 21, 53, 60
sea views 68, 72, 78, 82-83
smugglers' haunts 76, 239
ten perfect country pubs 53-54
traditional country pubs 47, 50, 53-54,
57, 68, 208, 224, 233, 237, 239, 242
traditional town pubs 24, 31, 33,
134, 139, 140
witch trials venue 145
places:
Ashwell 56, 57
Beachy Head & area 244, 245
Brighton 16-17
Bristol 29-30
Broadstairs 77, 78
Cambridge 138, 139, 140
Dungeness 74
Grantchester 47
Leigh-on-Sea 86
Lewes & area 38, 208, 239, 240
Oxford 21, 24
Penshurst 242
Rye 33, 34
Uffington & area 49-50
West Wycombe 116
Whitstable 82-83, 84, 85
Windsor & environs 134, 135

R

radio heritage
first international broadcast 244
pirate radio forts 84
railways
full-size steam trains 173, 215, 230-232
funicular 81
miniature steam trains 74, 97, 232, 255
model railways 263
steam fair 256-257
restaurants & cafés
cuisine & special features:
afternoon teas 17, 38, 41, 47, 74,
82, 145, 147, 231-232, 240
Caribbean 24

INDEXES

child-friendly 30, 32, 255
fish & chips 34, 67, 74, 81, 82,
158, 159, 255
French 67
hotels 38, 57, 72, 74
Indian 29
Italian 24, 78
lunch at LASSCO 124-125
organic & farm produce 209, 211, 269
oysters 82, 84, 87-88
pies 29-30
pub food 34, 49-50, 53-54,
68, 135, 145, 172
retro coffee bars 14, 77, 78
seafood 15, 16, 32, 34, 67, 68, 72,
78, 81, 82, 84, 86, 87-88
tapas 16, 82
top foodie destinations 53-54, 60,
68, 72, 79-81, 87, 147, 155, 166
on a train 231-232
vegetarian 16, 29, 38, 140, 145
places:
Brighton 15, 16, 17
Broadstairs 77-78
Bristol 29-30
Camber Sands 71-72
Cambridge 138-139, 140
Cheltenham 154, 155
Dedham 145
Dungeness 74
Lavenham 147
Lewes 38
Littlehampton 79-81
Mersea Island 87-88
Oxford 20, 24
Rye 33, 34
Snape Maltings & area 158, 159
West Wittering 67-68
Westonbirt 105
Whitstable 82
Wisley 103
Woodbridge 31-32
riverside idylls
cycle route 241
Oxford meadows 20-21
pubs 21, 53, 60
walks 31, 46-47, 59-60

S

sculpture
five sculpture parks 160-161
Hambling's scallop 159
open-air (on cycle route) 240-241
seaside
beach huts 65, 79, 89
Botany Bay 76-78
Brighton 13-17, 85
Camber Sands 69-72, 85
child-friendly beaches 65, 69, 76,
79, 255
cliffs 76, 89
crabbing 66, 85
donkey rides 255
Dungeness 73-75, 85, 151,
153, 233
kite buggying 65
Leigh-on-Sea 86
lido 147
lighthouses 73, 74, 78, 122, 233,
243, 244, 255
Littlehampton 79-81
Mersea Island 87-89
modernist arts centre 146
nudist beach 85
Punch & Judy 78
rock pools 72, 76, 78, 85
sand dunes 66-67, 68, 69-72
smugglers' haunts 33, 66, 76, 78,
239, 243
sunsets 198-199
ten beach activities 85
traditional resorts 68, 78, 79, 81,
85, 253
watersports 65, 69, 76, 78, 79, 85
West Wittering 65-68, 85
Whitstable 82-84, 85, 233

ships (*see also* boat trips)
historic 25
wreck-diving 79
shops (*see also* markets)
five shopping extravaganzas 41-42
five one-off shops 19
places:
Bath 41
Brighton 13-17
Bristol 25, 30
Broadstairs 41
Canterbury 42
Cheltenham 155
Guildford 42
Henley-on-Thames 59, 60
Lewes 37, 39
Oxford 23, 24
Rye 33
Saffron Walden 242
Snape Maltings 158
Southwold 42
Windsor 135
Woodbridge 31
products:
antiques &
bric-a-brac 13, 17, 30, 33, 34, 37,
38, 39, 41, 59, 81
architectural salvage 124-125
art 16, 88
auctions 31
bakeries 41, 57, 81, 138
beauty products 37, 41
beer 37
books 23, 31, 33, 37, 41, 42, 59
butchers 33, 88
CDs & vinyl 33, 39
charity shops 33
cheese 37
children's 19, 41, 42, 119
chocolate 16, 60
confectionery 33, 37, 41, 42, 116
crafts 31, 37, 39, 42, 145, 158, 269
delicatessens 21, 30, 33
designer discount 24
farm shops 164, 208, 209, 211, 223
fashion 14-15, 23, 24, 41, 42, 209
fish 33
garden products 103, 105, 124-125,
158, 209, 211, 223
gifts 37, 42, 103
groceries 15, 32, 37, 145
haberdashery 39
herbal remedies 41
homewares 14, 17, 23, 42, 158, 209
jewellery 15-16, 42
kites 30
models 19
musical instruments 37, 42
pets & pet products 17, 19, 24
quirky & retro 19, 24, 41
sex toys 14
shoes 14
vintage clothes 14, 17, 24, 41, 81
whisky 19
wine 41, 42, 99
spas
Bath Thermae 188-189
Calcot Manor 200-201
Goodwood Hotel 166
Haybarn Daylesford 190-191
Pennyhill Park Hotel 192-194
Sequoia at the Grove 185-187
Vineyard Spa 195-197
sport (*see also* watersports)
clay pigeon shooting 174
five spectator sports 175
golf 164, 166, 169-170, 195
historic cricket pitches 100, 175
indoor snow sports 177
horseracing 164-165, 164-166
motorsports 164-166
polo 167-168
real tennis 174
rock climbing 171-173
stately homes & great houses
arrive by steam train 232

arts & crafts homes 146, 232
deer parks 109, 131, 134
Goodwood 160, 164-166
around Henley 59
medieval 242
outdoor sculptures 160, 161, 166
Rothschilds' home 125
ten recommended 129-133

theatre
Cambridge productions 139, 140,
141
festivals & events 23, 253
open-air Shakespeare 23, 132

V

views
best sunsets 198-199
from clifftops 81, 143, 243, 244
from hilltops 113, 134, 178, 233,
235, 244, 245
from a lighthouse 74, 233
from pubs 30, 68, 72, 78, 82-83
from a spa 188
from towers 21, 33, 38
from treetop walkway 96

W

walks
around Aldeburgh 158, 159
Beachy Head 243-245
Cambridge to Grantchester 46-47
Chichester Harbour 66-67
country parks 81, 258
five recommended 244
with llamas 112-113, 258
Mersea Island 89
riverside 31, 46-47, 59-60
Roald Dahl trail 260
Winchelsea Beach 72
Windsor Great Park 134-135
woodland 92-94, 96, 258
war & weaponry
Battle of Hastings
experience 126-127
ceremonial cannons 43
forts 84, 89
Greatstone sound mirrors 74
museum 146
Spencer's war paintings 151
World War I tower 255
World War II heritage 74, 84, 89, 94,
96, 122, 146, 233, 255, 263
watersports
kiteboarding 65, 69
kitesurfing 79, 85
lido 147
regattas 58, 60, 84, 88
sailing 78, 174, 234
surfing 76, 78, 79
windsurfing 65, 69, 78, 79
wreck-diving 79
wildlife parks
(*see also* animals; nature reserves)
Chessington Zoo 251, 252
New Forest 111
Port Lympne 253-254, 259
Wildwood 254
woodland
aerial adventures 253
arboretums 102, 104-105
best for autumn colours 94, 96, 100,
102, 104
Burnham Beeches 92-94
butterflies 96, 105, 109
conservation volunteering 106-107
cycle trail 242
foraging for mushrooms 220
Salcey Forest 95-96
wildlife parks 111, 254

INDEXES

A-Z Index

a

A1 Barnet Shooting
Ground 174
Abode 14
ADC Theatre 139, 140
Adnams ale 158
Agora at the Copper Kettle 138
Albion bookshop 41
Albion pub, Bristol 29
Aldbury 244
Aldeburgh 72, 156-159
Aldeburgh Festival 156
Aldeburgh Food & Drink
Festival 158, 224
Aldeburgh Museum 159
Aldeburgh Music 156
Aldenham Country Park 258
Alfriston 239
All Saints' Church, St Ives 43
All Saints Church, Tudeley 151
Allens Farm 222-223
Alton market 215
Amber Shop 42
American Air Museum 146
Anatolian Kebab 33
Angel on the Bridge 60
Anne of Cleves Museum 37-38
Apache Tears 42
Apple Festival 208
Apple Week 224
Arcadia 23
Armoire 42
Art & Travelling
Landscape 240-241
Art Café 88
Arts Restaurant 138-139, 140
Ascot Park Polo Club 168
Ascot Racecourse 180
Ashbee & Son 33
Ashdown Forest
Llama Park 258
Ashridge Estate 244
Ashwell 55-57
Ashwell Gallery 57
Ashwell Springs 56
Ashwell Village Museum 55, 57
Audley End House 129, 133,
242
Auntie's Teashop 138
Avebury stone circle 120, 198
Avon Boating 234
Axe & Compasses 242

b

B184 cycle route 242
Baby Love 42
Balloon Safaris 246
Bamford Barn 209
Barnards Farm 151-152
Barrow Sands 84
Barry Keane Gallery 59
Bartholomew House 38
Basketball League 175
Bath 41, 146-147
Bath Thermae Spa 188-189
Battle 126-127
Bayblast 84
Beach House, West
Wittering 67
Beachy Head 243-245
Bead Games Shop 24
Bee Antique & Teddy
Market 41
Beecroft Art Gallery 143

Bekonscot Model
Village & Railway 263
Bell's Diner 29
Bentley Wood 109
Better Food 211
Bicester Village 24
Bidgoods 34
Big Garden Birdwatch 265
Bill's Produce stores 15, 37
Birdies 82
Black Horse, Woburn 53
Blackdown 235
Blackdown Farm
Riding Club 235-237
Blackwell's bookshop 23
Bleak House 78
Bluebell Railway 230-232
Boathouse, East Wittering 67
Bodleian Library 20
Bohemia arts market 42
Bohun Gallery 59
Bonne Bouche 37
Bookthrift 42
Botany Bay 76-78, 85
Bottle Inn 224
Bottle Neck 41
Bracklesham Bay 85
Bracknell Bees 175
Brasserie Blanc,
Cheltenham 154
Bredgar & Wormshill
Light Railway 232
Brentwood Farmers'
Market 217
Bridge Cottage 144
Brighton 13-17, 85, 147,
148-149
Brighton Festival 13
Brighton Flea Market 17
Bristol 25-30
Bristol Farmers' Market 27
Bristol Festival 27
Bristol International
Balloon Festival 27
Bristol International
Kite Festival 27
Britannia, Dungeness 74
Britchers & Rivers 33
British Birdwatching Fair 265
British Open Crabbing
Championship 85
British Trust for
Conservation Volunteers 106
Britten, Benjamin 156, 159
Broadstairs 41, 72, 77-78, 81
Broadstairs Dickens Festival 78
Brooke, Rupert 47
Browsers 31
Bruditz 37
Bull, Fenny Stratford 43
Burnham Beeches 92-94
Bury, the 55
Bushel & Strike 56, 57

c

Café Coco 20
Cakeham Equestrian Club 65
Calcot Manor
Hotel & Spa 200-201
Camber Sands 69-72, 85
Cambridge 46, 138-141, 244
Cambridge Arts Theatre 138,
139
Cambridge Artworks 138
Cambridge Folk
Festival 140, 148

Cambridge Music Festival 140
Cambridge University
Botanic Garden 46
Cambridge University
Library 138
Canterbury 42
Canterbury Tales 251
Captain Digby Inn 76
Captain's Table 31
Caravan Café 31
Carfax Tower 21
Cartier International 167
Cass Sculpture
Foundation 160, 166
Castor + Pollux 16
Cellar & Kitchen Store 42
Chagall, Marc 151
Chalk Gallery 37
Champignon Sauvage, Le 155
Chandos Deli 30
Chapel of St Ledger 43
Charleston 129, 130, 146
Cheese Please 37
Cheltenham Literature
Festival 154-155
Cherhill white horse 120
Chessington World of
Adventures & Zoo 251-252
Chiappini's 77
Chichester Cathedral 68, 151
Chichester Harbour 66-67, 68
Chiltern Hills 59, 116, 124, 199,
232, 233, 244
Chilterns Gateway
Centre 178
Chinnor & Princes
Risborough Railway 232
Chris and Les Harper's
Siesta 42
Christ Church College,
Oxford 20, 23
Christ Church Meadow 20
Christmas at Christ Church 23
Clacton-on-Sea 244
Classic Bike Hire 229
Clergy House 239
Cliff Top Café 240
Cliffe Antiques Centre 37
Clifton Arcade 30
Clifton Sausage 29
Cliftonville 81
Cliveden 129-130
Coastguard Café 255
Collen & Clare 42
Comme Ça 67
Company Shed 87, 89
Constable, John 144-145
Corfe Castle
Model Village 263
Corn Exchange 139
Coronation Tap 29
Corpus Playroom 139
Coton Manor Gardens 109
Cowdray Estate 235, 237
Cowley Road Carnival 23
Crab & Lobster 68
Cranfield Golf Academy 169
Cricketers Arms, Alciston 208
Crockford Bridge Farm 223
Crooked Billet,
Leigh-on-Sea 86
Crooked Billet,
Stoke Row 60, 61
Cudmore Country Park 89
Cycle Experience 229

d

Daffodil 155
Darwin, Charles 121
Dashwood Mausoleum 116
Daylesford Organic 190,
209-211
Day's of Ashwell Bakery 57
De La Warr Pavilion 146
Dedham Art & Craft Centre 145
Dedham Vale 144-145
Delia's Diner 255
Denny of Southwold 42
Devil's Dyke 198
Dicing for Bibles 43
Dickens, Charles 78, 253
Dickens House Museum 78
Dickens World 253
Diggerland 253, 254
Ditchling Beacon 233
Dolls House Miniatures
of Bath 41
Dorset Nettle Eating
Championships 224
Dot to Dot Festival 148
Dover Castle 122
Dover cliffs 240, 244
Dover White Cliffs Tours 234
Down House 121
Downs Golf Course 166
Dream Car Hire UK 229
Duke of Cumberland Arms 53
Duke of Essex Polo Trophy 168
Dungeness 73-75, 85,
151, 153, 233
Dungeness Gallery 74
Dunstable 233
Dunstable Downs 178
Dunwich 85, 158
Dymchurch 85

e

Eagle, Cambridge 139
East Beach Café 79-81, 151
East Bergholt 144
East Mersea Stone 89
East Quay Shellfish 82
Eastbourne 72, 81, 143, 243
Eastoke 255
Elton Hall 130
English Women's Golf 170
Epping & Ongar Railway 232,
242
Epping Forest 94
Epsom Downs
Racecourse 178, 180
Essex Gliding Club 174
Essex Rose Tea House 145
Eton College 135
Exbury Gardens 97

f

Falkland Arms 53
Farmcafé & Foodmarket 211
Feed the Birds Day 264
Fenny Poppers 43
Fernhurst 237
Ferret 59
Festival of Speed 164
Fidra 16
Field & Fork 68
Fifteenth Century
Bookshop 37
Firle Beacon 53, 208, 239
Fish Café, Rye 34

INDEXES

Fishers Farm Park 258
Fitzwilliam Museum 138, 141
Flatford Mill 144
Flora Tea Rooms 158
Focus on the Past 30
Folkestone 241
Food for Friends 16
Fox & Hounds,
Englefield Green 134, 135
Fox & Hounds, Uffington 49-50
Freud's 24
Friend & Co 29, 30
Frinton-on-Sea 146
Frinton Park Estate 146
Friston Forest 245
Frogmore House 134
Fry Art Gallery 143, 242
Funland 255
Fusciardi's 72

Gardeners Arms 38
Garsington Opera 150
Garsons Fruit Farm 223
Gatton Park 111
George, The, Rye 34
George & Davis'
Ice Cream Café 21
George & Dragon,
West Wycombe 116
Georgian Coffee House 31
Get Cutie 14
Glass etc 34
Glorious Goodwood 164-165
Glynde 205-208, 240
Glyndebourne 208
Go Ape Experience 253
Golden Arrow Pullman
Service 232
Golden Galleon 159
Goods Shed 42
Goodwood Hotel 166
Goodwood House 160, 164-166
Goodwood Revival 165-166
Gorvett & Stone 60
Grammar School Records 33
Grantchester 46-47
Great Britain, SS 25
Great Dixter 98
Great Escape 148-149
Great House Restaurant
& Hotel 147
Great Missenden 260
Great Story Picnic Season 23
Greatstone sound mirrors 74
Green Gym 106
Green Man, Grantchester 47
Green Owl 72
Green Park Station 41
Greys Court 59
Grove Farm 223
Grove Hotel 185-187
Guards Club 167
Guerilla Galleries 29
Guildford 42
Guildford Farmers' Market 217
Guildford Heat 175
Guildhall, Windsor 135
Guildhall Market, Bath 41

Ham Polo Club 168
Hamford Water Nature
Reserve 111
Hampton Court Maze 266
Hannah Peschar
Sculpture Garden 160
Harrison's Rocks 171-172
Harvey's Brewery 37, 38-39
Hastings 81, 244
Hastings, Battle of 126-127
Hastings Castle 81
Hastings Country Park 81

Hatfield House Tennis Club 174
Hawkin's Bazaar 42
Haybarn Daylesford 190-191
Hayling Island 255
Hayling Island Donkeys 255
Haysden Country Park 242
Heatherwick,
Thomas 81, 151-152
Hell-Fire Caves 116
Henley Festival of
Music & Arts 60
Henley Food Festival 60
Henley-on-Thames 58-61, 234, 246
Henley-on-Thames
Farmers' Market 217-219
Henley Royal Regatta 58, 60
Henry Moore Foundation 160-161
Herbal Apothecary 41
Herne Bay 85, 233, 254, 259
Hever Castle 117-119, 266
Hi-Lo (Jamaican
Eating House) 24
High Rocks 172-173
Hitchin market 215-216
Hobbs of Henley 60, 234
Holkham Beach 198-199
Hollycombe Steam
Fair 256-257
Hop Gallery 37
Hope & Harlequin 14
Hope Gap 85
HOT Balloons 246
Huntsman 172
Hyde Hall 178-179

Imperial War Museum
Duxford 146
International Birds of
Prey Centre 174
International Women's
Polo Association 168
Ives Ice Cream Parlour 72
Ivinghoe Beacon 199
Iydea 15

Jane Wicks Kitchenalia 33
Jarman, David 37
Jarman, Derek 73, 151
Jerwood Sculpture 161
Jewel Thief 16
John Nike Leisuresport
Complex 175
Jonkers Rare Books 59
Joss Bay 78
Joss Bay Surf School 76
Julie Phipps 31
Junction, The 139, 141

Keble College 20
Kempton Park
Racecourse 180-181
Kenilworth Castle 122-123
Kensington Rocking
Horse Company 19
Kent Ballooning 246
Kent County
Cricket Club 175
Kettle o' Fish 34
Kettle's Yard 138, 141
Kichel throwing 43
King's College, Cambridge 138
King's College Chapel 139
King's Head, Wadenhoe 53
Kingsgate Bay caves 76
Kit Kat Café 72
Kitestore 30
Kitesurfing Championships 79

Knight's Antiques 59
Knole Park 109, 130-131
Koba 17

Lacys 24
Lakeland Plastics 42
Lamb House 33
Landgate Bistro 34
LASSCO Three
Pigeons 124-125
Latitude 149
Lavender Line 232
Lavenham 147
Lea, River 241
Leander Club 58
Lee Valley Boat Centre 229
Leeds Castle 122, 123, 266
Legoland 253, 266
Leicester Arms 242
Leigh Folk Festival 86
Leigh-on-Sea 86
Lemongrove Gallery 59
Leonardslee Gardens 111
Leopard 3 (yacht) 234
Lewes 35-39, 239
Lewes Arms 38
Lewes Bonfire Night 37
Lewes Castle 36, 38
Lick 15
Lickfold Inn 53
Light Railway Café 74
Lincoln Whisky Shop 19
Litlington 245
Littlehampton 79-81
Living Rainforest 267-269
Lizzie James 23
Lodge, The 264-265
London Golf Club 170
London Irish rugby
union team 175
Longleat Maze 266
Loseley Park 97, 98
Lounge on the Farm 149
Love Food 27
Lower Leas Coastal Park 253
Lumps Fort 263
Luna Caprese 24

Macari's 72
Macknade Fine Foods 211
Madejski Stadium 175
Magdalen College, Oxford 20
Malvern Hills 199
Man on the Moon 138
Manningtree 144, 145
Manningtree Local
History Museum 145
Manton white horse 120
Margate 78, 81
Margate Caves 78
Market Fisheries 33
May Day 23, 43
May's General Store 37
Mermaid Inn, Rye 33
Merry Harriers 112-113
Mersea Island 87-89
Mersea Island Vineyard 89
Mersea Museum 88
Mersea Regatta 88
Metfield Café 158
Middle Farm, Glynde 205-208
Midhurst 237
Minsmere nature
reserve 158, 265
Miss Ritzy 41
Mistley 144, 145
Model Shop 19
Modern Art Oxford 21
Montezumas 16
Morelli's 72, 81
Mrs Tee's Wild
Mushrooms 220
Mumford Theatre 138

Mummers' Play
& Sea Shanties 86
Munnings, Alfred 144

Nab Tower 255
National Collection
of Cider & Perry 205-208
National Malus Collection 151
Needlemakers 39
Neptune's Hall 77
Nettle Eating
Championships 224
New Forest 110, 220, 229
New Forest Otter, Owl
& Wildlife Park 111
New 2 You 33
NewArtCentre Sculpture
Park & Gallery 161
No Name 17
Noah's Ark Inn 53
North Foreland Lighthouse 78
North Kent coast 233
North Laine Antique
& Flea Market 14
Northward Hill
Nature Reserve 109-110
Novelli Academy 212-214
Nuffield Place 59
Nuts 4 Climbing 171-172
Nymans Garden 98-99

Oakwood Inn 244
Off Beat Coffee Bar 14
Old Bookbinders Ale House 24
Old Hall 144
Old House at Home 68
Old Lighthouse 74
Old Neptune 83, 85
Old New Inn Model Village 263
Old Vicarage, Grantchester 47
Olde Bell & Steelyard, Ye 53
Olde Smugglers Inne, Ye 239
Olney market
& pancake race 216
One Stop Thali Café 29
Orchard Tea Garden 47
Organic Farm Shop 211
Orwell Book Shop 42
Osborne, Richard 37
Osborne Bros Seafood
Merchants 86
Oscar Road Tea Rooms 41
Osteria Pizzeria Posillipo 78
Oxfam Bookstore 23
Oxford 20-24, 147, 246
Oxford Literaty Festival 23
Oxford Punting 21
Oxford Shakespeare
Company 23

Painshill Park 98, 99
Palace Cinema,
Broadstairs 78, 81
Pallant House Gallery 68
Pearson's Arms 82, 84
Pelham House Hotel 37, 38
Pennyhill Park Hotel 192-194
Penshurst Off Road
Cycling Centre 242
Penshurst Place 242
People's Republic
of Stokes Croft 29
Peppers 24
Petworth 129, 131
Pickerel Inn 139, 140
Pieminister 29
Pilot 74
Pintxo People 16
Pitt Rivers Museum 24
Place at Camber
Sands, The 71-72
Plough & Harrow 245

Plough & Sail 158
Pod 155
Pokeno's 14
Polesden Lacey 130, 132
Port Lympne Wild
Animal Park 253-254, 259
Port Meadow 21
Portland Arms 139
Portsmouth International
Kite Festival 179
Posh Frocks 23
Primrose Café 30
Prince of Wales, Bristol 30
Prospect Cottage 73, 151, 153
Punch & Judy 78

q
Queen Mary Sailing
Club & Sailsports 174
Queen's Hotel 154

r
Radcliffe Camera 20, 147
Ragley Hall 161
Rainbow Café 139, 140
Rainham nature reserve 265
Ram Inn, Firle 53, 240
Real Eating Company 38
Reculver 233
Red Lion, Fernhurst 237
Red Roaster 17
Red Sand forts 84
Reign 24
Rennie's Seaside Modern 19
Requena, Pablo 37
RHS see Royal Horticultural
Society
Richard Hayward's
Oysters 87-88
Richard Way Antiquarian
Books 59
Richmond Arms at the
Goodwood Hotel 166
Richmond Park Golf Club 169
Ridgeway National Path 49,
199, 244
River & Rowing Museum 60
Roald Dahl Museum
& Story Centre 260-261
Rochester Sweeps'
Festival 43
Rodings 242
Romford market 216
Romney Bay House Hotel 74
Romney, Hythe & Dymchurch
Railway 73, 74, 85, 232
Romney Sands 74
Rose & Crown, Ashwell 56, 57
Rossi's 72
Rousham Manor 99-100
Royal Albion 78
Royal Botanic Gardens,
Wakehurst Place 109
Hyde Hall 178
Wisley 101-103
Royal Mausoleum 134
Royal Oak, Critchmere 237
Royal Pavilion 13, 147
Aldeburgh guided walks 158
Dungeness Nature
Reserve 73, 74
The Lodge
(headquarters) 264-265
Northward Hill reserve 109-110
Stour Estuary reserve 108
Rushton Triangular Lodge 147
Ruskin Gallery 138
Russell-Cotes Art Gallery
& Museum 143
Rye 33-34, 244
Rye Arts Festival 33
Rye Bay Scallop
Festival 224-225
Rye Delicatessen 33

s
Saffron Walden 242
St Martin's church,
Fenny Stratford 43
St Mary the Virgin,
Dedham 144
St Mary's church,
Ashwell 56, 57
St Mary's church,
East Bergholt 144
St Mary's church, Rye 33
St Mary's church,
Uffington 50-51
St Mary's church,
Woodbridge 31
St Peter & St Paul,
Aldeburgh 159
St Peter & St Paul,
West Mersea 88
St Peter's church,
Dunstable 233
St Werburgh's City
Farm & Café 30
Salcey Forest 95-96
Saltdean Lido 147
Samphire Hoe 85, 240
Sandham Memorial Chapel 151
Sandown Park Racecourse 181
Sandy Point nature reserve 255
Savernake Forest 94
Savill Garden 134
Scarecrow Festival 255
Scudamore's 47, 139
Sequoia at the Grove 185-187
Seven Sisters 243, 245
Seven Sisters Sheep
Centre 110
Sharnfold Farm 223
Sheffield Park
Garden 100, 111, 231, 232
Shell Grotto 78
Shere 233
Sherman's Hall 144
Ship Inn, Itchenor 68
Shop on Jesus Lane 138
Silbury Hill 120
Silent Pool 233
Simply Italian 33
Sir Alfred Munnings
Art Museum 144
Sir Harold Hillier Gardens 100
Sissinghurst Castle
& Gardens 100, 131, 132
Sitooterie 151-152
Skandic Hus 155
Skaters' Meadow 46
Slapstick Silent Comedy
Festival 27
Slow Food Market, Bristol 27
Snail Trail 229
Snape Maltings 156-159, 224
SNO!zone Milton Keynes 177
Snooper's Paradise 14
Snow Centre 177
Snow Drop 240
Snow Hill Common 66
Snowshill Manor 131, 133
Soil Association
Organic Food Festival 27
South Downs
199, 233, 243, 245
South Downs
Way 233, 239, 245
South Downs white horse 245
Southcoast Exotics 19
Southdown Antiques 37
Southover Grange Gardens 38
Southsea Common 179
Southsea Model Village 263
Southwold 42, 158
Spa at Pennyhill Park
Hotel 192-194
Spa Valley Railway 173
Spencer, Stanley 143, 151
Spencers Farm Shop 223

Sportsman 53-54, 82
Standard Inn 33
Standen 146, 232
Stanley Spencer Gallery 143
Stonehenge 120
Stonor 59
Stour Estuary 108
Stowe Landscape Gardens 100
Strawberry Fair 140
Suffolk Horse Museum 31
Sugar Boy 42
Summer in the City 140
Summer Seashore Safaris 76
Sun Inn, Dedham 145
Sunningdale golf club 170
Super8 Film Festival 140
Surbiton Hockey Club 175
Surrey Hills 233
Surrey Hills Llamas 112-113
Sussex Border Path 236
Sussex Downs 246
Sussex Guild Shop 39
Sustrans 240, 241
Sutton Hoo 31
Swan, Tetsworth 124-125
Sweet Yesterday 41
Sylvester 23

t
Tash Tori Arts & Crafts 37
Tea Cosy 17
1066 Battle of Hastings,
Abbey & Battlefield 126-127
Thame market 216-217
Thames Barges 84
Thames Path 60
Thanet, Isle of 76-78
Thanet Coast Project 76
Thaxted 242
Thaxted Festival 242
Thaxted Morris Men 242
Thetford Forest Park 94
30A 17
Thorpe Park 251, 254
Thorpeness 81, 159
Three Chimneys 54
Three Pigeons 124-125
Three Tuns 56, 57
Tickled 14
Tickled Pink Tea Rooms 147
Tide Mill, Woodbridge 31, 32
Tiger Inn 244
Tiptree jam factory
& museum 145
To Be Worn Again 14
Tom Brown's School
Museum 51
Tonbridge Castle 241
Totally Tomato Show 225
Tower Hill Tea Gardens 82
Towner Gallery 143
Trevor Arms 208
Tribeca 15
Trout Inn 21
Trumpington Meadows
Country Park 47
Tuck Shop 42
Tudeley Festival 151
Tudor House Antiques 59
Two Brewers 134

u
Uffington White
Horse 48-51, 179
UK Boat Hire 234

v
Valley Farm 144
VC Jones 82
Vegetarian Shoes 14
Viking Bay 78
Viking Coastal Trail 78
Vine Tree 54
Vineyard Spa 195-197
Vista house 74

w
Waddesdon Manor 125
Wakehurst Place 109
Walberswick Nature Reserve 85
Walton-on-the-Naze 85, 244
Warwick Castle 123
Watercress Line 215
Waterfront Café 32
Waterperry Gardens 111, 125
Watts Cemetery Chapel 146
Wayland's Smithy 51
Weighing the Mayor 43
Wendover Woods 94
Wentworth golf club 170
West Beach Café 79, 81
West Dean Estate
& Gardens 225
West Hill Cliff Railway 81
West Kennett Long Barrow 120
West Lodge Rural
Centre 258-259
West Road Concert Hall 138
West Wittering 65-68, 85
West Wycombe 116
Westdean village 245
Westonbirt National
Arboretum 104-105
Wheelers Oyster Bar 82, 84
Whipsnade Tree Cathedral 94
Whistlestop Café 32
White Hart, Manningtree 145
White Horse Hill 48-51, 179
White Horse pub, Shere 233
White Lion, Bristol 30
Whitfield Farmers' Market 219
Whitstable 82-84, 85, 233
Whitstable Brewery Bar 83, 84
Whitstable Harbour Market 84
Whitstable Oyster
Festival 82, 84, 225
Whitstable Oyster Fishery
Company 82, 84
Whitstable Regatta 84
Whole World Café 241
Wickham Fruit Farm 223
Wickle 37
Wild Strawberry Café 31
Wildlife (sailing boat) 259
Wildwood 254
Williams & Brown 82
Willy Lott's Cottage 144
Wilton House 133
Wimborne Minster
Model Town 263
Winchelsea 72, 85, 244
Winchester Cathedral 152
Wind Farm 84
Windsor 134, 135
Windsor Castle 123, 134
Windsor Farm Shop 211
Windsor Farmers' Market 219
Windsor Great Park 134-135,
167
Windsor Racecourse 181
Windsor Royal Shopping 135
Wisley 101-103
Wittering Surf Shop 65
Woburn golf club 170
Woodbridge 31-32
Woodbridge Museum 31
Woodman Inn &
Restaurant 49, 50
Wordfest 140
World Pea Throwing
Championship 37

x
Xscape Leisure Centre 177

y
Ypres Castle Inn 33

z
Zazu's 30
Ziggy Pickles by the Sea 41

INDEXES

WORCESTERSHIRE

WARWICKSHIRE

NORTHANTS

GLOUCESTERSHIRE

OXFORDSHIRE

BUCKS

BERKSHIRE

AVON

WILTSHIRE

HAMPSHIRE

SOMERSET

DORSET

Locations by county

For key, see p280.

MAP KEY

Avon
1. Bath p41, p146, p147, p188
2. Bristol p25, p148

Bedfordshire
1. Biggleswade p229
2. Leighton Buzzard p223
3. Sandy p264
4. Tea Green p212
5. Whipsnade p94, p178, p233
6. Woburn p53

Berkshire
1. Ascot p180
2. Bracknell p175, p253
3. Cookham p143
4. Hampstead Norreys p267
5. Maidenhead p129
6. Newbury p195
7. Reading p175
8. Windsor p123, p134, p181, p219, p253, p266

Buckinghamshire
1. Beaconsfield p263
2. Buckingham p100
3. Burnham p92
4. Ivinghoe p199, p244
5. Great Missenden p260
6. High Wycombe p43, p116
7. Milton Keynes p43, p95, p177
8. Olney p216
9. Wendover p94

Cambridgeshire
1. Cambridge p138, p148, p244
2. Duxford p146
3. Elton p130
4. Grantchester p46
5. St Ives p43

Dorset
1. Bournemouth p143
2. Corfe p263
3. Marshwood p224
4. Wimborne Minster p263

Essex
1. Brentwood p217
2. Epping p168
3. Frinton-on-Sea p146
4. Halstead p223
5. Harwich p43, p108
6. High Ongar p242
7. Leigh-on-Sea p86
8. Loughton p94
9. Mersea Island p87
10. Rettendon p178
11. Saffron Walden p129, p143
12. Southend p72, p143
13. Walton-on-the-Naze p85, p111, p244
14. West Horndon p151

Gloucestershire
1. Broadway p133
2. Bourton-on-the-Water p263
3. Cheltenham p154
4. Kingham p190, p209
5. Newent p174
6. Tetbury p104, p200

Hampshire
1. Alton p215
2. Ampfield p100
3. Brockenhurst p229
4. Burghclere p151
5. Burley p110
6. Exbury p97
7. Hayling Island p255
8. Liphook p256
9. Lymington p220
10. Marchwood p111
11. Portsmouth p19
12. Southampton p234
13. Southsea p179, p263
14. Winchester p152

Hertfordshire
1. Ashwell p55
2. Barnet p174
3. Broxbourne p229
4. Chandler's Cross p185
5. Elstree p258
6. Hitchin p215
7. Much Hadham p160
8. Old Hatfield p174

Kent
1. Ashford p246
2. Biddenden p54
3. Broadstairs p41, p72, p76, p81, p85
4. Camber Sands p69, p85
5. Canterbury p42, p149, p175, p251
6. Chatham p253
7. Dover p122, p219, p240, p244
8. Downe p121
9. Dungeness p73, p85, p151, p233
10. Dymchurch p85
11. Eridge p171
12. Herne Bay p85, p254, p259
13. Hever p117, p266
14. High Halstow p109
15. Faversham p224
16. Folkestone p19, p234, p253
17. Lympne p253, p259
18. Maidstone p123, p266
19. Margate p81
20. Rochester p43, p253
21. Sevenoaks p109, p130
22. Sissinghurst p100, p132
23. Tonbridge p151, p241
24. Whitstable p53, p82, p85, p225, p233

Northamptonshire
1. Coton p109
2. Kettering p258
3. Northampton p19
4. Rushton p147
5. Wadenhoe p53

Oxfordshire
1. Chipping Norton p53
2. Garsington p150
3. Henley-on-Thames p58, p217, p234
4. Milton Common p109, p124
5. Oxford p20, p147
6. Stanford-in-the-Vale p229
7. Steeple Aston p99
8. Thame p216
9. Uffington p48, p179

Suffolk
1. Aldeburgh p72, p156
2. Brandon p94
3. Dunwich p85
4. East Bergholt p144
5. Henham p149
6. Lavenham p147
7. Snape p156, p224
8. Southwold p42, p81
9. Sudbury p174
10. Woodbridge p31
11. Walberswick p85

Surrey
1. Bagshot p192
2. Chertsey p254
3. Chessington p251
4. Chobham p168
5. Cobham p99
6. Cranleigh p229
7. Dorking p132
8. Epsom p178, p180
9. Esher p181, p223
10. Guildford p42, p98, p175, p217
11. Hambledon p112
12. Hampton Court p266
13. Long Ditton p175
14. Ockley p160
15. Reigate p111
16. Sunbury-on-Thames p174, p180
17. Weybridge p223
18. Wisley p101

Sussex, East
1. Battle p126
2. Beachy Head p243
3. Bexhill on Sea p146
4. Brighton p13, p85, p147, p148, p229
5. Devil's Dyke p198
6. Eastbourne p72, p81, p110, p143
7. Firle p53, p205
8. Forest Row p258
9. Hastings p81, p244
10. Hellingly p19
11. Lewes p35, p129, p146, p239
12. Pevensey p223
13. Rye p33, p98, p242
14. Sheffield Park p100, p111, p230
15. Winchelsea p85

Sussex, West
1. Ardingly p109
2. Bracklesham Bay p85
3. Fernhurst p53, p235
4. Goodwood p160, p164
5. Handcross p98
6. Littlehampton p79
7. Lower Beeding p111
8. Lurgashall p53
9. Petworth p53, p131
10. West Dean p225
11. West Wittering p65, p85
12. Wisborough Green p258
13. Worthing p72

Warwickshire
1. Alcester p161
2. Kenilworth p122
3. Stratford-upon-Avon p234
4. Warwick p123

Wiltshire
1. Avebury p120, p198
2. Longleat p266
3. Marlborough p94
4. Salisbury p161
5. Stonehenge p120
6. West Tytherley p109
7. Wilton p133

Worcestershire
1. Malvern p199